The Rise and Fall of Great Cities

The Rise and Fall of Great Cities
Aspects of urbanization in the Western World

Edited by Richard Lawton
Emeritus Professor of Geography,
University of Liverpool

Belhaven Press,
(a division of Pinter Publishers)
London and New York

© The editor and contributors 1989

First published in Great Britain in 1989 by
Belhaven Press (a division of Pinter Publishers),
25 Floral Street, London WC2E 9DS

British Library Cataloguing in Publication Data
A CIP catalogue record for this book is available from the
British Library

ISBN 1 85293 050 0

Library of Congress Cataloging-in-Publication Data
The Rise and fall of great cities.
  Bibliography: p.
  Includes index.
  1. Urbanization – History. I. Lawton, Richard.
HT361.R57 1989   307.76'09   89-7030
ISBN 1-85293-050-0

Typeset by Book Ens, Saffron Walden, Essex
Printed and bound in Great Britain
by SRP Ltd, Exeter

Contents

List of figures

List of tables

Notes on contributors

Professor Gordon E. Cherry is a leading planning historian and currently head of the Department of Geography, University of Birmingham.

Dr Anthony J. Fielding, a specialist in migration studies of contemporary Western Europe, is Director of the Centre for Urban and Regional Research, University of Sussex.

Professor John B. Goddard, who has pioneered studies of the impact of information technologies on urban and regional development, is Director of the Centre for Urban and Regional Development Studies, University of Newcastle upon Tyne.

Professor Jean Gottmann introduced the term 'Megalopolis' to the study of the great city regions of North America and Western Europe: he is Emeritus Professor at the University of Oxford and associated with EHESS in Paris.

Professor Peter Hall has written extensively on urban and regional planning problems – present and future – in Western Europe and on great cities of the world: he is currently Professor of Geography in the University of Reading and at the Institute of Urban and Regional Development, University of California at Berkeley.

Dr Gerard Kearns, who has specialist interests in urban public health and administration in nineteenth- and early twentieth-century Europe, is Lecturer in Geography and a member of the Institute of European Population Studies at the University of Liverpool.

Professor Richard Lawton has worked on population trends and their impact on urban society in nineteenth-century Britain: he is Emeritus Professor of Geography in the University of Liverpool and, currently, External Professor at the University of Technology, Loughborough.

Dr Colin G. Pooley, an authority on social and public housing problems of nineteenth- and twentieth-century Western European cities, is Senior Lecturer and, currently, Head of the Department of Geography in the University of Lancaster.

Professor Brian Robson, who has written extensively on the development of nineteenth-century cities and on problems of developing policies for their economic and social revival, is Professor of Geography and, currently, Dean of the Faculty of Arts, University of Manchester.

Dr Gareth Shaw has made specialist studies of retailing and the economic structure and morphology of nineteenth-century cities: he is Senior Lecturer in Geography at the University of Exeter.

Professor Robert Woods is a leading historical demographer with special interests in the mortality and fertility transitions in England and their socio-economic and spatial significance: he was recently appointed to the Chair of Geography in the University of Liverpool.

Preface

This book was conceived at the 1987 Annual Conference of the Institute of British Geographers at Portsmouth Polytechnic. It was thought appropriate that the Institute should devote three plenary sessions at that meeting to a review of the development and problems – past, present, and future – of the great Western cities. For their help in bringing my idea to fruition I gratefully acknowledge the support of Barrie Gleave, the then Conference Secretary, and the various officers of the Institute's Historical, Population and Urban Study Groups.

Dr Iain Stevenson, the Editorial Director of Belhaven Press, was amongst the audience and I owe him and the Press a considerable debt of gratitude for their encouragement to bring together papers delivered at those sessions in this book of essays on 'The rise and fall of great cities'. Current concern with the state and future of cities is universal and has attracted the attention of many academics, planners, administrators and politicians. The unprecedented growth of urban living since the late eighteenth century has transformed most of the Western World, capitalist and socialist alike: a similar transformation is under way in the developing world but on a much greater scale and at a more rapid pace than any urban revolution of the past. We face a challenging future.

Modern urbanization is one of the 'grand themes' of history. It involves demographic, economic, technological, social, cultural, political, and even moral/philosophical issues; it already affects the lives of the bulk of mankind and, through an all-pervasive urban-focused culture, reaches out to the remotest areas of the world. Linked as we now are by fast global transport systems and instant electronic communications the vision (or nightmare – view it as you will) of writers such as H. G. Wells, Lewis Mumford and Arnold Toynbee of a virtually wholly urbanized world is not a distant dream but may well be the reality of the early twenty-first century. It is not surprising, therefore, that this has been reflected in a spate of academic and planning literature on the city since the 1960s and that urban studies embrace disciplines ranging from architecture and building science, through economics, sociology, political science and administration to many aspects of environmental and business studies. Moreover, urban historians and historical demographers find in the study of city development a veritable laboratory of the human experience.

The themes of the essays in this book are, inevitably, highly selective. As explained in Chapter 1, we have not attempted to cover all aspects of the development of cities and their past, present and future problems. We have also focused on the cities of the Western world, principally in Western Europe and North America, though their relationships with and possible lessons for the rapidly-growing cities of the developing world are alluded to from time to time. The essays are representative of a number of aspects of urban studies to which geographers, including the authors of these essays, have made both research- and policy-related contributions. For the choice of these themes I must bear sole responsibility: they are, I believe, of interest not only to geographers but to other social scientists and planners and, indeed, to all students of cities.

The credit for this book must, however, go principally to the individual authors. I have not sought to impose constraints on their approach to the themes suggested to them other than in the interest of coherence within the text. To them I extend my warmest thanks for their co-operation and forbearance. But the book is also the product of many other hands – notably those who in various places typed the manuscript and drew the illustrations – and other eyes, especially Sara Wilbourne and Vivienne Robertson of Belhaven Press who read, checked and guided a complex manuscript through the press. My special thanks go to them and to Iain Stevenson for his constant encouragement and patience.

But this is, I believe, a book not only created by heads, hands and eyes: it also comes from the heart. All of us are deeply concerned with the fate and future of cities and their millions of citizens throughout the world. To them we dedicate our efforts.

Richard Lawton
Marton, North Yorkshire
12 April 1989

1 Introduction: aspects of the development and role of great cities in the Western World in the nineteenth and twentieth centuries

Richard Lawton

Urban origins

Cities are as old as civilization: indeed they *are* civilization. The timeless fascination which has drawn people to them throughout history is as potent as ever. Witness the massive contemporary migrations to the mega-cities of the developing world; the continuing lure of the great metropolitan centres of Western civilization; and the intense concentration of a global transactional society around the glittering skyscrapers of the major international business centres both old – London and New York – and new – Tokyo, Hong Kong and Singapore.

Yet the revulsion which many feel for the city has never been far from the surface, even among city-dwellers. It erupts periodically in massive demonstrations of urban unrest, and is implicit in the continual tensions of urban existence. The 'anomie' and 'alienation' found in the city by Durkheim (Weber, 1958) has its counterpart in the pastoral idyll which draws city-dwellers to the countryside: whether to the patrician estates of imperial Rome; the villas of Palladian Venice; the country estates of English *nouveau riche* – from Elizabethan merchant venturer to Victorian industrialist; or, more recently, the mock-Tudor semi-detached of the inter-war commuter and, now, the country cottage of the week-ending business-man or the middle-class drop-outs from the urban rat-race.

The ambivalence of the city thus reflected, and so well encapsulated in Brian Robson's review of current concern over the future – indeed the very existence – of big cities (Chapter 4), has its roots in the very real tensions of city life and the conflicts, as well as the complementarities, of urban and rural society. For urban societies have tended to dominate their rural neighbours or, as they are often seen, dependencies. What Hans Bobek (1962) has described as 'rent–capitalism' had its origins in the control of both wealth and political power of early hydraulic civiliz-ations. These were, argues Paul Wheatley (1969, p. 7), ' . . . the style centre[s] in the traditional world, disseminating social, political, technical, religious and aesthetic values, and functioning as an organizing principle conditioning the manner and quality of life in the countryside'. In that sense it is as misguided to make a false dichotomy between 'pre-industrial cities' (Sjoberg, 1960) and 'industrial cities' as it is to focus on the European-dominated style of city life and urban structure of recent times. Rather, we should recognize that, in Europe for example, the understanding of city origins and the impact of their economic and demographic processes on urban society requires ' . . . a lengthy look backward in time' even to answer many of the questions concerning contemporary cities (Hohenberg and Lees, 1985, p. 1).

The need for historical understanding stressed in the Marxist dialectic, has recently been significantly extended by David Harvey (1985a, 1985b) to the spatial implications for Western capitalist urbanization, underlining the ' . . . study of that process as it unfolds through the production of physical and social landscapes and the production of consciousness' (Harvey, 1985a, p. xvi). In recognizing the centrality of the urban experience in the capitalist world not only to economic and political processes but also to social and spatial structures, Harvey has reminded us in new ways of the centrality of that urban experience for mankind.

Prior to the nineteenth century, however, despite the influence wielded by great cities over the political, commercial and cultural life of their territories, they seldom dominated territorially or in population numbers. To be sure, some headed vast empires (military and commercial) and were great centres of cosmopolitan cultures and polyglot societies: Babylon, Nineveh, Alexandria, Rome, Constantinople, Sravasti, Patna, Chang'an, Hangchow, Nanking, Peking, Cairo may all have topped 100,000, and in some cases half a million at various stages of their history. Others, such as Athens, were much smaller in territory and population, but powerful in democratic and intellectual identity and influence. But it was not until the dawn of the age of European commercial expansion in the fourteenth century that big city growth began to assume substantial and continuously developing proportions. With the entry into the world urban system of the capitals of nation states – Paris, London, Madrid – and the centres of international trade in the Mediterranean – Venice, Genoa, Milan, Florence, Cadiz – and the Low Countries – Bruges, Ghent – populations of over 50,000 and, in some cases, 100,000 were reached and the foundations of the modern urban system of Europe were laid. European discovery, exploration and settlement of the New World and rapid commercial penetration established a progressively global trade system and an international urban hierarchy from the late sixteenth century in which the great ports, commercial centres and imperial capitals were dominant. Western Europe, once an area of mainly small cities with market areas limited by access from their agricultural hinterlands (classically in the German city-states) became a region of rapid city growth within powerful nation states (Italy and Germany excepted).

The rapid increase in the population of Elizabethan London and many of its attendant problems – including the sustaining of growth in the face of disease, housing and food supply – epitomizes the impact of political and commercial forces (Finlay, 1981). Such cities as Rotterdam and London, as Jan de Vries (1984) has convincingly demonstrated, depended heavily on migration for their continuing growth with national and even international hinterlands of labour recruitment. Not until the problems of containing, then conquering, urban disease did large cities begin to provide the natural increase for their own demographic future (Woods, chapter 6). And the containment of disease and ordering of the urban environment, through public health administration (Kearns, chapter 7) and planning of urban layout (Cherry, chapter 3) and housing (Cherry; Pooley, chapter 8), formed an important part of the story of the emergence of large modern cities.

The full impact and ultimate dominance of Western urbanism in the European world and, in time, near-universally, awaited the concentration of capital and production brought by the industrial and commercial revolutions. The ability to harness motive power to mass production progressively destroyed the 'handmade' world of rural and urban handicraft workers alike and drew the surplus army of labour to the new points of production at sources of power, raw materials and around transport nodes, whether at ports or key points in inland communications networks. The rise of large manufacturing centres transformed the scale and pattern of world cities by the mid-nineteenth century, and confirmed Western Europe's lead in the new urbanization.

The changing role and pattern of urbanization

By 1800 there were relatively few great world cities, arbitrarily defined as those with a population of over 100,000, a figure which was exceptional prior to the fifteenth century (table 1.1). The total rose rapidly from 65 to 106 between 1800 and 1850, and nearly trebled again by 1900. Moreover, whereas in 1800 Peking was the only 'million city' (narrowly defined), by 1850 it had been joined by London and Paris and by 1900 there were 16 such cities – mainly in Europe and North America, a tribute to the triumph of the Atlantic economy – and another 27 of over half a million. As Adna Ferrin Weber observed in his pioneer and still unique statistical study of the population of urban areas throughout the world, ' . . . the most remarkable social phenomenon of the present century is the concentration of population in cities' (Weber, 1899, p. 1), a concentration which he attributed to the 'era of steam and machinery' and the way in which ' . . . all the agencies of modern civilization have worked together to abolish . . . rural isolation; . . . the railways, the newspaper press, freedom of migration and settlement . . . cause the spread of the ideas originating in the cities and lift . . . the rural districts out of their mental stagnation' (ibid., pp. 7–8).

It was this view of urbanization as the dominant economic, political, cultural, social and moral force which, half a century previously, had led Robert Vaughan (1842, p. 1) to proclaim 'Our age is pre-eminently the age of great cities' and to contrast the strength and universality of city life with its more exceptional and exiguous nature in the past. Vaughan's sub-title 'Modern Civilization viewed in its relation to Intelligence, Morals and Religion' pointed to the significance of urbanization not so much in economic terms as in its implications for society – in science, the arts, and in relation to 'popular intelligence' and culture. It was a per-

Table 1.1   Large cities of the world, by major region, 1800–1950

Region	Size-range	1800		1850		1900		1950	
		Number of cities by size-category							
Mediterranean,	(a)	-		-		-		9	
North Africa	(b)	1	15	1	21	5	36	8	48
and Middle East	(c)	14		20		31		31	
North Western	(a)	-		2		7		13	
and Central	(b)	2	9	-	28	8	96	21	82
Europe	(c)	7		26		81		48	
Eastern Europe	(a)	-		-		2		3	
and USSR	(b)	-	2	1	4	1	27	16	68
(Russia)	(c)	2		3		24		49	
	(a)	-		-		4		13	
North America	(b)	-	0	1	5	3	39	12	67
	(c)	-		4		32		42	
Latin America	(a)	-		-		-		7	
and the	(b)	-	1	-	4	2	12	5	37
Caribbean	(c)	1		4		10		25	
	(a)	-		-		-		1	
Sub-Saharan	(b)	-	0	-	0	-	3	1	9
Africa	(c)	-		-		3		7	
	(a)	-		-		-		2	
Australasia	(b)	-	0	-	0	-	4	-	7
	(c)	-		-		4		5	
South and	(a)	-		-		1		8	
South East	(b)	-	15	1	19	3	36	11	55
Asia	(c)	15		18		32		36	
	(a)	1		1		2		14	
Far East	(b)	2	23	4	25	5	46	11	61
	(c)	20		20		39		36	
	(a)	1		3		16		70	
WORLD TOTAL	(b)	5	65	8	106	27	299	85	434
	(c)	59		95		256		279	

The three size-categories are (a) over 1 million; (b) ½–1 million; and (c) 100,000–500,000 (1950, 200,000–500,000).

Source: Chandler and Fox, 1974

ceptive and prescient view: perceptive because it saw the challenge as well as the difficulties of rapid urban growth; prescient because it pointed to processes already sweeping through Europe which, he thought, were likely to become universal as 'The Anglo-American people [spread] rapidly from the pole to the equator, and from the Atlantic in the eastward to the Pacific in the westward . . . above all to that new land of promise . . . South Australia' (ibid., pp. 96–97) and which would, in Vaughan's view, maintain ' . . . the momentum which is now in action on the side of a progressive course of things . . . the great tendency of modern society toward the formation of great cities' (ibid., p. 100).

That phase of European hegemony – political, commercial and industrial – was reflected in its growing status amongst the world's great cities over the next century. Whereas in 1800 large European cities were still exceeded by those of the Orient (table 1.1), by 1850 they had moved ahead in numbers and by 1900, in both numbers and aggregate size, they dominated the composition and ranking of their respective urban hierarchies, as Weber's statistical tables clearly show. In both the size-range and the proportion of their populations living in large cities, the European world was far ahead of other culture areas, notwithstanding the beginnings of rapid modernization and urbanization in Japan. In England – the most urbanized country in the world – four-fifths of the population were urban-dwellers: moreover in both the United States and Australia the rapidity of city growth is striking testimony to the increasing dominance of modern, industrialized, Western society by city life in which towns were 'fast becoming the "prime producers" of wealth in the world' (Vance, 1977, p. 356).

Nowhere is the transformation more apparent than in the structure of the 'top 100' cities of the continents as identified by Chandler and Fox (1974) (table 1.2). In 1800, 34 of Asia's 100 largest cities had populations of over 100,000 as compared with 22 in Europe; by 1850, the proportions were roughly equal (at 45 and 49, respectively); but by 1900, Europe had 57 towns of over 200,000 as against 40 in Asia, while 'Europe overseas' in the Americas and Australasia had another 30. By 1950, the size and number of large towns in Europe and the USSR had greatly increased, not least due to the surge of urban growth in the Soviet Union after the revolution: of 184 cities of over 200,000 population, 23 had more than one million inhabitants and 41 between one-half and one million. The Americas, too, had become a society largely dominated by 'million cities' – 13 in North America and 7 in Latin America – and with 100 or so towns of over 200,000, reflecting in particular the surge in North American manufacturing industry and commerce.

The dominance of the world map of large cities in 1850 by Western Europe and the north-eastern USA persisted into the mid-twentieth century. In the mid-nineteenth century, the largest cities were generally the capitals and big commercial centres, especially the great ports, but there were many large industrial towns on the coalfields (figure 1.1). Linked by a growing network of inland waterways and, in this age of steam, by railways, a new urban-focused way of life was spreading across large areas of Western Europe and north-east America, already pointing to the emerging conurbations of the early twentieth century. As Halford Mackinder acutely observed:

Table 1.2   The 'top 100' cities over 10,000 by continent, 1500–1950

Continent		1500	1800	1850	1900	1950
EUROPE	a	-	3	4	22	23
and	b	6	19	45	35	41
RUSSIA/	c	63	78	51	43	36
USSR	d	31	-	-	-	-
	a	-	-	-	7	13
NORTH	b	-	-	1	13	12
AMERICA	c	-	-	5	16	42
	d	-	4	11	54	-
LATIN	a	-	-	-	2	7
AMERICA	b	1	1	5	5	5
and the	c	4	18	16	7	25
CARIBBEAN	d	2	5	NA	31	-
	a	-	3	6	11	22
ASIA	b	2	31	39	29	24
	c	13	66	55	50	54
	d	64	-	-	10	-
	a	-	-	-	1	3
AFRICA	b	2	3	2	1	3
	c	18	14	29	6	14
	d	2	8	7	11	-
	a	-	-	-	-	2
AUSTRALASIA	b	-	-	-	2	1
	c	-	-	1	2	4
	d	-	-	1	7	-

The 100 cities over 10,000 population are shown in four size-categories: 1500–1850 a = ½ million, b = 100,000 – ½ million, c = 25–100,000, d = 10–25,000 (1850, 20–25,000); for 1900 a, b, c and d are, respectively, over ½ million, 200,000–½ million, 100–200,000 and under 100,000 (minimum in Europe and Russia 126,000); and for 1950 over 1 million, ½–1 million and 200,000–½ million, respectively. The minimum size within the 'top 100' in 1900 was 89,000 in Asia and 126,000 in Europe; and in 1950 241,000 for Asia and 328,000 for Europe.
NA = not available
Source   T. Chandler and G. Fox, 1974. Supplementary data for Australasia from Weber (1899) and Briggs (1963)

In a manner all south-eastern England is a single urban community; for steam and electricity are changing our geographical conceptions. A city in an economic sense is no longer an area covered continuously with streets and houses. The wives and children of the merchants, even of the more prosperous of the artisans, live without – beyond green fields – where the men only sleep and pass the Sabbath. The metropolis in its largest meaning included all the counties for whose inhabitants London is 'Town', whose men do habitual business there, whose women buy there, whose morning paper is printed there, whose standard of thought is determined there. [Mackinder, 1915, p. 258]

That metropolitan tendency – which Mackinder identified in what he called 'metropolitan England' – was increasingly dominated by commerce and business providing goods and services to ever-increasing city-regions linked in a complex fashion by expanding rail and, from the early twentieth century, road commuter networks. The era of the great industrial town was passing. The focusing of industry into highly specialized regions and centres of production – Bradford for worsted; Halifax for heavy woollens; Bolton or Lille for cotton; Sheffield or Solingen for steel – which characterized the first industrial revolution was giving way to more diverse patterns of industrial location, progressively freed from close dependence on coal to fuel the steam-powered factories by easily transportable electricity, and geared to wide markets for mass-production, consumer industries.

That transition is well observed by Peter Hall (chapter 2) and, in the particular case of Manchester, by Gareth Shaw (chapter 5). It gave advantage to the larger cities with more diverse, market-oriented industries, new sources of labour, especially semi-skilled machine operatives and, increasingly, female factory workers, and green field or suburban sites with space and road access for the assembly lines of the Fordist era. The ensuing sprawl of large cities in which cheap rapid rail transport and then the automobile broke the close nineteenth-century relationship between workplace and residence gave access for many more people to suburban living and posed new problems of regional as opposed to city planning (Cherry, chapter 3). But it also brought more into contact with the cultural and entertainment amenities which large cities alone can provide (Robson, chapter 4) while allowing city-dwellers to escape to the recreation of the country and seaside. It is not surprising, therefore, that planners thought in terms of city regions (Geddes, 1915) and that these became the focus for a substantially expanded urban geography in which 'urban fields' and accessibility to cities for work, shopping and services reflected the changing scale and function of towns and their relationships to one another (Smailes, 1953; Dickinson, 1947).

At the head of their respective urban hierarchies the major metropolitan centres – national and regional – were nearly all cities of over 500,000 by 1900 and they and their urbanized hinterlands frequently exceeded one million population. By 1950, cities of this size were commonplace and, more significantly, were distributed much more widely throughout the world's major settlement areas (figure 1.2). Not only were the great Western European and North American conurbations in excess of one million with a number – New York, London, Paris, Chicago, the Ruhr – over four million, but many cities of rapid early twentieth-century growth had joined them – Tokyo, Shanghai, Moscow, Buenos Aires and

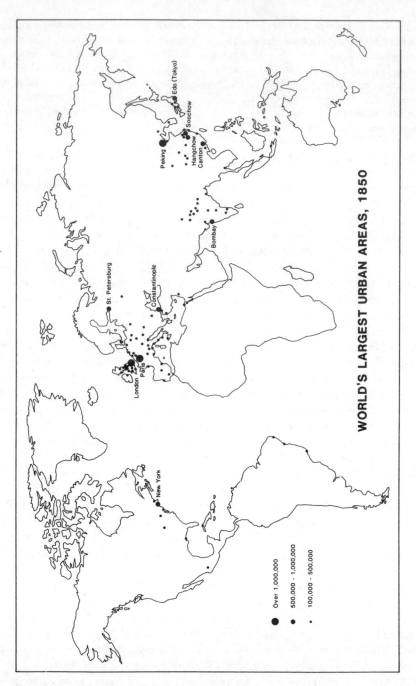

Figure 1.1 Great cities of the world *circa* 1850. Cities of over 100,000 are shown in three size-groups. *Source:* Based on T. Chandler and G. Fox, 1974 'Data sheets' pp. 20–68 and 'World's largest cities', p. 328

Calcutta, to mention only those with more than four million inhabitants. The intense urbanization of the southern hemisphere's areas of European settlement had produced six 'million cities' in Latin America, two in Australia and one in South Africa. In the third world a combination of an older-established commercialization associated with European-induced trade and industry and a swelling tide of migration from the crowded countryside had generated seemingly uncontrollable urban growth and the beginnings of a progressive Europeanization in which Japan led the way. Indeed, by 1950 South and South-East Asia and the Far East had almost as many cities over one million as Europe, the Mediterranean and the USSR combined (table 1.1). Hence the emphasis in city growth has inexorably shifted from the developed to the developing world where, over the past fifty years, the accelerating growth of city populations has outstripped even its own explosive general population increase. Secondly, in Western cities growth rates have slowed, with a catastrophic fall in the number of inhabitants of what we have come to call the 'inner city', and a widespread dispersal of people and work to the outer areas of city regions and, from the 1970s, into their rural periphery. This may well be a phase of counter-urbanization, as discussed for Europe by Tony Fielding in chapter 9, which has been more pronounced in North America, according to Brian Berry (1976); but it may represent, rather, a new form of urbanism as Jean Gottman implies (chapter 11).

The mega-cities of the late twentieth and twenty-first centuries are taking shape principally in the developing world. They exhibit, in a frequently heightened intensity and rate of change, many of the problems which characterized Western cities in the nineteenth century: under- and unemployment; homelessness; shortage of public utilities; problems of health and sanitation; crowded residential and working conditions; polluted environments; and the continuing pressure of population on public services, such as schools, hospitals and transport, and private amenity (above all space for the individual family) alike.

While forecasting of demographic and socio-economic trends in the rapidly evolving societies of the developing world is hazardous, there is little doubt that there, in contrast to the falling populations of large cities in developed countries, people continue to flood into the cities. The combined force of intensive, often nation-wide, migration from the countryside and peripheral regions to the core metropolitan areas and of high national growth among their youthful populations is putting third world cities under intense physical, economic and psychological pressure and severely testing the political process in often unstable societies. In 1980 there were more million cities (119) in the developing than the developed world (103) containing, in each area, around one-third of the total urban population. Over the next half century that proportion is expected to remain about the same in the developed areas but to increase to nearly one-half in the developing areas (Habitat, 1987, p. 29, table 3.3 and figure 3.2). Moreover, the number of very large cities of over four million people is likely to rise to 114 in developing countries (out of a world total of 135), nearly 30 per cent of their urban population, in contrast to a decline in such cities in developed areas, especially Europe and North America, to around one-eighth of the total in cities (figure 1.3).

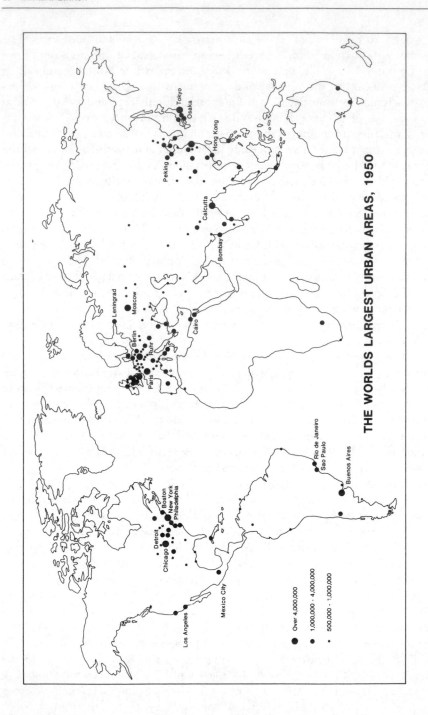

Figure 1.2 Great cities of the world *circa* 1950. Cities of over 500,000 are shown in three size-groups. *Source*: Chandler and Fox, *ibid.*, pp. 337–38

**URBAN POPULATION INCREMENT
1955-2015 (MILLIONS)**

**URBAN POPULATION TRENDS BY REGION
1950-2025 (MILLIONS)**

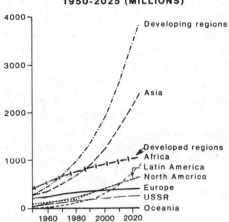

**PERCENTAGE OF URBAN POPULATION
IN 1+ MILLION CITIES, 1960-2025**

**PERCENTAGE OF URBAN POPULATION
IN 4+ MILLION CITIES, 1960-2025**

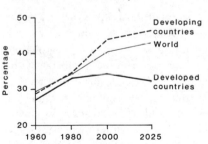

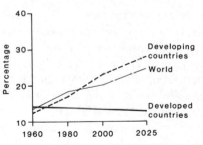

Figure 1.3 Urban growth *circa* 1960–2025
(**top left**) Urban population increment in developed and developing countries in 15-year periods 1955–2015
(**top right**) Urban population trends by region, developed and developing countries 1950–2025
(**bottom left**) Percentage of urban-dwellers in cities of over 1 million, developed and developing countries and world-wide 1960–2025
(**bottom right**) Percentage urban-dwellers in cities over 4 million 1960–2025
Source: Based on Habitat, 1987, *Global Report on Human Settlements*. United Nations Centre for Human Settlements (Habitat), New York, figs 1, 2a and b, 3.2 and 3.3

The change in rank order of world cities since mid-century has been striking. The New York metropolitan area fell from first to second between 1960 and 1980 but, with a virtually stagnant population, is likely to rank only sixth by the year 2000. London, already in sixth place as compared with second in 1960, is unlikely to be in the top 25 cities by 2000. Of the great 'western' cities, only Tokyo is likely to grow significantly in population (from 18 to over 20 million) and to retain the third place it held in 1960 but be displaced from its present leading position by either Sâo Paulo or Mexico City. Indeed, whereas in 1980 only three of the ten mega-cities of over 10 million were in the developing countries, by the year 2000 of 22 such cities '. . . all but 4 . . . will be in developing countries. The largest, Mexico City and Sâo Paulo, could have populations of around 25 million' (Habitat, 1987, pp. 29–30).

It is in the developing world that the population of large cities is growing faster than that of urban areas as a whole and the gap between the largely-urbanized developed world that at present accounts for two-thirds in the least and nine-tenths in the most urbanized areas and the still mainly rural developing world (Latin America excepted) is narrowing rapidly. Indeed, Latin America, with two-thirds of its population in towns, is more urbanized than some developed countries. But even Africa, until recently the least urbanized continent, and Asia – still dominated by village life not least in India and China – are likely to have half their populations in cities by the third decade of the twenty-first century. How these new citizens – an extra 2700 million of them – will be fed, housed and employed is one of the greatest challenges of our time and our children's time.

Historical problems and contemporary issues

This vast problem lies outside the immediate scope of this book. Our focus is on the stagnant, in some ways declining, cities of the West, particularly those of Western Europe and North America. Though the questions posed by their rapid growth in the nineteenth and early twentieth centuries *may* be relevant for many of the problems of third world cities in the late twentieth and twenty-first centuries, they are unlikely to offer solutions to – or even policies for – cities of different cultural, economic and technological contexts in which the scale of population, social and environmental problems is of a different, and much higher order than that experienced by even the largest of Western cities during their peak of growth.

Yet, as Lewis Mumford (1961, p. 11) has rightly observed, 'If we would lay a new foundation for urban life, we must understand the historic nature of the city'. And it is in the large industrial, commercial and political centres of Europe and its overseas dependencies that 'modern' cities emerged, not least the metropolitan and megalopolitan centres that are the most striking features of twentieth-century urbanism. Here, according to many commentators, can be seen the seeds of decay and potential collapse, due not least to a poverty of leadership which has failed to produce imaginative ideas and policies to renew their vibrancy and excitement as places in which to live and work. Yet given the opportunity and, perhaps, freed from unsympathetic and inappropriate corporate planning, city-dwellers themselves could well reinvest 'Dull inert cities [that] contain the seeds of their own destruction and little else' with the drive and initiative coming from ' . . . lively, diverse, intense cities [that] contain the seeds of their own regeneration, with energy enough to carry over for problems and needs outside themselves' (Jacobs, 1961, p. 462).

There is nothing new in this dilemma. Rome, Constantinople, medieval Paris and, more recently, the great cities of Victorian Britain were prey to disease, poverty, overcrowding, and social and political instability from within, let alone from the barbarian at the gate. Often relatively newly established, the large cities of the industrial revolution grew so fast as industry, trade and communications created new bases for rapidly-increasing populations that they experienced many of the old problems in intensified form, but also encountered many new ones. Acute economic, environmental, social, political and moral crises engendered great ambivalence in the minds of many contemporaries and, as in ancient times, for many the city was – and has continued to be – a place of decadence, a modern Sodom and Gomorrah: the real strength of society, the true *Wealth of Nations*, was in the countryside.

For others – the young and ambitious, the innovative and creative, the seekers after wealth and power – the city was the hub of life, a place of progress and pleasure where people could escape from the constrictions of an established rural order into a more flexible, opportunistic society with possibilities of advancement. It was also a place of risk: risks of poverty in a competitive labour market; of loss of identity in a class-structured, secular society; of hazards to health in poor housing and environments; of loneliness and isolation away from kith and kin. This ambivalence remains, though now manifest in the desire to escape from the stress of the city into an alluring – if unreal – rural idyll. Is this a portent of the death of great cities or, as Brian Robson (chapter 4) and Jean Gottman (chapter 11) argue, a challenge to their remaking in the context of changing patterns of production and communication and the new lifestyles of the late twentieth century, a challenge to which, arguably, the city beautiful, the garden city and suburb, the modernist vision of the skyscraper and cities in the sky and the spreading commuter suburbs of the earlier twentieth century are no longer regarded as providing satisfactory answers.

The processes involved in these questions of city organization – economic, social and physical – are still those identified in many studies of the major metropolitan centres of the late nineteenth and twentieth centuries as summarized by Jean Gottman (1978): demographic forces, especially the relationships between natural and migrational trends; economic forces affecting standards of living (and affordable space) and modes of employment, especially with the shift from manufacturing to services, not least those of the specialist quaternary sector; technological change and its impact on both the centralizing and decentralizing tendencies of transport and modes of production; and cultural variation – the most difficult to measure but that which ultimately shapes the values and attitudes of urban societies and the design and appearance of cities.

I shall not attempt to summarize – merely to highlight – discussion of these processes as they feature in the following chapters. These fall into four main, but overlapping, sections. Chapters 2–4 are concerned with the transition from the great cities of the late nineteenth century to those of the present with an emphasis on economic, population, planning and societal change. Chapters 5–8 deal with some of the (largely) historical problems of the emergent great cities: employment structure and the location of economic activity, with its consequences for urban land use (Shaw); the demographic problems of providing the supply of people for the city in the face of high mortality and low fertility (Woods) reflected in the dependence of the city on the countryside for recruitment of much of its labour force and – in the view of some commentators – for the reinvigoration of its stock; the burning issues of adequately providing for sanitation and health of rapidly growing, overcrowded populations with sharp social and economic cleavages and the political and moral, as well as economic, issues raised by the 'sanitary problem' (Kearns); the enormous strain of providing adequate housing, especially for the poorer working class (Pooley).

Chapters 9 and 10 are concerned with the changing role and structure of the twentieth-century cities in terms of both urban form and regional relationships in the face of greatly-changed patterns of mobility, workplace and residence, and the growth of a leisure society with national and even international horizons (Fielding); a feature, too, of the modern city economy in which both technological and organizational innovation and the global integration of information, economic activity, skilled technical and business workforces, and financial markets are combining to favour a few major international centres but where there will be, perhaps, more losers than gainers among the older regional capitals of Europe and North America (Goddard).

These are not, of course, separate issues. They are interdependent in time and space and the ways in which they reflect the complex interplay of forces which have both shaped the evolution of modern western cities and which underlie many of their current problems. Thus Peter Hall (chapter 2) finds in the turbulence and economic and social malaise of the cities of the 1980s a counterpart of the not dissimilar anxieties of the 1880s, reflecting the waxing and waning of long waves of economic and technological change also noted by Gareth Shaw (chapter 5). In the sprawling cities of the 1920s and 1930s, with ominous signs of decay in their pre-First World War cores, Gorden Cherry (chapter 3) shows the failure of permissive planning legislation to get to grips with problems of land-use, transportation and integrated regional planning. Despite failures pointed out by Lewis Mumford (1961) and Jane Jacobs (1961), planning has achieved much, not only in the control of urban form but in regulating standards of housing, environment and working conditions and in seeking to balance – however imperfectly – the interests of competing groups within the city and between city and countryside (whether by restriction of urban dominance or through integrated regional planning). But some form of planning also continues to be vital for health provision, as Gerry Kearns shows (chapter 7), and for stimulating and shaping economic activity as John Goddard implies in chapter 10 and has forcibly argued in relation to the regeneration of Britain's northern cities (*The Times*, 10th April 1989, p. 3).

People are central to the vitality and future of the city. They must, as Brian Robson argues (chapter 4), *all* be involved – individually and collectively – if the life, work and culture of our great cities are to survive and be reinvigorated. The corporatism of the 1950s and 1960s did not succeed in that task and is unlikely to do so without more flexibility in planning and government which will allow for individual initiatives and responsibility, not least at the level of the local community. It is essential, too, to open opportunities to *all* sectors of society – black and white, better-off and poor – through better access to facilities for education, work training, recreational and cultural activity, and above all, to financial resources. Only thus will the present 'poverty in prosperity', the gulf between inner city deprivation and outer suburban wealth, between private affluence and public squalor be alleviated. Hall finds little new in this – it has been with us since the nineteenth century – but it will demand both political will and individual commitment to correct it in the interest of both social justice and national well-being.

The economies of regional cities of the late nineteenth century described by Shaw (chapter 5) were very different from those of the global cities of the late twentieth century outlined by Hall (chapter 2) and Goddard (chapter 10). Legacies from the past – physical, economic, and social – are among the chief impediments to their rehabilitation, though they may offer in old mills or refurbished waterfronts a heritage industry to add new dimensions to their activities in an age of increasing leisure.

Their demographic heritage is very different from the excess mortality but deficient fertility which led cities to rely on migration to provide growth well into the nineteenth century (Woods, chapter 6). Now, stagnation and decline are more the result of ageing populations and declining fertility, a far cry from the mushrooming city populations of the developing world. This brings a twist to the age-old rural/urban demographic complementarity in which shortages of labour in the factories and more menial service jobs in the 1950s and 1960s brought immigration from the developing world and from the poorer to the richer countries of Western Europe just as a baby boom was leading to a period of higher natural growth. The reaction against such 'new citizens' in the growing labour surplus and unemployment of the 1970s and 1980s may well be moderated in the face of renewed labour shortages in the 1990s, though the emphasis is more likely to be on skilled labour – especially in the information and knowledge industries – of an international migratory élite as Goddard and Gottman both indicate.

Nevertheless, while big cities are no longer a graveyard as well as a place of opportunity, they remain more hazardous than rural areas, psychologically and physically, just as they were at the time of the public health debates of the nineteenth century (Kearns, chapter 7). Whereas the environmentalist debate has changed in nature, cities still levy a considerable toll in higher morbidity and mortality. Though preventive and curative medicine avoid their payment of the full cost (in both the developed and developing world), they may be put further at risk, as Kearns argues, by the current political debate in many Western countries over market forces in the pricing of natural monopolies and the debate over private *versus* public management of environmental, health and social services.

In one significant area of that debate, housing, the nineteenth century failed to come to grips with the problem which, as Colin Pooley shows (chapter 8), was tackled with full vigour only from the 1920s. That problem has not ended with the apparent matching of housing supply to household needs. Problems of unequal demand, of access to housing, and of poverty create gaps in provision in both capitalist and socialist cities and in the private and public sector. The problem is reflected in a spate of literature in the 1970s and 1980s, in growing homelessness in major cities – the many sleeping rough on subway grids in New York, under railway arches in London, or on park benches in Sydney. The purchase, even the renting, of a decent home is still beyond the means of many in the unfairly structured societies of the large cities of the world (Badcock, 1984, especially Part III). There is need for more and better-distributed resources to provide greater equity in the housing market: and there are warnings, as well as lessons, for the developing world from the Western experience.

For many more prosperous citizens, however, housing choice has progressively widened from the first suburban rail and then tramway networks of the nineteenth century, making possible the divorce of home and workplace. In Belgium, for example, cheap railway passes increased from some 14,000 in 1870 to 6.4 million by 1908, permitting many urban workers to retain their rural residences and to commute daily or weekly (Vandenbroeke and Deprez, 1989, table 10.8). Typical of many great cities, London's commuter hinterland was 65–80 km (40–50 miles) across by 1961 when 1¼ million people travelled daily to work in central London and the total inward commuter flow to all metropolitan boroughs was nearly two million, 75 per cent of their workforce (Lawton, 1967). Since then the scale and complexity of daily travel – to work, school, shopping and recreation – has greatly increased. In a highly mobile society, the outer limits of city regions are extending greatly with 'de-urbanization' reflected in falling populations in both inner cities and many of their early twentieth century suburbs (Fielding, chapter 9). Whether that decline represents true 'counter-urbanization' with a return of both people and jobs to small towns and rural areas or new forms of more widely-spread urbanization in more loosely-knit metropolitan areas is more debatable. It certainly reflects changes in the location of some small industries and services and has affected housing markets up to 200 kms (125 miles) from major cities like London. In a more mobile society access to motorways and fast inter-city trains may carry one 100 kms (60 miles) in the time it takes to drive from the suburbs to the centre of large cities. But to what extent such de-centralization may spell the end of the modern city is uncertain.

Uncertain futures

That the nature of large cities has changed and continues to change is clear. From the late nineteenth century major metropolitan centres increasingly have become transactional cities. The typewriter, the telephone, the internationalization of business and politics – while but harbingers of the mass communication and information technology revolutions of the late twentieth century – set in motion a transformation of Western-style cities. The essence of these 'modes of life', as Jean Gottmann (1978) has persuasively argued, is the shift from manufacturing industry and even some of the basic service industries to a quaternary sector of informational and high-order services. These reflect changes in the forces shaping urban growth – demographic, economic, technological and cultural – and are reflected in the jobs, tastes and lifestyles, and action spaces of their inhabitants. The interpretation of the impact of such recent, far-reaching changes has given rise to considerable speculation and controversy (as Gottmann shows in his conclusion to this volume, chapter 11). Does the de-centralization of industry described by Peter Hall (chapter 2) and, more recently, apparent in certain commercial activities, as indicated by John Goddard (chapter 10), betoken a break-up of modern cities into a post-industrial, post-modernist society leaving our big cities vulnerable to social and political breakdown, as Brian Robson debates (chapter 4)? Or will we see transitions to new forms and patterns of urban livelihood and living, with more flexible relationships between work and leisure already reflected in changes in residential patterns and population distribution? Will the 'greening' of the urban economy benefit the cause only of inner-city gentrification, or will the spin-offs help the cause of employment and rehabilitation of inner-city working-class areas?

John Goddard sees hope of continuing strength in such major city economies as those of New York and London despite strong challenges from Tokyo and such relative newcomers as Singapore and Hong Kong. Many cities in South-East Asia and Latin America now operate on three levels: as traditional centres of indigenous culture with distinctive craft industries, cultural monuments, and touristically attractive townscapes; as outliers of international industry with cheap labour for the manufacture of textiles, clothing and consumer, especially electrical, goods; but also as sophisticated Western-style cities with growing international hotel and shopping complexes and business centres. Such cities as Bangkok and Singapore figure on the routes of major international airlines and are recent additions to the network of world cities, as Jean Gottmann shows (chapter 11).

They also reflect the internationalization of capitalist economies. With the progressive collapse of distance by modern communications, multi-national corporations have extended their operations to take advantage of low-cost production on a world-wide basis, to the loss of manufacturing throughout the West. Developments in the information economy, such as computer networking and on-line information systems, feed into a globally-integrated system described by John Goddard which will tend to place further power in the hands of large corporations and in fewer cities. Will this benefit the West, given its control of important financial institutions and of the dominant language of business, or shall we see a similar surrender of leadership of the quaternary sector to new leaders in Japan or, even, Singapore as that in much of secondary industry? Will we, indeed, see two types of mega-city: giants of international high-tech and information technology in advanced nations; and centres of secondary activity with a big informal sector in third world countries? Or will the cities of the future be part of a globally integrated system, the coming world city or Ecumenopolis envisaged by Constantinos Doxiadis (1968) (see also Toynbee, 1970), dominated by a few super-cities but also containing many large industrial and service centres, the home for an increasing proportion of the people of all regions (Dogan and Kasarda, 1988)?

The form taken by individual cities will depend not only on economic forces (as indicated by Hall, chapter 2) but the political philosophies and administrative controls which shape their planning (Cherry, chapter 3) and the will of governments and society to make them succeed (Robson, chapter 4). Accessibility to and from their immediate hinterlands (Fielding, chapter 9) as well as within the international system discussed by Goddard and Gottmann will also surely be reflected in their landscapes and structure. These may become more complex but, perhaps, more Western-dominated in concept, style and culture. It would, however, be a pity further to diminish regional identity in a world crying out for the enrichment brought by cultural diversity.

One key to the structure of future cities, as indicated by Hall and Gottmann but not the subject of a special essay in this book, is that of mobility. It would be ironic if transportation, which nurtured large modern cities and enabled them to break the bonds of distance, were to prove inadequate for its future task. Frequent reports of traffic congestion, with tailbacks of up to 25 km (15 miles) on London's M25, reduced average speeds of movement in large cities since the turn of the century, and suburban and underground railway systems under pressure, notably in London, are an unhappy augury (Hall, 1989). On the other hand, the inauguration of mass transit systems has done much to ease accessibility and improve the urban environment in cities such as San Francisco, Toronto, Washington, Moscow, Tokyo and, most recently, Singapore (Hall, 1988). In such matters, important for urban regeneration and growth, political will and a balance between private amenity and public good will continue to be as essential for shaping the future of great cities as they have been in guiding their past, as many of our contributors show.

References

Badcock, B. (1984), *Unfairly Structured Cities*, Basil Blackwell, Oxford.
Berry, J.B.L. (1976), 'The counterurbanization process: urban America since 1970', in B.J.L. Berry (ed.), *Urbanization and Counterurbanization*, Sage, Beverly Hills.
Bobek, H. (1962), 'The main stages in socio-economic evolution from a geographical point of view', in P.L. Wagner and M.W. Mikesell (eds), *Readings in Cultural Geography*, University of Chicago Press.
Briggs, A. (1963), *Victorian Cities*, Odhams Press.
Chandler, T. and Fox, G. (1974), *3000 Years of Urban Growth*, Academic Press, New York.
de Vries, J. (1984), *European Urbanization 1500–1800*, Methuen.
Dickinson, R.E. (1947) *City, Region and Regionalism*, Routledge, Oxford.
Dogan, M. and Kasarda, J.D. (eds) (1988), *The Metropolis Era* (2 vols). See especially *Vol. 1: A World of Great Cities*, Sage, Beverly Hills.

Doxiadis, C.A. (1968), *Ekistics – an Introduction to the Science of Human Settlements*, Hutchinson.

Finlay, R.A.P. (1981), *Population and Metropolis: the demography of London, 1580–1650*, Cambridge University Press.

Geddes, P. (1915), *Cities in Evolution*, Ernest Benn.

Gottmann, J. (1978), *Forces Shaping Cities: A Jubilee Lecture*, Department of Geography, University of Newcastle upon Tyne.

Habitat (1987), *Global Report on Human Settlements 1986*, UN Centre for Human Settlements, Oxford University Press, New York.

Hall, P. (1988) *Cities of Tomorrow*, Basil Blackwell, Oxford.

Hall, P. (1989) *London: 2001*, Unwin Hyman.

Harvey, D. (1985a), *The Urbanization of Capital*, Basil Blackwell, Oxford.

Harvey, D. (1985b), *Consciousness and the Urban Experience*, Basil Blackwell, Oxford.

Hohenberg, P. and Lees, L.H. (1985), *The Making of Urban Europe 1000–1950*, Harvard University Press, Cambridge, Mass.

Jacobs, J. (1961), *The Death and Life of Great American Cities. The Failure of Town Planning*, Random House, New York (Pelican Books, 1965).

Lawton, R. (1967), 'The journey to work in Britain: some trends and problems', *Regional Studies*, 2, 27–40.

Mackinder, H.J. (1915), *Britain and the British Seas* (2nd edn, reprinted; 1st edn, 1902), The Clarendon Press, Oxford.

Mumford, L. (1961), *The City in History*, Secker and Warburg (Pelican Books, 1966), especially chapters 16–18.

Sjoberg, G. (1960), *The Preindustrial City: Past and Present*, The Free Press, New York.

Smailes, A.E. (1953), *The Geography of Towns*, Hutchinson.

The Times (4 April 1989) 'Spectrum: 1979–89 the British Revolution? A fragile prosperity'.

Toynbee, A. (1970), *Cities on the Move*, Oxford University Press.

Vance, J.E., Jr. (1977), *This Scene of Man. The Role and Structure of the City in the Geography of Western Civilisation*, Harper's College Press, New York.

Vandenbroeke, C. and Deprez, P. (1989) 'Population growth, population distribution and the urbanization of Belgium during the period of the demographic transition', chapter 13 of R. Lawton and W.R. Lee (eds), *Comparative Urban Population Development in Western Europe from the Late-eighteenth to the Early-twentieth Century*, University of Liverpool Press.

Vaughan, R. (1842), *The Age of Great Cities*, reprinted by the Woburn Press, 1969.

Weber, A.F. (1899), *The Growth of Cities in the Nineteenth Century. A study in statistics*, Cornell University Press, New York (reissued 1965).

Weber, M. (1958), *The City* (translated and edited by D. Martindale and G. Neuwirth), The Free Press, New York.

Wheatley, P. (1969), *City as Symbol*. An inaugural lecture, University College London.

2 The rise and fall of great cities: economic forces and population responses

Peter Hall

People, not least geographers, worry a great deal nowadays about the fate of great cities. Many of them always have done. They were worrying about them fifty years ago, when a group of IBG members met to prepare evidence to what was originally known as the Royal Commission on the Geographical Distribution of the Industrial Population (Taylor et al. 1938). And, as Andrew Lees has reminded us in his recent book *Cities Perceived*, some – especially in Europe, less so in the United States – were worrying about them a century and more ago (Lees, 1985). The central question must be: what is new? Are we hearing the same record all over again? Despite the monumental economic changes of the last hundred years, is it true that the world's great cities suffer from permanent economic and social malaise which simply manifests superficially new symptoms from time to time? Or are there new features that represent a novel threat to the vitality of the great cities?

Let us start, then, in the world cities of a century ago. As Lees and many others have eloquently testified, from 1885–90 there was a perceived urban crisis that makes our present discontents seem positively wimpish: a real fear in every city – in London and Paris, in Berlin and New York – of the perceived threat from the submerged urban underclass. The Parisian working class had been decisively defeated in the uprising of 1871, and – as David Harvey reminds us – the Third Republic determinedly worked to expunge all record of it (Harvey, 1985). But in Chicago, the Haymarket Riots of 1886 – culmination of a bitterly fought strike – culminated in the execution and martyrdom of four of the leaders; and in London, after months of marches and rioting, on Bloody Sunday (13 October, 1887) the unemployed fought with police in Trafalgar Square and invaded the service at Westminster Abbey (Stedman Jones, 1971; Wohl, 1977; Hall 1984a, 1988). In every city, respectable newspapers contained dire warnings of the imminent breakdown of society. In comparison with the 1880s, the 1980s are a tranquil decade indeed.

London's economy starts to fail

Yet there are strange similarities. The troubles in London were the result of a deep depression in the British economy, which prompted the appointment of a Royal Commission. It concluded that the problem was not merely the trade cycle, but a structural weakness in British industry compared with its major competitors, above all Germany: Britain was losing its hold on traditional markets and was failing to win new ones, and the reputation of British workmanship was not as good as it was. Despite the forebodings of some witnesses, trade unions and labour disputes were not the cause, so the Commissioners determined (R.C. into the Depression . . . , 1886).

The real problem, as emerged in the course of a great national debate over the following two decades, was the failure to make the critical transition to a new stage of industrial production. Britain's industrial leadership, the basis of her early urbanization, was based on innovations in the first hundred years of the industrial age: what Schumpeter (1939) called the first Kondratieff long wave of cotton and iron and the second Kondratieff of steam and steel. It faltered at the start of the third wave, 'the Kondratieff of electricity, chemistry and motors', which he dated from 1898 (ibid., p. 170). This wave had two key characteristics. First, the new industries were based on systematic applied research and development. Secondly, and associatedly, they involved a quantum leap in the scale of production: though some of the critical techniques had been developed several decades earlier, in the engineering shops of the Connecticut Valley between 1840 and 1870, these were the first truly mass production industries.

In contrast, much of the industrial production of Britain still came either from small factories and workshops, or from larger units that specialized in one-off bespoke craft production as in the Tyne and Clyde shipyards. As Reyner Banham once put it, the average factory before 1914 had less power in it than a modern kitchen. But, as we need to remember, this was the characteristic mode of urban industrial production up to the 1880s not merely in London, but everywhere. The great metropolitan cities were dominated by small-scale artisan production, mostly catering for the demands of the metropolitan community and hidden away in small-scale workshops (Hall, 1962, 1987a; Roncayolo, 1987).

The new industries also happened to be urban, distinctively localized in great cities. Between 1870 and 1914 Berlin, the Philadelphia–New York–Boston corridor and Chicago became the great high-tech urban regions – the Silicon Valleys – of their day. They were distinguished by huge, often new production complexes that sometimes seemed to spring fully-fledged out of the ground, but that drew on the older craft-workshop tradition and on the unique supplies of skilled technical labour associated with it: such were Siemens and AEG in Berlin, and Bell-Western Electric in New York and Chicago. Only one, General Electric, moved early from the city to a smaller town, Schenectady, with the deliberate aim of avoiding the labour unions. The overwhelming reason for this concentration on large cities was that here were the great concentrations of research and development skills, here the reservoirs of skilled labour and the inherited technical capabilities, here the sources of venture capital. In such international competition, London – always the unique high-tech production centre of the British economy – lost out badly. Hamstrung by lack of government support in the form of higher technical education and research, as well as by a fragmented supply system, it failed grievously to compete in the new electrical industries; only in the 1930s, with early advances in electronics, did it begin to catch up (Hall and Preston, 1988).

The overwhelmingly powerful image of the London economy in these years, is already therefore of a failure to compete on the world stage. Indeed, in some ways the economy remained almost pre-industrial, dominated by small weakly-capitalized workshop industries clustered in traditional industrial quarters, and relying either on traditional artisan craft skills or on an immigrant lumpenproletariat who formed a literal ghetto labour force. We must not exaggerate this, because similar traditions can be found in Berlin or in New York; indeed, from 1880 to 1914 those cities absorbed poor immigrants from Eastern Europe at a far higher rate than ever London did. The critical difference was that in London the workshop economy continued to dominate until the 1920s and 1930s, while in Berlin and New York the mass production economy continually gained on it. London still depended on its huge unskilled labour pool, constantly augmented by in-migration from the provinces, by the downwardly-mobile and by displaced soldiers and sailors, and which was trapped in the dense inner-city slums (Stedman Jones, 1971). The theory was that this was a permanent underclass, biologically unfit for work. Only the First World War, which rapidly emptied the workhouses, was to disprove that theory.

Yet, despite the depression of the 1930s, London's economy flourished between the wars. Belatedly, the newer mass-production industries of the third Kondratieff developed along the arterial roads of north and west London. They had an insatiable desire for semi-skilled labour, which could be filled by the sons and daughters of the workshop proletariat. Thus, as workshops failed to compete with larger-scale mass production – small Jewish workshops in Whitechapel and Bethnal Green were no match for Burton's giant suit factory in Leeds, or Harris Lebus's furniture factory in Tottenham – factories, some started by the more successful among the workshop entrepreneurs, took up the slack. By belatedly shifting into mass production, the London and Birmingham economies enjoyed relative prosperity throughout the depression, while Tyneside and Clydeside suffered.

Restrictions on alien immigration, coupled with a decline in movement from the countryside and a falling birth rate, meant that there was no longer a reservoir of unskilled labour. Similar factors may have aided the Berlin and New York economies too. Only one perceptive voice in the wilderness warned that the end of the era of urban mass production was nigh. In an extraordinary paper of 1925, entitled 'Dinosaur Cities', the American planner Clarence Stein warned that

when smaller centers are, in spite of their poorer financial and business facilities, able to make their industrial advantages felt, the great city's industries will have to migrate or face bankruptcy. We are still in the day of postponement; but the day of reckoning will come; and it behooves us to anticipate it [Stein, 1925, p. 138].

New patterns of location

That day was indeed postponed, for at least one good reason. The larger industrialists could obviate the disadvantages of the metropolis – traffic congestion, cramped sites – by moving to its periphery. In Berlin the great electrical concerns had pioneered this process even before the First World War: Siemens had gone north-west to build their model settlement Siemensstadt next to Spandau: AEG had gone in the opposite direction down the Spree to Oberschöneweide. The New York Regional Plan of 1927–31 actually encouraged the same process, in particular identifying the Hackensack meadows of New Jersey as a prime site for industrial deconcentration, and thereby earning the undying hostility of Stein and his fellow-members of the Regional Plan Association of America. In London the same process produced the new factory zones along the arterial roads of west and north London, which so much alarmed the equivalent group of planners there. Everywhere it was the successful high-tech firms of the day – above all in the electrical and the infant electronic industry – that led this process. Already, fifty to seventy years ago, we can see the critical distinction between the general metropolitan economies of agglomeration, which continued to operate through education, research and development, and – often enough – government defence contracting, and the micro-economics of location, which, as they grew, drove larger and some smaller firms to the metropolitan periphery.

In a recent series of seminal papers Allen Scott has embodied these historical processes in a new synthetic theory of metropolitan industrial location (Scott, 1982; 1983; 1985) in which, beginning around 1900 – the start of the third Kondratieff – inner-city areas have a comparative advantage for labour-intensive industries, peripheral areas for capital-intensive ones: what he calls a spatially-structured Heckscher-Ohlin effect (Scott, 1982). The labour-intensive complexes are characterized by division of labour, vertical disintegration of functions, specialized services and subcontracting, which – sometimes from very random origins – lock each of them into a 'self-confirming focus of specialised entrepreneurial activity', further cemented by the development of specialized skills and even an entire culture of production (Scott, 1985, p. 496). But, as this occurs, over time the complex creates barriers to its own further growth in the form of high land prices, union organization, high wages and what neoclassical economists distinguished as agglomeration diseconomies; and the more competitively-successful producers react by substituting capital for labour, increasing scale of production, internalizing externalities and escaping from the inner city to the periphery. As we have seen, this was already beginning to occur – in London, in Paris, in Berlin – around 1900.

The rise of the salariat

Labour-intensive industry was one main engine driving the metropolitan economies of the early twentieth century. The other was the early development of the white-collar service industries. However, caution is needed here. The steady growth of service employment in all advanced industrial countries, in which the great metropolitan cities led the way, was first commented on in the 1930s. Whilst service industry already accounted for close on 40 per cent of London workers as early as 1861 and 49 per cent in 1921 (Hall, 1962), many of these were casually employed industrial labourers; 25 per cent of London's labour force in the mid nineteenth century were in what we today call miscellaneous services, the great majority of them domestic servants; professional services, public administration and banking, insurance and finance – the major sources of white-collar employment – accounted for less than 10 per cent of the workforce in 1861, against perhaps 15 or 16 per cent just before the Second World War (Hall, 1962) and close on 40 per cent in 1981 (Hall, 1987a).

This early white-collar salariat resulted from the first stage of what, in Scott's eclectic location theory, is the other part of his metropolitan model: as production functions migrate outwards, other functions – financial, controlling, managing, relating to government – split off and are, from the beginning, heavily concentrated in central area offices. Each city (save for New York, which lacked an office quarter) had one distinctive financial district around the exchange and the major banks, and another in the governmental quarter. From the 1850s, a distinctive radial pattern of transportation evolved; from the 1880s onward, the new electrical technologies massively aided this process, allowing the new middle-class workforce to be drawn in from distant suburban villas. This process is very clear in London, Paris, Berlin and New York between 1890 and 1910. As Brian Robson (1986) has recently shown, at this time London began rapidly to gain dominance over the previously-autonomous provincial institutions for such functions: London banks began to dominate and take over the provincial ones; London media spread their tentacles to threaten and finally envelop provincial ones, a process massively aided by Reith's centralized BBC of the 1930s and, finally, by the virtual demise of the provincial daily press after World War Two.

As a result, segmented labour markets developed. Certain sectors and rings of the city, in a process later analysed precisely for American cities by Homer Hoyt (1939), became high-income areas linked to centrally-located jobs by radial public transport. Certain others – especially along rivers, railways and major highways – became the great industrial districts: in London, what Young and Willmott (1973) have called the Great Cross formed by the river and its tributaries the Lee and the Wandle; in Paris, the 'Red Belt' from Boulogne-Billancourt to Aubervilliers; in Berlin, the Spree from Spandau through Moabit to Wedding and then, on the other side of the city centre, downstream to Köpenick; in New York, the Jersey shore and the outer parts of Brooklyn and Queens. Here, local blue-collar labour markets developed, largely segregated from the mass metropolis-wide labour market of the white-collar workers, as Westergaard noticed long ago for London (Westergaard, 1957). And, within these same belts, the traditional inner-city working-class tenement and workshop districts – areas like Hackney and Tower Hamlets in London, the 11th and 19th and 20th *arrondissements* in Paris, the Kreuzberg area of Berlin, the Lower East Side of New York – continued as homes of an older style of production and an older, almost pre-industrial way of life: nineteenth-century industrial relics in the twentieth-century city.

The post Second World War era: new location patterns

Much of this urban structure has been rudely shattered since the Second World War. In one extreme case, Berlin, a whole urban economy has been divided and then effectively destroyed. Berlin is no longer, in any sense, one of the great high-tech industrial cities of the world; one of the two great combines that gave it that position has today vacated West Berlin altogether, leaving a series of abandoned industrial monuments plus a sorry-looking nationalized residue in the eastern half of the city. Governmental, financial and headquarters functions for a whole nation-state have gone elsewhere, save for the part that functions in East Berlin for the DDR, a small fraction of the former whole; Wilhelmstrasse, Berlin's Whitehall, is symbolically cut in half by the Wall.

Of course, Berlin's fate was unique. But London has suffered almost as grievously from world peace as Berlin did from world war. The performance of its economy in the 1970s was as bad as that of any of Britain's major provincial cities, despite the supposed resilience of its service sector. It lost nearly half a million workers, some 12 per cent of its labour force, between 1971 and 1981. Three-quarters of the loss was concentrated in Inner London, where the decrease of 15 per cent was exceeded only by Liverpool (Hall, 1987a). More extended analysis shows that between 1961 and 1984 London lost over 800,000 jobs, of which manufacturing losses made up the overwhelming majority (calculated from Buck et al., 1986). The authors of this analysis rightly comment that 'the problem of employment decline in London is a chronic one, which has been in operation for around a quarter of a century, and not an acute crisis induced by the recession of the late 1970s and 1980s' (ibid., p. 179). Contrary to popular myth, services have failed to compensate: in fact during many years in the 1970s, they too were shedding jobs. London has declined despite its over-representation in the 'growth' sectors of the service economy; its differential performance is therefore very bad indeed (ibid. p. 66).

The contrast with the New York economy is instructive. New York City – which can be regarded as somewhat comparable with Greater London – lost some 516,000 jobs during 1970–76, no less than 400,000 of them in the central business district which includes much of the old workshop manufacturing area (Hall, 1984b). But subsequently, from 1977 to 1983, it had a net gain of 159,000 jobs, whereas between 1978–83 London lost 314,000. The reasons were instructive: while New York continued to lose manufacturing jobs, it more than compensated by service job creation (256,000 against 108,000); London, in contrast, lost in both sectors (Hall, 1987b). Arguably, growth in services is now the key criterion of economic success or failure in the world's great cities.

These changes may be reinterpreted in terms of Scott's general model. He concludes that during the course of the twentieth century as capital intensification proceeded, and as capital-intensive firms moved outwards on a huge scale, there arose concomitant changes in the distribution of people and in the transportation infrastructure which changed the distribution of comparative locational advantages and thus the spatial form of the Heckscher-Ohlin function. Large, capital-intensive plants could operate effectively at increasing distances from the metropolitan core, and even right outside it. This process Edison initiated so uncannily in the 1880s when he located General Electric at Schenectady: nowadays large multi-national companies can increasingly locate whole processes and whole plants in cheap labour enclaves in newly industrializing countries.

Further, even the seedbed innovative function may transfer to the metropolitan periphery, as is evidenced by the development there of new agglomerative production complexes: Highway 128 outside Boston, Silicon Valley outside San Francisco, Orange County outside Los Angeles, or – on a more minute scale – the Western Crescent around London (Saxenian, 1985a, 1985b; Scott, 1986; Hall et al., 1987; Hall and Preston, 1988). As Scott shows in his case study of Orange County, such complexes display all the essential features of their nineteenth-century inner-city equivalents; the point is that they do not develop there. Instead, as Soja and his colleagues show for Los Angeles, the inner-city locales continue to nurse the relic sweatshop economy, fed by new generations of Third World immigrants (Soja et al., 1983; Soja, 1986; Scott, 1985). The same process can be seen in London's Whitechapel: over the past thirty years the classic clothing quarter has survived, but in the course of that time nearly all the Jewish names have been replaced by Bengali ones.

The critical role of services

The critical point, however, is not what is happening in inner city industrial areas, but what is happening to the service functions which survive in the metropolitan core. The work of Stanback and Noyelle on the American urban system shows clearly that in the global cities – what they term the national nodal centres – only four (New York, Chicago, San Francisco, Los Angeles) have continued to augment their service functions, though less rapidly than the next level of the hierarchy, which they label regional nodal centres (Boston, Philadelphia, Atlanta, Houston, Minneapolis, Phoenix); the traditional manufacturing headquarters cities (like Pittsburgh and Detroit), which they term 'functional-nodal' centres, have lost ground badly (Noyelle and Stanback, 1983; Stanback, 1985).

We do not have similar work for Europe, but some intriguing parallels are suggested. At least two separate processes seem to be occurring (Hall and Cheshire, 1987; Cheshire and Hay, 1988). One is de-centralization of people and jobs from cities to suburbs, leading eventually to de-urbanization: the second is the decline of population and activity in entire urban regions or Standard Metropolitan Areas. This is not new: outward movement of people from cities to suburbs has been observable in the United Kingdom and United States since the 1950s, and had progressively spread to much of Western, Northern and Central Europe by the 1960s and to France, Italy and Spain by the 1970s (see chapter 9). After a time lag, it was followed by outward movement of jobs which, in the largest urban regions, could finally result in a movement outside the metropolitan area altogether into other smaller urban systems such as, for example, the ring of such systems between twenty and fifty miles from London, or the smaller urban systems just outside the Dutch Randstad. All this corresponds fairly well to the Scott model of industrial relocation and does not present a problem in itself; it does so only if accompanied by structural decline of the entire urban economy.

The problem is that this has happened with especial force, simultaneously, to many of the larger major city regions of Europe. These are concentrated in a narrow band from Genoa and Torino through eastern and northern France, the Saar and Ruhr and Southern Belgium to the Midlands, North West and North East England, and finally north to Glasgow and Belfast (Cheshire and Hay, 1988). They have suffered both massive de-industrialization and failed to develop compensating service functions (Hall, 1987a; Gillespie and Green, 1987; Green and Howells, 1987). Most of these places – Essen and Dortmund, Liverpool and Manchester – are the European equivalents of Noyelle and Stanback's functional–nodal centres. In contrast, the equivalents of their regional-nodal cities – strong provincial cities like München or Frankfurt, Grenoble or Norwich, and smaller national capitals like Brussels or Copenhagen – are performing conspicuously well.

The extraordinary anomaly, in all this, is London: the national-nodal, in fact international-nodal, city *par excellence*. By all the rules, it should not be in the club of declining cities: the fact that it is, unless it is a temporary aberration like New York a decade before, may portend some even deeper weakness in the British economy. However, recent analysis confirms a paradoxical feature of the London economy in decline: there has been virtually no differential effect on overall unemployment rates, which have remained marginally below the national average. Because the labour force has proved very mobile, the decline in jobs and the decline in the workforce have kept in step. People have moved out for housing reasons, but once out of London many eventually find jobs there (Buck et al., 1986, p. 97).

The problem of mismatch

But there is a sting in the tail. Unemployment rates have risen in line with national rates: in the process, the burden has disproportionately been borne by the young, the less skilled and less qualified, the non-white and the inner-city residents generally who, because of increasing competition for jobs, get left at the end of the job queue with their unemployment rates rising much faster than the average (ibid., pp. 106–7). What emerges is 'a growing polarization of society characterized by concentrated poverty, dependence, unemployment, and deterioration of the built environment for those left behind in the cities', wherein 'secular stagnation of the economy accentuates the results of the current redistributions, designating places and people within them as either "winners" or "losers" ' (Begg et al., 1986, p. 36).

The policy implications of this are disturbing. They are that whatever cities do to create jobs, most of them are likely to be filled by suburban and exurban commuters who are better qualified than the remaining inner-city inhabitants. Though the latter will always be at the end of the queue, the consequences for them are most severe in declining urban economies. Moreover, since they tend to be the least mobile, the only really good way to help them would be to reflate the economy: failing that, the alternatives are either to try to preserve the jobs they have, or to assist them to move to growth areas (Buck and Gordon, 1987).

The disturbing point about this analysis is that it confirms a host of results from the United States. There, determined attempts have been made over a long period to regenerate the urban economies, to provide comprehensive education and training, and to fight racial discrimination. Despite this, the percentage of blacks in poverty has begun again to increase. In fact America's black population has itself polarized: part has rapidly raised itself into the middle-class salariat; part is sunk ever deeper in the urban underclass (Wilson, 1978; Farley, 1984). This has occurred during the second half of the 1970s, a period when the American economy, too, was in recession.

Some American observers, indeed, believe that it is more than a cyclical phenomenon: it is structural. As long ago as 1968, the economist Charles C. Killingworth identified what he labelled the 'twist' in labour demand: a long-term fall in demand for low-skill, unqualified, poorly-educated labour and a long-term rise in demand for high-skill, well-educated labour, shifts that have been occurring faster than the corresponding shifts in the supply of labour. Demographic phenomena, the result of the 'baby boom' in the United States from 1946 to 1958 and in the United Kingdom from 1955 to 1965, may have exacerbated this, some believe, by leading to a secular fall in educational quality and the development of a youth culture inimical to learning. On top of a simple glut of these generations on the labour market of the 1970s and 1980s, low-skill jobs have been destroyed rapidly in the inner urban areas, many in industries like manufacturing and warehousing which have suffered particularly grievous losses in the inner cities.

If the problem is long term and structural, even reflation of the economy will not deal with it. There is a strong indication of this from the United States, where in the mid 1980s a fairly buoyant national economy has retained pockets of stubborn urban unemployment. Kasarda and Friedrichs (1986), in comparing these phenomena in the New York region and in German cities, have confirmed a problem of mismatch between labour demand and supply: the urban economies, they argue, are no longer supplying the entry-level jobs that could be performed by an unskilled, unqualified labour force.

Thus there develops, in typical urban labour markets, the phenomenon of simultaneous high rates of unemployment, concentrated in certain groups, and high numbers of job vacancies: the one in no way matches the other. Another key indicator, very evident in London in recent years, has been huge variations in local residential unemployment rates between nearby inner and outer boroughs such as between Hackney (24.5 per cent in September 1986) against Redbridge (8.7), or Lambeth (20.4) against Croydon (8.6) and Sutton (6.4) (SERPLAN, 1987). We are dealing here with segmented labour markets; the irony is that many of the employed from the outer boroughs commute through the high-unemployment inner boroughs to their central area jobs. Exactly the same phenomenon occurs in New York, where rail commuters from Connecticut daily gaze on the 'bombed-out' urban disaster area of the South Bronx on their way to their Manhattan offices.

What are the policy conclusions? Kasarda and Friedrichs conclude that 'under conditions of sustained national economic growth, a locality with a moderate amount of unemployment has much better prospects of economically rebounding and further reducing its unemployment rate than a locality with substantially larger portions of its labour force unemployed' (Kasarda and Friedrichs, 1986, p. 245). However, this is contradicted by parallel British research on a relatively successful urban economy, that of Bristol. Here too manufacturing employment has declined, but service jobs have more than compensated. Yet still the high-risk groups – the less-qualified young, the minorities – fail to get the jobs; here, too, employers are free to pick and choose, and they pick those whom they find suitable not merely in technical but also in social terms. The result is that the Bristol labour force, also, is polarized (Boddy et al., 1986, pp. 207–12). Nevertheless, the fact remains that these high-risk groups would have a better chance of a job in a growth area such as Bristol, or a new town, or one of the faster-growing towns around the metropolis (Buck and Gordon, 1987) than in a declining city in the periphery.

Yuppies to the rescue?

Paradoxically the hope may lie in a process now much noticed in the United States: the gentrification of the city by the yuppies, coupled with the process that there is coming to be called its Rousification, as exemplified by Quincy Market in Boston, South Street Seaport in New York and the Inner Harbor in Baltimore (Hall and Cheshire, 1987). The arrival of the yuppies, those suburban-born children of the emigrés from the city of the 1940s and 1950s, is creating a boom in consumer-led service employment and in associated construction, which may at last provide the basis for broad-based economic revival with jobs for a wide spectrum of skills and talents. But, it should be noticed, it is based on the successful transition to the service economy that is notable in these cities, already discussed.

The question now is how many such cities can join in the process, and on what basis. Recent evidence suggests that in America more cities are being affected, including some earlier identified as problem cities (such as St. Louis). But what will count, more than ever, is the general cultural and physical environment. In this process, Europe's historic cities should have a head start, if only they exploit it. To do so will need new kinds of urban planning skills, hardly now taught at all in the planning schools, as well as new forms of public-private partnership. In that respect, without doubt, the American cities are now leading the European ones, perhaps because many of them experienced the problems of structural decline before any of the others did so.

References

Begg, I., Moore, B. and J. Rhodes, (1986), 'Economic and social change in urban Britain and the inner cities', in V.A. Hausner, *Critical Issues in Urban Economic Development*, Vol. I, Oxford University Press.

Boddy, M., Lovering, J.H. and K. Bassett, (1986), *Sunbelt City: A Study of Economic Change in Britain's M4 Growth Corridor*, Oxford University Press.

Buck, N. and I. Gordon, (1987), 'The beneficiaries of employment growth: an analysis of the experience of disadvantaged groups in expanding labour markets', in V.A. Hausner, (ed.), *Critical Issues in Urban Economic Development*, Vol. II, Oxford University Press.

Buck, N., Gordon, I. and K. Young, (1986), *The London Employment Problem*, Oxford University Press.

Cheshire, P. and D. Hay, (1988), *Urban Problems in Europe*, Unwin Hyman.

Farley, R. (1984), *Blacks and Whites: Narrowing the Gap*, Harvard University Press, Cambridge, Mass.

Gillespie, A.E. and A.E. Green, (1987), 'The changing geography of producer services employment in Britain', *Regional Studies*, 21, 397–411.

Green, A.E. and J. Howells, (1987), 'Spatial prospects for service growth in Britain', *Area*, 19, 111–22.

Hall, P. (1962), *The Industries of London*, Hutchinson.

Hall, P. (1984a), 'Metropolis 1890–1940: challenge and response', in A. Sutcliffe, *Metropolis 1890–1940*, Mansell.

Hall, P. (1984b), *The World Cities* (3rd edn), Weidenfeld and Nicolson.

Hall, P. (1986), 'National capitals, world cities and the new division of labour,' in H.-J. Ewers, et al., *The Future of the Metropolis: Economic Aspects*, Walter de Gruyter, Berlin.

Hall, P. (1987a), 'The anatomy of job creation: nations, regions and cities in the 1960s and 1970s', *Regional Studies*, 21, 95–106.

Hall, P. (1987b), 'Perspectives on post-industrial society: Britain, America and the world', in J. Brotchie, P. Hall and P. Newton (eds), *The Spatial Impact of Technical Change*, Croom Helm.

Hall, P. (1988), *Cities of Tomorrow: An Intellectual History of City Planning in the Twentieth Century*, Blackwell, Oxford.

Hall, P., Breheny, M., McQuaid, R. and D. Hart, (1987), *Western Sunrise: The Genesis and Growth of Britain's Major High Tech Corridor*, Allen and Unwin, London.

Hall, P. and P.C. Cheshire, (1987), 'The key to success for cities', *Town and Country Planning*, 56, 50–1.

Hall, P. and P. Preston, (1988), *The Carrier Wave: New Information Technology and the Geography of Innovation, 1845–2007*, Allen and Unwin, London.

Harvey, D. (1985), *Consciousness and the Urban Experience: Studies in the History and Theory of Capitalist Urbanization*, Johns Hopkins University Press, Baltimore.

Hoyt, H. (1939), *The Structure and Growth of Residential Neighborhoods in American Cities*, Government Printing Office, Washington DC.

Kasarda, J. and J. Friedrichs, (1986), 'Comparative demographic-employment mismatches in U.S. and West German cities', in H.-J. Ewers et al. (eds), *The Future of the Metropolis: Economic Aspects*, Walter de Gruyter, Berlin.

Lees, A. (1985), *Cities Perceived: Urban Society in European and American Thought, 1820–1940*, Manchester University Press.

Noyelle, T.J. and Stanback, T.M. (1983), *The Economic Transformation of American Cities*, Rowman and Allanheld, Totowa.

Robson, B. (1986), 'Coming full circle: London versus the rest 1880–1980', in G. Gordon, (ed.), *Regional Cities in the U.K. 1890–1980*, Harper and Row.

Roncayolo, M. (1987), 'Long-term trends and problems of metropolitan Paris', in H.-J. Ewers, et al. (eds), *The Future of the Metropolis: Economic Aspects*, Walter de Gruyter, Berlin.

Royal Commission into the Depression of Trade and Industry (1886), *Final Report* (C. 4893), (BPP 1886, XXIII), HMSO.

Saxenian, A. (1985a), 'The origins of Silicon Valley', in P. Hall and A. Markusen, (eds), *Silicon Landscapes*, Allen and Unwin.

Saxenian, A. (1985b), 'Silicon Valley and Highway 128: regional prototypes or historic exceptions?', in M. Castells, (ed.), *High Technology, Space and Society* (Urban Affairs Annual Reviews, 28), Sage, Beverly Hills and London.

Schumpeter, J.A. (1939), *Business Cycles*, 2 volumes, McGraw Hill, New York, (reprinted 1982, Porcupine Press, Philadelphia).

Scott, A.J. (1982), 'Locational patterns and dynamics of industrial activity in the modern metropolis', *Urban Studies*, 19, 114–42.

Scott, A.J. (1983), 'Industrial organization and the logic of intra-metropolitan location: I. Theoretical considerations', *Economic Geography*, 59, 233–50.

Scott, A.J. (1985), 'Location processes, urbanisation and territorial development,' *Environment and Planning A*, 17, 479–501.

Scott, A.J. (1986), 'High technology industry and territorial development: the rise of the Orange County Complex, 1955–1985', *Urban Geography*, 7, 3–45.

SERPLAN (The London and South East Regional Planning Conference) (1987), *Regional Trends in the South East: The South East Regional Monitor 1986–87* (RPC/800), SERPLAN, London.

Soja, E., Morales, R. and G. Wolff, (1983), 'Urban restructuring: an analysis of social and spatial change in Los Angeles', *Economic Geography*, 59, 195–230.

Soja, E.W. (1986), 'Taking Los Angeles apart: some fragments of a critical human geography', *Environment and Planning D*, 255–72.

Stedman Jones, G. (1971), *Outcast London: A Study in the Relationship between Classes in Victorian Society*, Oxford University Press.

Taylor, E.G.R. et al. (1938), 'Discussion on the geographical distribution of industry', *Geographical Journal*, 92, 22–39.

Westergaard, J.H. (1957), 'Journeys to work in the London area', *Town Planning Review*, 28, 37–62.

Wilson, W.J. (1978), *The Declining Significance of Race: Blacks and Changing American Institutions*, University of Chicago Press.

Wohl, A.S. (ed.) (1977), *The Eternal Slum: Housing and Social Policy in Victorian London*, Edward Arnold.

Young, M. and Willmott, P. (1973), *The Symmetrical Family: A Study of Work and Leisure in the London Region*, Routledge and Kegan Paul.

3 Public policy and the morphology of western cities: the example of Britain in nineteenth and twentieth centuries

Gordon E. Cherry

Urban morphology has been a popular theme in geographical study, developing periodic fashions, with trends set by influential writers. Gordon (1984), for example, reminds us that Conzenian town plan analysis has provided a model for many to follow: the examination of burgage patterns has been important for the study of medieval towns; patient empirical work has told us much about the morphology of Welsh towns; and a more modern approach has looked at the relationships between urban development and urban rent theory (Whitehand, 1987).

An overarching explanatory thrust in the creation of urban landscape would emphasize the general importance of prevailing economic, social and political forces, and more specifically the role of key actors and decision-takers. In this framework of analysis historical geography, urban geography and planning history all depend heavily on the social sciences and behavioural studies for their insights. The lesson is that if we regard townscape as a palimpsest, we can only interpret the various morphological layers in terms of the cultural values, the power structures and the decision-making procedures of the society that gave rise to them.

This approach is usefully confirmed by Konvitz (1985) who identifies three periods of city building in Europe, each characterized by a different set of operative criteria. From the early Middle Ages to the late seventeenth century he observes that cultural factors determined city space, producing environments that everyone could use and understand. In the eighteenth and nineteenth centuries economic considerations dominated, enhancing the city as a place of production and exchange. Speculation made city building more complex and riskier, transforming relationships among lenders, owners, builders and occupants. From the late nineteenth century another change took place as city building became subordinate to political and social institutions. The function of space allocation was progressively taken over by bureaucracies and, as a consequence, the question as to who controls city space (and how it is controlled) became a volatile political and social issue. The distinction between the three periods is very clear: in the cultural mode, emphasis is on the user; in the economic mode, it is on the investor; and in the political, on the regulator.

Over the last two centuries western cities have acquired their present shape, structure and aspect through processes of regulation, devised and enforced as responses to economic and technological change and the associated building cycles. Contrasts between cities and between countries have of course been marked, as even a few illustrations from the nineteenth century make clear. The British regulatory hand over urban affairs was cautious and incremental, much concerned with housing conditions and related health matters, and in many ways British cities in 1914 were no nearer solving some of their urban problems than they had been in 1850. But consider the contrast between, for example, Paris and London. Paris was carved by Haussmann's grand manner surgery, but London witnessed a piecemeal addition of a few new thoroughfares and street widenings. For an explanation, we have to reflect that British politics distrusted the concentration of arbitrary power wielded by the Prefect of the Seine; it baulked at the heavy expenditure which his schemes entailed; and it feared the social disruption and possible community disturbances that might ensue.

This is no place to attempt a comprehensive review of the pattern of morphological change in the western industrial city, but the point can be emphasized that social and political conditions varied considerably between countries, with some striking individual consequences. In France, Paris was not the only city to embark on urban surgery with the authority of Napoleon III; in Lyon, for example, two new streets were cut running the length of the city's central peninsula in a programme of public works which included hospital building and public facilities such as quays, bridges and parks. In Germany, Hamburg was the only large city to be rebuilt in mid-century. After the fire of 1842 William Lindley, a British-born engineer who had come to Hamburg to assist in railway construction and land drainage, carried out sweeping reforms and provided modern sewerage systems, waterworks and housing and street networks. Thereafter, throughout the growing German state, urban regulation was much concerned with public health and traffic movement. By comparison, in America, where wood was often a principal building material, the issue of fire protection was important in matters of urban regulation, as the fires of New York in 1835 and Chicago in 1871 readily testified.

Contrasts in city rebuilding are nicely drawn out by Olsen in his study of London, Paris and Vienna, all of which underwent particular upheavals in the nineteenth century in ways which altered their urban structures and established firm patterns for future change. In London there was the cutting through of Regent Street at the time of George IV; in Paris there were Haussmann's avenues and boulevards; and in Vienna the laying out of the Ringstrasse. The three cities performed differently:

Each pursued a characteristic method for housing its expanding population: in Paris and Vienna, the block of flats adapted to the special requirements of the two societies. Each responded to the aspirations of its dominant classes with institutions and built environments intended to serve their interests and reinforce their values: in London the gentleman's club and villa suburbia; in Paris the boulevard with all its attendant pleasures; in Vienna the creation of a vast stage set on which its more fortunate citizens could pursue their daily lives in a manner that partook of the quality of grand opera [Olsen, 1986, p. ix].

The point has been made: city form, structure and appearance are heavily dependent on social and political institutions. London was different from other European capitals: it had none of the adornments which absolutist rulers elsewhere could bestow, and English aristocrats built country seats rather than splendid town residences. London's material progress in the nineteenth century was much more prosaic: in water supply, drainage systems, street lighting, paving and urban transport. In the twentieth century power by monarchs has been replaced by the power of governments, and again we might note how cautious London has been, as Appleyard (1979) reminds us. Post-war commercial development in the capital has been remarkably scattered compared, say, to Paris where the new large centre of La Défense was created in an effort to cluster new development and avoid scattered destruction. Brussels, on the other hand, tore down much of the old city for new development so that it could rank as the capital of Europe. Rome planned a Centro Direzzionale to the east of the historic centre, a project on similar lines to La Défense, but it never materialized – perhaps in itself a commentary on Italian institutional frailties.

It is against these observations that this analysis of the shaping of the British city over the last two centuries – more precisely over the years 1835 to 1985 – is focused. It is agreed that during this period decisions, policies and programmes of the State (local and central government and public institutions) have contributed an increasing dimension to the internal layout and patterns of the urban townscape, confirming recent studies in both geographical and planning literature of the way in which problems of urban growth have been interlinked with the development of planning policy (Cherry, 1972; Hall, 1974). From urban history too we have ample evidence that the relationship is well recognized as Yelling's (1986) study of the clearance of London's Victorian slums or Rodger's (1979) study of the operation of the Dean of Guild Courts in Scotland and their contribution to the evolution of urban form both testify. Hence, from various points of view, over the relatively recent past a number of highly significant legislative measures have provided the basis for the effective public regulation of the urban environment, and these have had a profound bearing on the course of townscape change.

The British political background

In developing this perspective it is important to recognize the political background to public regulation, to appreciate how little of it there was in the early years and what grudging steps were taken to extend State involvement. With the exception of the Poor Law no great interest was displayed by local authorities or government during the years at the beginning of the nineteenth century with regard to enviromental matters or conditions of life. Intervention in public health, for example, was largely confined to the general law of nuisance. But the burgeoning growth of the new manufacturing cities and London, itself a major manufacturing city, soon brought public authorities face to face with an environmental crisis. The State had no immediate experience of environmental regulation.

Towns were growing virtually without control, though a large number of Improvement Commissions, perhaps 300 in number, were charged with performing particular tasks – such as paving, lighting, drainage – or perhaps limited programmes of development. But overall the pattern of local government was merely a patchwork quilt of overlapping bodies responsible for a variety of environmental matters; the institutions of local government were too haphazard and imperfect to meet the new scale of urban problems.

For this reason the story begins in 1835, since public regulation of the environment effectively commenced with the Municipal Corporation Act of that year, legislation which reformed the existing corporations, creating boroughs which were given the powers previously held by Improvement Commissioners. Oligarchic bodies were replaced by elected councils, albeit on a franchise restricted to those with significant property qualifications. At this point a new pattern of central–local relations was forged, one which provided a new decision-making context for environmental affairs. Parliament increasingly imposed certain functions upon the corporations, and many more were made permissible, with freedom of local choice; in addition the corporations could seek their own powers through Private Acts of Parliament.

The framework of decision-taking was crucially important for the ways in which townscape was subsequently fashioned. For example, a second Reform Act in 1867 radically changed the structure of political power, with the working classes first entering the constitution, registering an increase in the male electorate of Britain from about 717,000 in 1832 to 2,226,000 after 1867. The political parties had to adjust their presentations to an electorate tripled in size. It is in this context that after the 1860s we see the emergence of popular politics and party machines, with some key cities throwing up new dynamic, populist leaders: look no further than Birmingham and the mayoralty of Joseph Chamberlain in the 1870s, when the dramatic cutting of Corporation Street through the slums of the central wards gave the city an urban feature around which the central area still revolves, while in the same period civic leadership in Glasgow also contributed to major projects of city development.

Throughout the nineteenth century the State response to environmental and social problems was cautious and slow, though it ultimately quickened. There was powerful resistance to taxes, and the very notion of extensions to public regulation could excite moral indignation. Gladstonian Liberalism, believing in minimal State action and opting for the lowest levels of taxation and expenditure, long prevailed against the sensitivities expressed in Disraeli's 'two nations' and the caring image of Tory paternalism.

Nevertheless, from the later nineteenth century, assisted by more favourable electoral support, public sector intervention took a succession of seemingly irreversible steps by which local and central government were drawn into widening areas of environmental regulation. As the electorate was extended, the principles of social collectivism advanced. Working class unrest may have reached a peak just before the First World War, though the Third Reform Act of 1884–5 widened the franchise to just under five million. Local authorities became much more powerful, but so too did central government which prodded them into action and, on occasion, had to restrain them. A new political party (Labour) mobilized the working class vote and articulated a more general approach to a comprehensive view of the welfare responsibilities of the State. In 1918 the Representation of the People Act, which gave the vote to all males over 21 and to women over 30 (with equality only from 1928), increased the electorate to over 20 million.

Between the wars the extent of State regulation continued to grow and with it political participation in an unchartered sea of lobbies, special interest groups and reformist pressures. All political parties became committed to welfare programmes and after the Second World War the tentacles of State regulation were omnipresent. Whilst a leftward surge in British politics was soon restrained, the hold of the State on virtually every aspect of life remained. Not until the 1970s were arguments, unfashionable for decades, heard again proclaiming the merits of withdrawing the State from increasing areas of social and economic activity and looking much more at the virtue of private markets against public intervention.

This backcloth of the history of State powers and the development of the institutions and practices of urban governance provides the setting against which the objectives, methods and consequences of environmental regulation have been played out (Checkland, 1983). Historical geographers, as much as the planning historians, wishing to explain how and why urban townscapes have been fashioned can do so only with full reference to the formative influences of national and local politics, social movements, and the continual process of response to pressures for change from many directions.

All that is possible in this essay is to sketch out a kind of working model for further study; the building blocks are expanded considerably in Cherry (1988). First let us look at the chronological sequence and the characteristics of particular periods. For completeness such a review should include all land uses: buildings, open space, parks, playgrounds and so on, but I will concentrate exclusively on housing and residential areas.

Principal formative periods in town planning in Britain

The half century, 1835–85, forms the phase of Britain's first lurching steps into measures of public regulation of environmental affairs. In response to problems of sanitation, water supply, health and housing, central and local government were drawn both into investment for engineering works on a new scale and into interference with property rights. The State's legislative measures, as reactions to the questions of urban health, proved to be far-reaching, not least in their consequences for townscape.

Britain had experienced no bubonic plague since the late seventeenth century (see chapter 7) and national death rates fell from the 1740s to the 1820s. In the 1830s, however, that decline was arrested by a resurgence of disease attributed by medical opinion to overcrowding and poor, or absent sanitation in urban areas.

Pressures for reform came from the ranks of an increasing number of British phys-icians and professional administrators, now usefully armed with statistics (Flinn, 1965). The Public Health Act of 1848 established principles of sanitary improve-ment from which there was to be no retreat, though it was not until 1875 that a full public health service administration covered the whole country, with authorities empowered to regulate the construction of new streets and buildings under the supervision of the Local Government Board (Frazer, 1950).

The greatest technological contribution to urban Britain at this time was in large measure underground in the form of pipes and sewers, but the overriding concern for health had its effect also on house construction and layout. The cellar dwellings of Liverpool and Manchester were relatively short-lived phenomena and by the 1870s their unwelcome notoriety had largely passed. Back-to-back dwellings in Lancashire and particularly West Yorkshire were harder to eradicate, however: although they seriously violated the objectives of effective ventilation, they were cheap and warm and disliked neither by the poorer classes who inhabited them nor by the speculators who built them.

Housing reform gathered pace, encouraged by a groundswell of opinion which fed on moral concern, the advance of technical information, visionary perspectives and practical experiments. Progress, though slow, was eventually made on two fronts: building control and bye-laws (Gaskell, 1983); and action against insanitary hous-ing through local improvement schemes (Tarn, 1973). Model bye-laws published in 1878 were adopted by all large municipalities in the 1880s, with the terms 'bye-law house' coming to suggest an environmental uniformity, a regulated order and a mechanistic rationing of space in the new suburbs and other speculative devel-opments of the later-Victorian city. Such townscape features can only be understood against half a century of sanitarianism, with all its socio-political dimensions. The performance of individual cities varied (and therefore calls for careful local study), but generally speaking the bye-laws conferred lasting features on the late-Victorian urban townscape. Streets exceeding 100 feet in length were to be at least 36 feet wide. For house construction a complete scale of specifi-cations was prescribed. Space around dwellings was carefully measured: an open space of 24 feet between the frontage and the opposite lands and premises, and 150 square feet of open space at the rear was required.

When it came to the removal of insanitary housing, hard political battles were fought. The Artizans' and Labourers' Dwelling Act, 1875, introduced the idea of dealing comprehensively with unfit housing on an area basis, the earlier legislation of 1866 being concerned only with individual dwellings. Although shackled by its com-pensation clauses, it was none the less an important precedent whereby another bridgehead of public action was established for the remorseless advance against the residual area of private interests. The local authority could now demolish slum and unhealthy areas and then (usually) sell the land to other bodies (for example the large model dwelling companies) for rehousing. The State's action amounted to the compulsory exchange of one form of social geography for another and for a century Britain has followed this principle in its various renewal schemes. The Act was no great success: in one city at least, Birmingham, the legislation was used to create commercial development in Corporation Street, no replacement housing being provided in that scheme.

The next period, 1885–1914, is that fascinating era around the turn of the century when the rigid principles of bye-law control governing streets and housing collapsed in favour of an altogether more flexible set of arrangements for housing layout and the design of dwellings (Cherry, 1979). For a long time the housing reform movement adhered to its old targets: the removal of insanitary housing: the limitation of overcrowding; and the reduction of high densities. The goals of fresh air, sunlight and space were confirmed. Protest literature, the fruits of investigative journalism, and the painstaking product of data collection by social scientists still fuelled the flames of concern.

The essential problem related to the provision of adequate housing for the working classes. The scale of the problem was certainly daunting. Philanthropy and the model dwellings movement had done well but together had probably achieved as much as they could. Improvement schemes were slow, as witness the Boundary Street scheme in Bethnal Green which, when it was finally opened in 1900 by the Prince of Wales, seemed to be closing the end of an era rather than ushering in a new golden age of improvement. Land prices were high: too high for private builders in the centres of cities. Finally, political resistance to local authority building remained stubborn. In fact the one way forward was to the suburbs where cheap land offered the possibility at least of cheaper houses, more spaciously spread out and controlled by local authority town planning schemes. To this the Liberal Government was sympathetic and the first town planning legislation entered the statute book in 1909.

The new public hand on the environment came from the advocate of low density housing, schemes well provided with gardens and served by a free-flowing road layout. Raymond Unwin's New Earswick at York, his and Barry Parker's design for Letchworth Garden City and his Hampstead Garden Suburb showed the way. The garden city as advocated by Ebenezer Howard, and adopted by his Association, confirmed this approach in the strategic setting of a totally new Social City in the form of a cluster of satellites. Unwin's little pamphlet of 1912 with the intriguing title Nothing Gained by Overcrowding! seemed to say all. The agents for change were now the architects of a new school, aided and abetted by a group of earnest liberal reformers, philanthropists and churchmen, motivated by visions of social progress and man's fulfilment, in which housing quality and the eradication of environmental squalor meant so much. The promise of town planning took on an almost Messianic fervour, and neither big business nor politicians seemed to object too much to what was proclaimed in its name.

Public recognition of these influences can usefully be seen in one case: the work of the London County Council housing architects before 1914 (Beattie, 1980). The Progressives (an alliance of Liberals and early Socialists) controlled the first two LCC administrations (1889–92 and 1892–5). Within the Architect's Department a Housing of the Working Classes Branch was set up where energies were mostly expended on the Boundary Street Estate in Bethnal Green, a large East End Scheme of nineteen block dwellings. The Millbank estate, Westminster, and others followed when after three years in opposition the Progressives were returned to power. This coincided with a switch in housing design to the building of suburban cottage estates as at Totterdown Fields (Tooting), Norbury (near Croydon), White Hart Lane (Tottenham) and Old Oak (East Acton). The earliest estates followed a bye-law grid pattern but later the design was freer under the influence of Unwin's pioneering work, with imaginative groupings of houses, culs-de-sac and curving roads.

We can now turn to *the period between the wars* when measures of public regulation over the urban environment were considerably extended, and in ways which had a dramatic impact on townscape and the spatial structure of cities. This was the time of the beginning of the spatial spread of cities and with it the growing lobby of planning advocacy, particularly in the form of the Garden Cities movement, though this was often confused with garden suburbs and low-density development generally. But the immediate problem concerned the country's housing stock. There were two main problems: first, a housing shortage because so few dwellings had been built during the war; secondly, a low standard of accommodation for the working classes which, together with Lloyd George's promise of 'homes for heroes', had to be addressed.

By 1939 we can see the response. No less than one-third of the nation's dwellings had been built since 1918 – four million new homes between the wars, one-quarter provided by local authorities. A new tenure structure to British housing had emerged and with it a new townscape feature, the council house estate. The critical influences were the Tudor Walters Report of 1918 and, in the first instance, the Housing and Town Planning Act, 1919.

Fifteen months before the end of the war, in the full flood of plans for post-war reconstruction, the President of the Local Government Board set up a committee of enquiry into the whole question of the provision of working-class housing under the chairmanship of Sir John Tudor Walters. Raymond Unwin was a member and his hand in the report was very much in evidence (Miller, 1981). The recommendations, accepted by the Government, were amplified in detail by the *Housing Manual, 1919* in which a range of house plans and layouts was illustrated. The revolutionary effect on house plans and urban form extended to both public and private sectors. The narrow-frontage terrace house was ousted in favour of the wide-frontage cottage built in groups of two, four or six and generously endowed with gardens; the setting was one of tree-lined roads, gently winding around contours, though in the public sector complex and wasteful geometric patterns were adopted. In time the private speculative developer settled on the semi-detached house as a compromise between economy and individuality. The Tudor Walters model laid its distinctive imprint on urban Britain for a quarter of a century, if not more, marking a complete break from the housing environment of the Victorian bye-law era.

The Housing and Town Planning Act, 1919, and subsequent legislation, assisted in this process in two ways (Cherry, 1974). First, the vital principle of giving subsidies to local authorities was introduced, to build houses for the working classes. The extent of the subsidy and the nature of the precise standards of houses to be built varied from time to time in accordance with the legislation of the day and the vagaries of national economic conditions. Though interesting local variations in dwelling stock resulted from the subsidies and space and design standards then obtaining, British cities henceforth were to look very different: morphologically they were to expand territorially in large estates, sharply divided by social class. The other aspect of the legislation was that it overcame the limitations of the permissive nature of the 1909 Act and obliged local authorities of over 20,000 population to prepare schemes for their developing, suburban areas. Housing provision was therefore linked to land planning in the suburbs and applied to both local authority and private builders. There was, in fact, no chance that all local authorities would proceed to prepare schemes – a shortage of trained manpower would see to that – and small councils remained constrained by fear of compensation demands on refusal of planning permission. But a start had been made on the practice of statutory planning, and the conscious shaping of city growth had begun in earnest. The Town and Country Planning Act, 1932 (the first legislation to include the word 'country'), restored the permissive aspect to the preparation of planning schemes, but extended the coverage to all local authorities. Against a background of scheme preparation, the practice of interim development control (a kind of informal pressure) gained wider acceptance. Local authorities grew bolder in establishing policies for urban growth: in London, for example, land was bought up in the form of estates for green belt purposes, a practice confirmed and given legal recognition in the London Green Belt Act, 1938. A new major public contribution had been made to metropolitan morphology, much more significant and longer lasting than the consequences of the Restriction of Ribbon Development Act, 1935.

Before the inter-war period ended, public attention had returned to the older city and the removal of unfit dwellings. Housing legislation in 1930 and 1935 signified a return to former concerns, with the result that before the outbreak of the Second World War the heart of some of our cities was affected by slum clearance and redevelopment, giving new additions to the townscape and a changing morphological pattern. The Housing Act, 1930 introduced new subsidies for slum clearance and the Housing Act, 1935 extended the subsidies for the rehousing of overcrowded families. Some locally spectacular schemes emerged, as at Quarry Hill, east of the markets area of Leeds.

The final period of the post-war years contains some important sub-divisions. Nevertheless, during these years the influence of the State on urban form and the housing environment has been all-pervasive. Common ground was established amongst the professions, developers, public administrators and politicians that the State was the wisest regulator of the environment and provider of community facilities – a consensus which has finally broken in a resurgence of individualism and private interests, marked by the politics of the New Right. At risk of being superficial, three points must be established.

First, Britain's bifurcated planning system was thoroughly established with the Town and Country Planning Act, 1947, and is enshrined in two aspects (Cherry, 1974): first, the making of plans for development; and, secondly, the granting or refusal of planning permission to develop. It is a subtle blend of public control, democratically placed both in the hands of popularly elected councils, and of individual freedom. A remarkable and workable consensus has emerged. For the individual, land ownership confers no right to develop: the private sector is buoyant but submits readily enough to public regulations: public authorities pretend to effect a hold on development, but rarely deflect well-established trends. A succession of development plans for all urban areas has provided a continual map for the lines of future growth. In some cases whole towns together with their component housing have been planned from scratch, the New Towns programme providing 28 from Stevenage in 1946 to Stonehouse in 1972 (subsequently aborted). Elsewhere towns have been extended in Town Development Schemes, spectacularly at Swindon, Basingstoke, towns in East Anglia, in the West Midlands and elsewhere. Around the big cities the housing sectors of urban growth have been sharply curtailed through green belt policies. These belts have been significantly extended in area over the last ten years, so that green belt designation now covers 11 per cent of the land surface of England. Within towns, a primary feature has been the conscious grouping of residential areas into clusters, heavily influenced by neighbourhood planning first seen in the New York Regional Plan of 1928. The difference between the speculative private development of the Victorian suburb with virtually no public regulation save street widths, house construction and space around dwellings, and the public sector-approved estates of post-war Britain could not be greater in terms of townscape and morphology.

The second feature is in the influences on design which the public sector adopted, and which inevitably affected the private sector too. The Dudley Report on the design of post-war houses, published in 1944, was intended to do for post-war housing what Tudor Walters had done in 1918 for inter-war housing (Burnett, 1978). Its recommendations were embodied in the *Housing Manual, 1944*, and addressed the problems of an alleged lack of variety in dwellings and in adaptation of space to modern needs. Tudor Walters was superseded: mixed development, with a break away from the semi-detached home and a greater emphasis on variety in housing, followed with – importantly – an implied zoning of densities from 120 persons to the acre in city centres to 30 persons in the suburbs. Modifications followed in later manuals, but a new feature of public regulation had been introduced and a later report on house design – the Parker Morris Report, 1962 – had the effect of once more emphasizing terraced housing.

A major departure came with the marked increase in the proportion of flats built by local authorities. Tall blocks first impinged on the urban landscape in the 1950s as part of mixed development schemes, but their subsequent fashion stems from a very complex set of factors which owed as much to the political conflict between land-hungry cities and the resistant shire counties beyond as to anything else: the 'save agricultural land' lobby was never terribly convincing as an argument against city growth.

Finally the public hand was exercised massively in a renewed attack on slums. The 1951 census had been stark enough in its revelation of the still inadequate national housing stock: 37 per cent of the houses of England and Wales had no fixed bath and more than one million dwellings had no flush toilet. The Housing Repairs and Rents Act, 1954 signalled the return to concern for overall quality of dwellings as opposed to simply the addition of new stock. Between 1945 and 1954 only 90,000 houses were demolished or closed. But at flood tide in the 1960s and into the 1970s annual clearance rates were never less than 61,000; in Scotland in the same period a further 296,000 dwellings were demolished or closed. The social consequences were profound. In the 20 years from 1955 to 1974 in England and Wales more than three million persons were moved from their homes as a result of redevelopment schemes – the sharp end of the process envisaged by Abercrombie in Greater London, Clydeside, the West Midlands and elsewhere in his deceptively simple schemes for the planned reduction of densities and redistribution of population. A totally new landscape of urban renewal followed, halted symbolically as far as tall blocks were concerned by the collapse of Ronan Point in Newham, east London, in 1968 and the gradual adoption of the principle of rehabilitation of stock rather than its clearance. In terms of social geography these high-rise areas were largely given over to an urban underclass with a mixed population including – in many cities – considerable ethnic concentrations.

In the preceding chronological review there may well be no great surprises in the topographical and morphological features identified. But the analysis serves to emphasize the strength of the public sector hand in the shaping of the British urban environment and offers a useful model, or contextual framework, within which further research might be conducted.

Explanations

The essential point to draw out from the canvas depicted is that the unfolding public regulation of the British urban environment has mirrored the changing socio-political conditions of the time. After 1835 the Government did not simply embark on a course of intervention out of philanthropy; urban management in the nineteenth century and town planning in the twentieth did not loftily follow an ordained path from Coketown to Milton Keynes: rather, public regulation was extended because various people (largely outside Government) wanted the things that would flow from it. Our model of explanation, therefore, is one of special interest, reform and response; an interactive process in which policies are agreed and action is taken in the context of pressure, negotiation, bargaining and the formation of alliances. Public regulation does not just happen, neither should we regard it as an inevitable product of enlightenment; and when we consider town planning, neither is it simply the high-minded product of one profession. The process is much more uncertain and open-ended; much more bound up with the interplay between competing forces (Cherry, 1982).

The geographer's interest in landscape, whether natural or man-made, leads to a concern with processes as well as product. The historical geographer, with an interest in townscape and urban morphology, needs to be well-informed about the processes of change, the machinery of governance and, in particular, the role of the key actors in a system characterized by interaction.

The British governmental system is typified by a capacity for response to demand for reform and innovation in which there are three interactive elements. First, there is the bureaucracy (local government and the civil service), in part professionalized, overall well established, and inherently conservative in outlook. Then, secondly, there are the active pressure groups who challenge, who are reformist by nature and who exert leverage on issues. Thirdly, there are the elected politicians who take decisions and activate particular programmes: some may have distinctive ideologies but most will seek centre ground. So environmental regulation in the social democracies of the West becomes a deeply political act. A particular policy that is followed may demonstrate not so much its own intrinsic merit, but rather the strength of the protagonists in whose interests it is being promoted. It is in this context that in Britain we see the fascinating interplay of forces for health reform, for model dwellings, for low density suburbs, for council estates and for planned renewal: forces which have done so much to shape the country's urban environment.

At a time when the public sector hand is currently being withdrawn from urban regulation in a number of different ways, it is interesting to speculate to what extent over the next quarter- or half-century urban morphology will continue to be shaped by public policy; or what new consortia of private interests will take the key role? I go back to one of my favourite sources. In 1936 Winifred Holtby wrote in her novel, South Riding, of the world of local government (Sheail, 1985): Alderman Snaith, a rich businessman, tempts the haulage contractor and lay preacher, Councillor Huggins, into speculating in land values in an area where a new road and garden village are planned by the county council – this was urban governance, warts and all, fifty years ago, illustrative of a city building process of uncertainty and conflicting aspirations. In fifty years' time the issues of conflict of interest and exercise of power will still apply: but perhaps the regulatory public hand will be less in evidence in the form and structure of the urban environment.

References

Appleyard, D. (ed.) (1979), The Conservation of European Cities, MIT Press, Cambridge, Mass.

Beattie, S. (1980), A Revolution in London Housing: L.C.C. Architects and their Work, 1893–1914, The Architectural Press.

Burnett, J. (1978), A Social History of Housing, David and Charles, Newton Abbot.

Checkland, S. (1983), British Public Policy 1776–1939: An Economic, Social and Political Perspective, Cambridge University Press.

Cherry, G.E. (1972), Urban Change and Planning: A History of Urban Development in Britain since 1750, G.T. Foulis, Henley on Thames.

Cherry, G.E. (1974), The Evolution of British Town Planning: A History of Town Planning in the United Kingdom during the 20th Century and of the Royal Town Planning Institute, 1914–74, Leonard Hill, Leighton Buzzard.

Cherry, G.E. (1979), 'The town planning movement and the late Victorian city', Transactions of the Institute of British Geographers, N.S., 4, 306–19.

Cherry, G.E. (1982), *The Politics of Town Planning*, Longman, Harlow.

Cherry, G.E. (1988), *Cities and Plans: The Shaping of Urban Britain in the Nineteenth and Twentieth Centuries*, Edward Arnold.

Flinn, M.W. (1965), Introduction to Edwin Chadwick, *Report on the Sanitary Condition of the Labouring Population of Great Britain, 1842*, Edinburgh University Press.

Frazer, W.M. (1950), *A History of English Public Health*, Balliere, Tindall and Cox.

Gaskell, S.M. (1983), *Building Control: National Legislation and the Introduction of Local Bye Laws in Victorian England*, Bedford Square Press.

Gordon, G. (1984), 'The shaping of urban morphology', *Urban History Yearbook*, Leicester University Press.

Hall, P. (1974), *Urban and Regional Planning*, Pelican, Harmondsworth.

Konvitz, J.W. (1985), *The Urban Millennium: The City Building Process from the Early Middle Ages to the Present*, Southern Illinois University Press, Carbondale, Ill.

Miller, M. (1981), 'Raymond Unwin, 1863–1940', in G.E. Cherry, *Pioneers in British Planning*, The Architectural Press.

Olsen, D.J. (1986), *The City as a Work of Art: London, Paris, Vienna*, Yale University Press, New Haven and London.

Rodger, R. (1979), 'The law and urban change: some nineteenth century Scottish evidence', *Urban History Yearbook*, Leicester University Press.

Sheail, J. (1985), 'South Riding: a portrayal of local government between the wars', *Local Government Studies*, 11, 65–74.

Tarn, J.N. (1973), *Five Per Cent Philanthropy: An Account of Housing in Urban Areas between 1840 and 1914*, Cambridge University Press.

Whitehand, J.W.R. (1987), *The Changing Face of Cities*, Blackwell, Oxford.

Yelling, J.A. (1986), *Slums and Slum Clearance in Victorian London*, Allen and Unwin.

4 Premature obituaries: change and adaptation in the great cities

Brian Robson

A recent outstanding production of William Wycherley's *The Country Wife* at Manchester's Royal Exchange Theatre used a modern adaptation and staging to give a fresh edge to the rumbustious timelessness of the Restoration comedy and in an interesting reflection of prevailing twentieth-century attitudes, underplayed the anti-rural views that Wycherley held in common with his contemporaries. Wycherley was in fact somewhat less overtly vituperative and damning about the limitations of rural life than were most of his contemporaries: for example, Farquhar, in *The Beaux Stratagem*, puts these words into the mouth of Mistress Sullen:

Country pleasures – racks and torments! Dost think . . . that my limbs were made for leaping of ditches and clambering over styles? Or that my parents, wisely foreseeing my future happiness in country pleasures, had early instructed me in rural accomplishments of drinking fat ale, playing at whisk, and smoking tobacco with my husband . . . brewing of diet drinks and stilling rosemary water?

The latter description could serve for the rural idyll as seen by today's health-food and goat's-milk communard in the rural fastnesses. The tone of derision, however, is the authentic voice of the seventeenth century, and would be shared by few today.

Since the seventeenth century, views of the country have been turned on their head. In Britain, especially since the industrial revolution, the myth of the country has played, and continues to play, a powerful role in shaping our views of what is thought desirable. The first suburban settlements in nineteenth-century London and in the Manchester of the 1830s were led by the bourgeoisie aping the landed gentry both in architecture (with scaled down versions of the country house) and in location. The twentieth-century inter-war rash of Elizabethan Tudor in the ribbon developments of the first mass growth of owner-occupation was prompted by similar sentiments (Green, 1988). The post-war move to small towns and 'rural' villages has reflected only slightly different impulses – to re-establish roots with nature and to recreate the small dense mesh of social community that rural village society is supposed to have had. The combination of environmentalism with the social cachet that stems from our long association of rural landownership with status has proved a powerful pull. That such residential pressure for rural and small-town locations is beneficial to the development industry – to developers themselves, to financial agencies such as banks and building societies, and to such exchange professionals as estate agents and solicitors – has ensured that institutional and financial interests have added a powerful reinforcing thrust to sustain the myth of rural life. The outer London area in particular has been the scene of a continuing sequence of development proposals within and just beyond the Green Belts of London and Oxford. Consortium Developments, a group of the nine largest housebuilders, have had the first of their country-town proposals, at Tillingham Hall in Essex, rejected; Foxley Wood in Hampshire will be the subject of a public enquiry in the summer of 1988; plans for Stone Bassett east of Oxford were submitted at the end of 1987 (Schoon, 1987); and Wilburton in Cambridgeshire is in the pipeline along with further possible developments in Braintree and Ashford. Proposals for new homes in Brenthall Park at Harlow from a partnership of Croudace, Countryside Properties and Wates have been approved by the Department of the Environment despite opposition by local authorities and the ring of development pressure around London has been further filled in by proposals at Caddington and Bishops Park in the north, Chafford Hundred and Leybourne in the east, Maiden Bower and Southwater in the south and Hook, Great Lea and Bracknell in the west.

Martin Wiener in his seminal book *English Culture and the Decline of the Industrial Spirit* (Wiener, 1981) offers a compelling reminder that a powerful strain of Victorian anti-urbanism came from those very people whose way of life was essentially urban, a truth borne out by the modern predilection for the so-called country cottage which has to be provided with every modern amenity as well as two or more cars to enable families to move to the facilities of the urban areas as often as they wish, and by the developers' exploitation of this image in their creation of a patina of village-ness to the new developments of the last few years – the Daffodil Dells, Lark Rises, Glebe Copses and the like, which help to pander to that seductive image of the countryside (Short et al., 1986, pp. 78–80). There is great power in the manipulated false consciousness of rural romanticism which we have allowed to dominate our contemporary urban society. The more we indulge in nostalgia and longing for a world of country living that never was – except for a favoured wealthy few in reality and a mythical many in literary imagination – the worse grows our view of the city.

Any doubts about the material deprivations and the poverty of spirit of real rural life, even in the twentieth century, for those outside the privileged few can rapidly be dispelled by accounts from those who bore the brunt (Blythe, 1969). Yet, for those whom the Bishop of Liverpool in his Dimbleby lecture castigated as 'comfortable Britain', it is the city which has become the symbol of all that is wrong in these latter days. Riots such as those of 1980 in Bristol, of 1981 in London, Liverpool, Manchester and their echoes in 1985 in Birmingham, London and Liverpool, confirm a widespread fear of the city. Such major riots are but the tip of a larger recurring pattern of unreported disturbances and minor incidents known only to those involved or those living in inner areas: Chapeltown in Leeds, Salford, Moss Side in Manchester, and most of the inner areas of our large cities endure recurring disturbances which only occasionally attract the attention of journalists or which are helpfully suppressed by the police. All such incidents help to confirm our very real dread that a bloody and despairing revolution will roll down these 'mean streets'.

Apart from all the other solutions currently being peddled to avert this happening, there is a growing tendency to blame 'the city' as an evil in itself. Both sides of the bitter wars being waged over development in the South East and the possible breaching of the London Green Belt – a controversy made acidly public by political jostling such as that between Michael Heseltine and Nicholas Ridley – are obsessed by the same hysterical belief that there is something magical in the few square miles of ploughland, grass and the odd copse. Such rural fantasies feed the views of many ex-urbanites who were early on the bandwagon of village living. Both those who wish to hold to the status quo and those who wish to share the supposed delights of moving out of the city are convinced of the joy in breathing pure country air, composed as it often is of the smell of manure and of burning stubble. Only time and experience will show whether an escape from the city actually does free the young from unemployment or ensnaring by the alcohol or drug culture; or the old from loneliness and dementia; or whether marriages are preserved and burglaries diminished. The auguries are not good: the problems of modern society are man-made and are as likely to flourish in or out of the urban context, as anybody will testify who has knowledge of the misery, the isolation, the poverty and the boredom of rural life for those who belong to the less affluent groups of contemporary society. It may well be that some perverted form of wishful thinking *wants* the city to die, or more precisely wants what is seen as the worst aspects of the city to disappear. Few of those who search for nirvana in the leafy suburbs or the supposedly quaint villages really want to be without the amenities of the large urban centres: shops, theatres, concert halls, museums, leisure centres are desirable; riotous youth, graffiti-strewn vandalized buildings, crime and violence are not. We all want the icing but not the rather problematic cake whose preparation and cooking we have handled so inexpertly.

Rural distress

The rural myth has helped to concoct a continuing anti-urban bias which has stimulated the flight from the city both by households and by secondary and tertiary activities. Yet, is the country so idyllic, so safe, so stimulating to the senses, so appropriate an arena in which to bring up young families? Do we not magnify or indeed build the ideas of urban-rural differences on demonstrably false bases? Take the issue of safety. All our preconceived notions are reinforced by media coverage given to urban riots – that is where they *should* be, among the blacks, the poor and the ungovernable whom we hope to remove from endangering 'comfortable Britain' by corralling them in the inner city. Yet much of the recurring unrest over holiday seasons of the last few years, was in places such as Lincoln, Stroud, High Wycombe (Helm, 1988) and in Newport Pagnell (Oxley, 1988). Looking back, Newport Pagnell recurs astonishingly frequently as a place of small-town riot and disturbance – virtually a Newport-Pagnell syndrome. Kilroy-Silk (1987) writes of a conspiracy of silence about such 'white riots' in small towns and cites additional battles in Shrewsbury, Fletching (Sussex), Chertsey, Weston-super-Mare and Llanelli. That violence in a rural setting can be more horrific than the often casual disturbances of gangs or urban youth was never more poignantly or tragically illustrated than by the massacre in Hungerford.

Take the case of the supposed stimulus of rural life. As farming becomes larger in scale and areas of recreation and open access become more formalized and restricted in extent, how will this effect the stimulus for children growing up in the rural areas? Marx was ever dismissive of 'the idiocy of rural life'; Ebenezer Howard, in justifying his notion of the garden city, wrote of the lack of society in rural areas: can this have somehow changed? It seems unlikely. Colin Ward, that most stimulating anarchist writer, convincingly recognized the stimulus of urban life in his book *The Child in the City* (Ward, 1978). It may be more dangerous to live in the city – for example from the point of view of traffic and the casual violence of a more massed population – but an essential part of childhood is precisely a coming to terms with the cut and thrust of a lively but potentially dangerous environment. If we could but fashion into more productive channels the liveliness of the urban child – whether Cockney or Scouse or the many other metropolitan versions – how much more alert and enterprising a nation might we be.

Decay or change?

Recognition of the persistent appeal and enduring quality of urban life – despite every act to the contrary – should be our starting point. To paraphrase Voltaire: if there had been no city it would have been necessary to have invented it. It may be that this is a dream-world of small-scale urban settlement, the vision of a Plato or a St. Augustine – a covert 'Tillingham Hall view' of Utopia or academics for Barratt. Not so. No *a priori* judgement is offered as to what is an ideal settlement in size, shape or situation. Rather, the proposition is that the obituaries of the great city have been written prematurely and that, contrary both to widespread opinion and to the sense of much academic wisdom, the large city *can* have a future. In no small way, we are blind to that future by attachment to the rural myth and by an unwillingness to accept that a realistic future can be built on service activities rather than solely on the so-called 'productive' activities of secondary manufacturing.

In 1977 one of the Inner Area Studies – of Liverpool – was entitled, interrogatively, 'Change or decay' (Department of the Environment, 1977). That question has still not satisfactorily been answered. In America, it seems that the urban issue may have become one of change rather than of decay and that a partial urban renaissance is helping to create new forms of metropolitan area. To set against the move to the sunbelt and away from large cities, the older cities of America are showing remarkable new resilience. Alongside the squalor of their inner areas and alongside levels of dereliction which are invariably infinitely worse than their British counterparts, many large American cities have expanded their labour markets despite the loss of manufacturing industry. For example, of the older industrial cities during the years 1959–1983 Chicago lost almost 150,000 manufacturing jobs but gained 440,000 service jobs, an overall rise of almost 33 per cent; Detroit lost 140,000 manufacturing but gained 200,000 service jobs to rise by 23 per cent; Cleveland lost 70,000 but gained over 100,000 in services to gain by 21 per cent; even in the 'rust city' of Pittsburgh the loss of manufacturing and gain of service jobs more or less balanced. Pittsburgh, indeed, is perhaps the most salient example: a smokestack city which has now begun to stake a claim as a 'think centre' – a variety of 'software valley' – based on its university complexes, with Carnegie-Mellon now developing software engineering for the Defense Department and the University of Pittsburgh having taken over Gulf Oil's research complex which is now being developed by U-Parc (the University of Pittsburgh Applied Research Centre) as a commercial venture and high-tech startup for infant industries. Add this to the major rehabilitation schemes involving the private and public sectors in the East coast cities – in Philadelphia, Boston, and Baltimore, in which 'yuppy' populations have been involved in the recycling of old housing, warehouses, port and sea frontages – and even the older American cities seem well placed to make a continuing contribution to growth despite the effects of counter-urbanization and inner decay (see chapter 2).

In Britain, by contrast, the received wisdom on the question of urban change is generally that cities have decayed and will continue to decay; that we face a future of dispersed smaller-scale settlement and that their inexorable decline means that the question is merely one of how best to render tolerable the demise of great cities. We seem too ready to agree, with hopeless resignation, that Liverpool is unsaveable, large cities as a category are doomed to long-run decay, and that all have become or want to become part of a new rural bourgeoisie: the death of the city is at hand.

However, there is no reason why the future of British cities could not be vastly different from this gloomy scenario and that the Pittsburgh story is one which could also apply to Britain. What cannot be suggested is that there is some inexorable logic which drives British cities to follow the lead of America, with a decade's time lag. The contexts of the United States and Britain are significantly different. It is too easy to forget the impact of contrasts in the sheer size and density of the two countries which have led, amongst other things, to Britain's stronger planning framework and the sanctity which is still accorded to the constraints of Green Belt planning (see chapter 3). Likewise, the very different pattern of jurisdictional fragmentation in America has helped to underpin the flight from the cities and the segregation of affluent white suburbs. The role of public enterprise is equally different, with a far lower role for public investment – with correspondingly much greater scope to the private sector – in the United States. Finally, the relations of central and local government are vastly different with Britain being a much more centrally-dominated society, revolving ever more around the great wen of Whitehall and Westminster, as against the continuing strength of states' rights and anti-trust legislation in the United States of America.

Developments in America need not necessarily be reflected, eventually, in the

British context. Britain needs more consistent and proactive policies through which urban fortunes can be turned around and from which can stem a willingness to believe in an urban future. Despite the differences we can learn from some of the successes of certain of the older American cities, not least something of the way in which the very differences have helped to create a context out of which urban regeneration has occurred in America. The decentralization of control – through such anti-trust laws as the MacFadden legislation on banking – and the greater involvement of *local* business to the locality in which it operates has clearly helped to bolster local private economic development. The relative success of American cities has owed much to the combination of public and private initiative which has been given scope both in Urban Development Action Grants and in the small-scale base of community enterprise. None of this has made substantial inroads into the distribution of economic and social benefit. The reliance on privatism and on commercially-attractive investment has merely reinforced the evidence that 'trickle-down' does not operate unless there are public resources and a specific targeting of those resources and benefits to the most disadvantaged population groups. The balancing of the goals of economic development and social justice remains a continuing unattainable chimera even in the boom conditions and the contract compliance policies of Boston which continues to show evidence of degrees of segregation of rich and poor and of levels of social degradation which would appall even the worst of British cities (Parkinson et al., 1988; Ward, 1988).

What, then, is the future for the great cities in Britain which date from the industrial past. Looking at examples of cities which *are* coming to terms with their new commercial social and economic environments, the range of examples is more impressive than the proponents of gloom might lead us to expect. Glasgow is one of the most impressive instances both of the improvement of its decayed environment and in the creation of what could be a self-sustaining momentum to create a new form of city. Significantly, what is emerging is a city which draws increasingly on recreation, on services and on culture (for which it will celebrate its year as 'cultural city of Europe' in 1990). Much of its success has been a result both of the ability of its regional structure of administration to better focus ideas and resources to support the city, through the activities of the Scottish Development Agency, and of the very scale of the public resources that have been put, for example, into housing and environmental rehabilitation through the involvement of small-scale local housing associations (Maclennan, 1987).

But Glasgow is by no means unique. In Manchester, for example, some remarkable successes have been achieved: the old cotton exchange has been converted into a highly successful theatre erected symbolically within the vast space of the old temple of cotton itself; the old Liverpool Road railway station (the first passenger station in the world) has been converted into an industrial museum linked to the conversion of the Castlefield surrounding area (which contains an old Roman fort, a second museum, a complex of canal basins and of older commercial buildings which have been converted into a heritage centre) into a complex of tourist and recreation activities. Manchester has also gone some way to halting the demise of peak retailing trade in the central area by an imaginative programme of commercial upgrading and advertising so that the proportion of Christmas trade in the centre has now grown significantly faster than in the competing suburban shopping centres over the last five years. It has converted the abandoned Central Station into G–Mex, a commercial exhibition centre, rehabilitated one of the decaying large station hotels into an up-market hotel complex and converted a textile warehouse into another high-status hotel. It has attracted a private/public consortium to collect funds for a Phoenix project to continue the upgrading of a large sector of the decayed central area with office and entertainment complexes.

The neighbouring authority of Salford – ideologically much more prepared than Manchester to proclaim its readiness to work with the private sector – has rehabilitated a considerable number of council flats into private properties which have generated a lively residential market and has taken the lead in the highly successful public-private promotion of the residential, recreational and commercial development of Salford Quays at the head of the Manchester Ship Canal.

Urban policy, with its increasing emphasis on the private sector and its consequent focus on commercially-attractive schemes, has as yet done little to address the needs of the most impoverished – indeed the very focus on schemes in the more commercially amenable areas has deepened the relative poverty of those in greatest need – but the commercial and environmental improvement has laid a potential base for more equitable regeneration. Each of these examples suggests the combination of commerce, quaternary activity, cultural complexes, recreation and tourism, and commercially-related hotel development that spell out the new role that cities can play if they are able and prepared to adapt themselves to the demands of a post-industrial society in which recreation and leisure and tertiary and quaternary activities dominate secondary productive activities (see chapter 11). The future role of great cities is not that of attempting to recreate the narrow industrial base on which many of the great cities of the nineteenth century arose, but to fashion the cultural, recreational and information base on which to reap the benefits of their inherited infrastructure and from their potential as areas of densely massed opportunities.

Social policy

Such a prospect is predicated on a radical rethinking of what can or might be done to help those who both now and in the future are likely to suffer from the lack of traditional industrial employment. The social aspect cannot be divorced from economic and environmental refurbishment. Big cities will have no future if large numbers of their citizens are poor and disenfranchised by that poverty from the 'real' life of the majority. The threat of social unrest and the more wayward excesses of a minority of 'new left' authorities are built on the gross inequities which inner city social malaise reflects. One of the more ironical aspects of much currently fashionable thinking is the demand to return to some dream past of community where men and women, who slaved in factories, foundries and mines for a pittance, loved every minute of it. The fact that our post-industrial society has not yet come to terms with the need for a Rawlsian form of social justice (Rawls, 1971) is no excuse for trying to recapture a past which was never as rosy as it is all too often painted. It is unfortunately true that much city renewal mostly benefits those in well-paid jobs. The aim must be to reform state taxation and benefits so that those who, for long or short periods, find themselves without regular work are not faced with a clumsily inadequate system which condemns them not only to the mean mercy of the state but also draws them into the marginal and occasionally criminal world of the black economy. This thriving sub-world of odd-job men and women – familiar to all who genuinely know the inner city but which, as yet, has largely evaded the blunt hand of the researcher – would be better brought into the full light of day rather than lurking in the murky twilight where too often it merges into the handling of illicit drugs and stolen videos and cars. Any one of the increasing number of schemes which have been suggested for unification of the tax and benefit systems would enforce a crude but necessary redistribution of wealth without returning to the uniformity and inefficiency of universal benefits which have always been popular with the middle class – including many leaders of left-wing opinion – who are the principal beneficiaries of them. No doubt theirs would be amongst the voices raised loudest were genuine tax reform to include the abolition of most of the allowances with which we lard our present tax system, including the now-indefensible mortgage tax relief system. We need only look at the self-righteousness of professional parents when threatened with the loss of fee-paying student grants to see something of the obstacles that stand in the way of socially-just tax reforms, in contradistinction to the regressive abolition of higher-rate tax levels.

The need for reform will surely become even more pressing after the combined effects of recent tax changes, the proposed poll tax and the newly-instituted benefit scheme become evident in an unacceptable widening of the gap between affluent and impoverished.

Nor can urban areas hope to survive successfully without a more precise targeting of the monies which are poured into them. Whilst I have no doubts about the potential for *survival* of the city as such, it is important to listen to those people who live there, who know what they want but get little help in achieving their aims. A summary of the recently-published poignant story of the Weller Street co-operative (McDonald, 1986) should be sent to every politician, every civil servant in Westminster and every town hall in the country. We worry more about political accountability and yearly accounting – about the form and structure of government – rather than how to give people a freer hand to govern themselves. Community architecture may be but a thinly fashionable band-wagon, but self-help has deep and grand roots in the selfish individualism which both makes and mars us as a society (Marquand, 1988). Currently many groups from the ethnic minorities are seeking ways to make progress in their urban settings: too often, lively ideas and potentially viable schemes get lost because such groups find it difficult to get started. Little wonder that in some cases they have become acolytes of skilful local politicians who see the opportunity to buy up votes. These matters are too serious to be left to the ambitions of petty politicians who 'strut their hour upon the stage'. Each lurch of the electoral system results in the waste of a few more millions as some new gimmick is tried: for example, who can say how long the enthusiasm for low-rise houses will last? Twenty years from now they may well be regarded as unsatisfactory as the modern tower blocks. Behind the university in Manchester is a council estate of good-quality conventional housing conforming to all the now widely-bruited ideas of good design (Coleman et al., 1985): ironically it is beset by problems of vandalism and violence on a scale which dwarfs those of many high-rise housing areas. Its tenants struggle to make their voices heard, but too often they have been ignored. In that lies an important ingredient of the local problems. Alongside its grander schemes of urban renewal the city council should also embark on a decentralization plan which may meet the needs of such tenants.

The essence of such evolving schemes of urban renaissance is not dissimilar from the American experience. The monolithic dominance of municipal enterprise which has been a growing twentieth-century blight on responsive urban development has now been leavened by the healthy alliance between public and private enterprise and by an increasing preparedness to listen, and sometimes to respond, to urban residents. Increasing scope is being given to smaller-scale initiatives and control through community enterprise, the growth of tenant groups, the devolution of more localized control by neighbourhood groups and the increased role of locally-based housing associations.

A new political realism which has led to greater willingness of local authorities to work with Chambers of Commerce and the private sector in cities such as Birmingham, Sheffield and Salford could provide the basis for a more genuine three-sided partnership with central government. The long-term challenge is how to incorporate within the drive for economic and environmental renewal the interests of the poor and dispossessed in new forms of urban governance and in genuinely people-targeted policies. It is in the encouragement of such *variety* that the strengths of future urban initiative will be realized. The post-industrial city *can* play a valuable role as a centre of commerce, education- and knowledge-based activity, culture, recreation, tourism and leisure, so as to capitalize on its knowledge base, the strength of its mass of population and activities, and the variety of its visual, social and economic stimuli. Some of the great cities will undoubtedly contract if they fail to adapt to the challenge of change or fail to make their environments sufficiently attractive to retain and attract population and new investment. There is, however, no reason why – with a combination of municipal and private enterprise, alive to the needs of local people – many great cities should not find renewed greatness for the future.

References

Blythe, R. (1969), *Akenfield: Portrait of an English Village*, Allen Lane, Harmondsworth.
Coleman, A. *et al.* (1985), *Utopia on Trial*, Hilary Shipman.

Department of the Environment (1977), *Change or Decay: Final Report of the Liverpool Inner Area Study*, HMSO.

Green, O. (1988), *Metro-land* (1932 edn with an introduction by Oliver Green) Oldcastle Books.

Helm, S. (1988), 'Small-town tensions which led to a race riot', *The Independent*, 4 January.

Kilroy-Silk, R. (1987), 'Riots that go unremarked', *The Times*, 22 August.

McDonald, A. (1986), *The Weller Way: The Story of the Weller Street's Housing Co-operative*, Faber and Faber.

Macleinan, D. (1987), 'Housing reinvestment and neighbourhood revitalisation', in B. Robson (ed.), *Managing the City: The Aims and Impacts of Urban Policy*, Croom Helm.

Marquand, D. (1988), *The Unprincipled Society: New Demands and Old Politics*, Jonathan Cape.

Oxley, S. (1988), 'Publicans call for action on New Year riots', *Newport Pagnell and District Herald*, 9 January.

Parkinson, M. Foley, B. and Judd, D. (eds), (1988), *Regenerating the Cities: The UK Crisis and the US Experience*, Manchester University Press.

Rawls, J. (1971), *A Theory of Social Justice*, Belknapp Press, Cambridge, Mass.

Schoon, N. (1987), 'Developers reveal a private vision of Stone Bassett', *The Independent*, 16 December.

Short, J.R., Fleming, S. and Witt, S. (1986), *Housebuilding, Planning and Community Action: The Production and Negotiation of the Built Environment*, Routledge and Kegan Paul.

Ward, C. (1978), *The Child in the City*, Architectural Press.

Ward, C. (1988), 'Democratic vistas', *New Society*, 22 April, 24.

Wiener, M.J. (1981), *English Culture and the Decline of the Industrial Spirit, 1850–1980*, Cambridge University Press.

5 Industrialization, urban growth and the city economy

Gareth Shaw

Introduction

Recent interest in the future of metropolitan areas has in part led to the search for the historical dimensions of our present urban crisis. This in turn has had two important consequences. The first is the growing awareness of the common threads in the economic development of cities, as illustrated by the comparative studies of Berlin, Paris, London and New York (Ewers et al., 1986). The second has served to highlight the somewhat fragmented nature of the research on the economies of industrializing cities, with many themes receiving little or no attention.

In North America, despite much discussion of past urban growth, Muller (1977) complains that the processes of development 'remain obscured by the use of oversimplified explanations'. Similarly, Meyer (1983) argues that, although the spatial dynamics of industrialization during the nineteenth century have been examined at different spatial scales in the United States, 'no conceptual framework integrates' their different insights. Other workers, notably Persky and Moses (1984), have pointed to the lack of empirical work on the history of industrialized cities, with much of the past research on specialized industrial cities being at best anecdotal in nature.

The situation in Britain is of a relatively low level of research activity and few recent studies on industrialization in nineteenth-century cities. In some cases, especially retail distribution and marketing, work has made steady progress and gone a considerable way towards explaining the role that these played in the urban economy. By contrast, much basic work remains to be carried out on the industrial structure of nineteenth-century cities, as well as the growing service activities found in most large urban centres. Pioneer studies of urban economic patterns in London provided what Hall (1962) and Martin (1964) regarded as 'but an initial essay on the subject'. Unfortunately, such work has received scant attention from historical geographers and the limited progress that has been made owes much to the work of urban and economic historians. Checkland's (1964) initial agenda for research on the British industrial city strongly emphasized the importance of developing a spatial approach to the urban economy, an argument followed up by Forsyth (1982) in his study of the economic development of nineteenth-century Glasgow.

A broader expansion of some of Checkland's ideas, Carter and Wheatley on Aberystwyth, was more fully developed in their work on Merthyr Tydfil (1982) in a systematic approach which views the transformation of Merthyr in terms of a series of sequential changes based on industrial technology, developments in retailing, advances in transportation systems and, finally, changes in building technology. However, the small size of Merthyr raises obvious questions concerning the relationship between urban scale and economic growth. Few studies of such relationships exist within the British context and recent reviews of so-called 'regional cities' provide little more than a series of case studies. This contrasts with the situation in North America where Pred (1966) and, latterly, Conzen (1987) have discussed the growth characteristics of city systems.

Within such diversity we can recognize three broad perspectives. One involves the changing economy and a consideration of the relative importance of different economic activities and their employment structure over time. The second is concerned with the relationships between economic growth and urban expansion, often stressing the positive association between industrialization and urbanization (Lampard, 1955) and also relates to studies of regional development in either particular countries or individual regions (Miller, 1979). Finally, a number of writers have been concerned with the growth and internal characteristics of economic land use within individual cities, using a range of methodologies (Mayer and Wade, 1969; Olson, 1981).

Furthermore, whichever questions are posed concerning the economic development of urban areas, answers are restricted by the unsatisfactory nature of much of the source material. In Britain, for example, the historical studies based on occupational data from the population censuses are hindered by the ever-changing basis of classification. Data for cities are also limited with tabulations reflecting administrative areas rather than urban economic units. Moreover, local information on the location and character of individual economic activities is limited, street or trade directories often forming the only available sources. It is against this problematic background that attempts to reconstruct the economic rise of nineteenth-century cities must be made.

Industrialization and urbanization

The links between industrialization and urban growth are in one sense obvious, but in another difficult to disentangle. Many observers have argued that during the nineteenth century industrialization and urbanization were mutually self-perpetuating forces, although at different times the factors binding the two together may have been very different. Indeed, the impact of industrial growth on individual cities depends both on their size and, more importantly, their functional role within regional economies. As Pred (1966) argues, whilst industrial growth generates a local multiplier within a particular urban area, a non-local multiplier is also created within the region's metropolis where the cumulative effects of economic developments throughout the region are felt. Such ideas, however, only give a partial insight into the processes at work and inevitably generalize, even distort, both historical and geographical influences. ⇐

In terms of understanding the broad stimulus to urban economic growth, reference may be made to the importance of 'long-waves' of economic development. This approach highlights the economic cycles identified by the work of Kondratieff (1935), Schumpeter (1939) and Kuznets (1953), each of whom suggests that economic development has occurred in a wave-like fashion since the early industrial revolution. These economic waves are themselves composed of a series of phases reflecting prosperity, recession, depression, and then recovery to the next cycle or wave. Furthermore, Kuznets believes it is possible to identify Kondratieff waves over the period of industrialization, especially for Britain and the United States (see table 5.1, figure 5.1 and chapter 2).

A re-examination of these ideas has led Mensch (1979) to suggest that rather than economic growth being characterized by a wave-like motion, the processes are perhaps better described by his metamorphosis model in which, Mensch argues, economic development is more likely to happen 'through a series of intermittent innovative impulses that take the form of successive S-shaped cycles' (op. cit., p. 73). Such impulses are triggered by swarms of product innovations that have occurred at different time periods which mark the end of a period of depression and the beginning of a recovery phase (table 5.1).

These ideas are especially attractive to urban historians since they offer a framework for comparative studies, as well as providing a broad organizational framework within which urban growth can be considered. Such opportunities have been used by Sutcliffe (1986) and Hall (1986) in their different reviews of the economic growth of major metropolitan areas after 1890, whilst Gordon (1986) selected the third and fourth Kondratieff waves as the time period for an examination of British provincial cities. All of them agree that these economic cycles and innovation swarms have important spatial ramifications which can assist an understanding of the differential rates of urban growth. During the nineteenth century these innovations led to a range of new industries being created that often had locational requirements and constraints very different from those of existing industries.

Industrial expansion in nineteenth-century England is suggestive of these changing relationships, producing differential growth rates of urbanization in distinctive phases of development. The first of these, to the mid-1820s, witnessed a substantial increase in the number of urban areas. Growth was dominated by textile- and metal-manufacturing towns in northern and midland England. In this phase industries such as cotton textiles were concentrated in specific locations, whilst their scale of operation was increased through a series of manufacturing innovations. The application of steam power from the 1780s onwards favoured the growth of those towns which had good supplies of coal and water. Such trends were strengthened by the early dominance of steam power in the Lancashire mills, a trend which owed much to the development of a local engine industry (Musson and Robinson, 1959). In addition, Chapman (1972) has shown how towns were further favoured by relatively good supplies of labour compared with the factories

Table 5.1 Kuznets' scheme of Kondratieff cycles and Mensch's innovation phases

Economic characteristics	Kondratieff cycles				Mensch's innovation phases
	Prosperity	Recession	Depression	Revival	
1787–1842: 'Industrial Revolution Kondratieff': cotton textiles; iron; steam power	1787–1800	1801–1813	1814–1827	1828–1842	Pre 1787, 1814–28
1842–1897: 'Bourgeois Kondratieff': railways; steel; engineering; coal	1843–1857	1858–1869	1870–1885	1886–1897	1870–1886
1897 to date: 'Neo-Mercantilist Kondratieff': electricity; oil; chemicals; light engineering; cars	1898–1911	1912–1925	1926–1939		1925–1939

Source: Kuznets, 1953 and Mensch, 1979

in rural locations. The cost savings brought about by canals and improved inland navigations further shaped the contours of urban growth by giving additional locational advantages for manufacturing. The boost given to these industrial settlements may be measured in terms of population growth (figure 5.2).

A second phase of urbanization that corresponds with the revival stage of the first Kondratieff wave (table 5.1) was largely concerned with the consolidation and expansion of those urban areas which possessed the economic advantages and specialized functions associated with the larger industrial complexes. The cotton textile industry is illustrative of such changes, since it witnessed a series of technical innovations in the hitherto backward weaving sections (Farnie, 1979). The commercial application of power-loom weaving, especially after 1820, led to the evolution of a complete factory-based system and gave added impetus to the

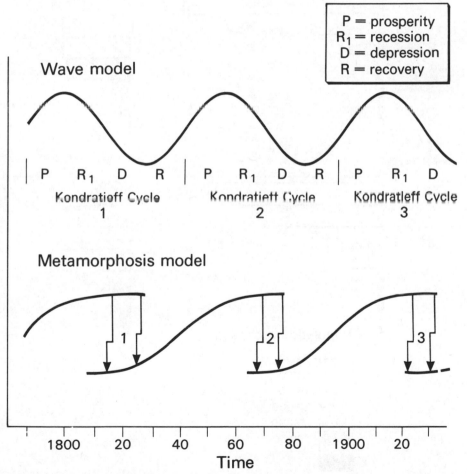

Figure 5.1 Wave model (Kondratieff cycle) and metamorphosis model (intermittent S-shaped cycles) of economic growth *circa* 1790–1939. *Source:* Kuznets, 1953 and Mensch, 1979

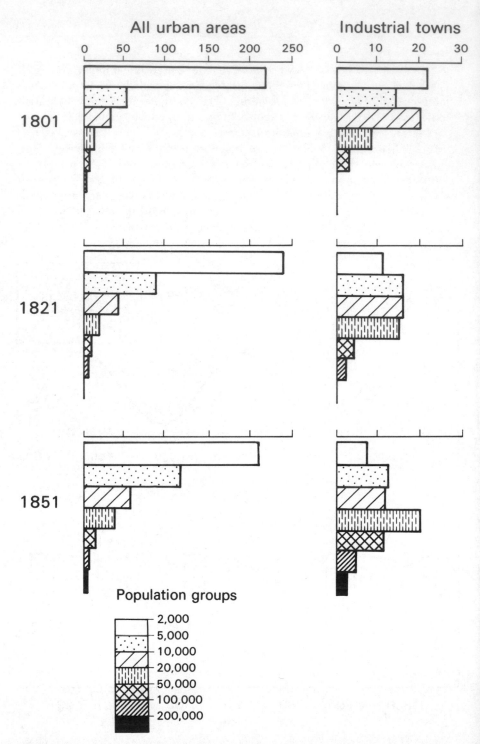

Figure 5.2 Population in all urban areas and in industrial towns of England and Wales 1801, 1821 and 1851. *Source*: Census

urban centres in south-east Lancashire. As Kenny (1982) shows, by 1850 these combined mills completely dominated the region, accounting for 64 per cent of employment and 82 per cent of looms. In other urban centres, the development of steel, engineering techniques and railways provided the necessary industrial base for rapid growth (figure 5.3).

The first half of the nineteenth century witnessed, therefore, a dramatic difference in the population growth of industrial centres as compared with other urban areas. Whilst the modal class of all urban areas remained in the population group 2,000–4,999 between 1801 and 1851, that for industrial towns had changed to 20,000–49,999 by 1851 (figure 5.2). Many of these industrial centres also expanded the service aspects of their economy, particularly retailing, to cater for the increased demand for food. In the early years of the nineteenth century retail provision was uneven as population and shops increased at differential rates, with the highest levels of provision in established market towns (table 5.2), but by 1851 shopping provision had become far more equalized as growing industrial towns developed their retail functions.

During the second half of the nineteenth century a third phase of urban growth can be recognized, bringing a wider economic base to urbanization processes. The main impetus of change was associated with a series of innovations, which Mensch identifies in the period 1870 to 1886 (table 5.1), the full impact of which on urban growth was to be felt over a much longer time span and produced marked locational shifts in economic growth.

Within the context of this changing economic base, previous studies have recognized the beginnings of a shift in employment away from the traditional manufacturing industries, whilst Lee (1984) has recently stressed the regional impact of the growth of tertiary activities. However, as table 5.3 shows rates of growth in manufacturing occupations compared favourably with increases in population between 1871 and 1911. Manufacturing appeared to be shifting from its dominant position in relative terms, with the growing importance of service and retail activities in overall employment (table 5.4).

These structural changes reflect a complex set of trends set in motion by technical and organizational innovations after 1870. Three main features may be identified. First, a group of traditional industries experienced a relative decline: clothing, wool, cotton, other textiles and metal manufacturing all grew at less than the national average, while their share of the workforce fell from 78.1 per cent in 1871 to 63.6 in 1911. Secondly, expansion took place in engineering, food, drink and tobacco manufacturing, printing, paper making, gas and chemical production in both relative and absolute terms from 21.9 per cent of the workforce in 1871 to 36.4 per cent in 1911. Thirdly, and of critical importance for the development of urban areas, was the spatial selectivity of such changes in manufacturing. In Britain this involved a significant south-easterly development of the new, expanding industries which were no longer tied so firmly to the coalfields (figure 5.4). A further dimension to this regional selectivity was through the service sector which, according to Lee, occupied some 40 per cent of the workforce by 1911 and concentrated strongly on London and the towns of south-east England.

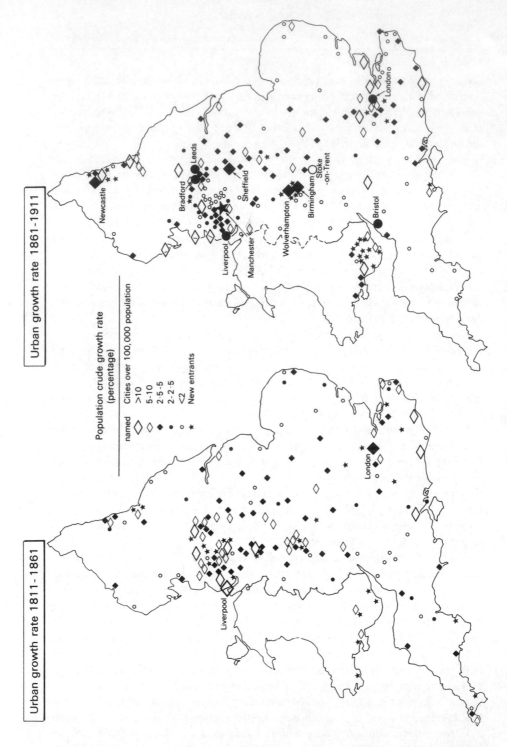

Figure 5.3 Percentage annual population growth in cities over 100,000, 1811–61 (left) and 1861–1911 (right). New entrants are those reaching 100,000 during the period indicated
Source: Robson, 1973

Table 5.2   Variations in shop provision for different types of English town, 1801–81

Settlement types	Population per shop			
	1801	*1821*	*1851*	*1881*
Industrial				
Leeds	340	89	61	51
Hull	97	73	60	72
Halifax	742	105	87	67
Huddersfield	429	103	69	53
Market towns				
York	57	70	83	48
Beverley	36	36	30	33

Settlements are marked according to size and data on shops have been interpolated to the nearest census date.

Selective urban growth and the rise of large cities

The previous description of the relationship between industrialization and urban growth serves to stress the role of technical change, but does little to explain the rise of large cities and the detailed processes of selective urban development. An understanding of these factors also involves a closer consideration of regional economic growth during the nineteenth century, and in particular the rise of regional industrial systems.

Much of the conceptualization of these processes in a temporal perspective has been by North American geographers, whose ideas range from place specific models to more general theories. Early work by North (1961) focused on export base theory in an attempt to explain regional industrialization processes in the United States during the antebellum years. North argued that regional specialization led to the growth of industrialization in the Eastern states, which produced manufactured goods for the Middle West and South, in return for plantation staples and foodstuffs. However, as Lindstrom (1978) has shown, such an approach is too narrow and fails to stress the importance of intra-regional trade in the economic growth of the Eastern states, whilst more recently Meyer (1983) sees these two approaches as complementary. It is these ideas of complementarity, rather than strict competitive relationships, that lie at the heart of the 'selective urban growth' hypothesis of North American urbanism within which Muller (1977) has identified three main periods of settlement evolution: the pioneer periphery; the specialized periphery; and the transitional periphery. Within each of these factors of site advantage, nodality, transportation and industrial development played different roles. Thus, whilst site advantages tended to diminish in relative importance over time, other

Table 5.3   Total population and the manufacturing workforce of England and Wales, 1871–1911

Year	Total population	Percentage increase p.a.	Manufacturing workforce	Percentage increase p.a.
1871	22,712,266		3,264,971	
1881	25,974,439	1.44	3,481,770	0.66
1891	29,002,525	1.17	3,954,146	1.36
1901	32,537,843	1.22	4,484,737	1.34
1911	36,070,492	1.09	5,148,623	1.48

Source: Censuses of England and Wales 1871–1911

Table 5.4   Percentage employed in industry and commerce in England and Wales, 1871–1911

Year	Industrial service	Dealers	Manufacturers
1871	4.52	18.93	76.55
1881	6.38	19.06	74.56
1891	7.26	20.32	72.42
1901	11.26	21.54	67.20
1911	9.90	23.36	66.74

Industrial service + dealers + manufacturers = 100

Source: Census of England and Wales, 1871–1911

factors, such as the growth of business institutions and transportation networks, served to stimulate further development in a particular city.

Both Meyer (1987) and Conzen (1987) have identified a series of regional industrial systems in the United States which had become pre-eminent during the second half of the nineteenth century. Probably the best documented of these systems is the emergence of Philadelphia, which was already well established as a regional centre by 1800 (Lindstrom, 1978). During the first half of the nineteenth century the city developed as a major manufacturing centre for consumer goods and producer durables for its regional market. Its service functions served to bind together more specialized manufacturing centres, such as Trenton, Camden and Wilmington. Cities, such as Philadelphia, were characterized not only by a considerable range of manufacturing output, but also by a few dominant industries. The

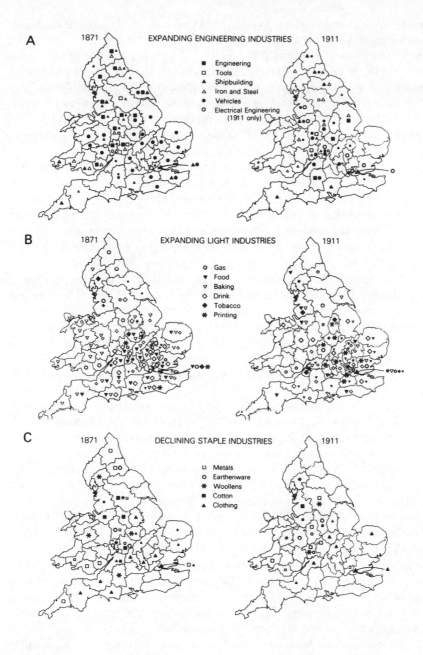

Figure 5.4 Expanding industries (A – iron and steel and engineering; B – light industry) and declining industries (C – metals, earthenware and textiles) in England and Wales 1871 and 1911. Thanks are due to Miss Alison C. Tipper for material for this and figures 5.6 and 5.7. *Source*: Census of population for England and Wales 1871 and 1911

textile industry, for example, accounted for 33 per cent of all industrial workers in Philadelphia in 1850.

More recent work by Groves (1987) has drawn attention to some of the internal characteristics of the North-East regional systems, and identified three distinctive types of centres: the large cities, New York, Baltimore, Boston and Philadelphia, which were originally built on a mercantile base and developed into major manufacturing centres; a second group of mere processing centres, such as Albany and Rochester; and a third type of small to medium-sized, specialized manufacturing towns, as represented by Lowell and New Bedford.

Two central themes emerge from such American research: first, the importance of regional industrial systems in the development of large cities; and, secondly, the role played by complementary urban economies. Muller, Meyer and Groves all stress the importance of these intra-regional support processes in the growth of a regional metropolis. Evidence from Britain, however, hints that processes of competition were equally important at least in the early growth of regional centres as Vigier (1970) has argued in his study of Liverpool and Manchester.

Many writers suggest that urban economic growth depended on the adoption of critical innovations, a feature heavily stressed by Robson (1973). Others believe that it is diversification, rather than specialization, that causes economic growth to be sustained (Jacobs, 1969; Rodgers, 1957). Cities grew initially at the expense of rural centres, as illustrated by Leicester and Northampton which progressively dominated their hinterlands in the production of hosiery and footwear until, by 1900, this means of growth was exhausted and the process was repeated with an urban competitor, the east end of London (Vigier, 1970). It would seem, therefore, that the growth of regional centres and of a regional urban system progressed through two stages: the first dominated by the processes of competition, as one centre attempted to become pre-eminent; the second characterized more by complementarity as the subdued towns supported their regional centre.

In geographically more complex regional systems, as found in parts of nineteenth-century England, inter-city rivalry continued to play an important role even in phase two. Liverpool's competition with Manchester is such a case of rivalry within, as Waller (1983, p. 87) points out, 'a situation of inter-city dependency'. Thus, Liverpool controlled both flows of cotton into Manchester and the export of finished products, and Liverpool merchants were often seen as manipulating the market in raw cotton to the detriment of manufacturers in Manchester (Biggs, 1895). To the people of Manchester, Liverpool merchants lived off the backs of their labours, and there is no doubting the importance of cotton to Liverpool's economy, since the shipping of raw cotton accounted for 40 per cent of the value of the port's trade in the first half of the nineteenth century.

So far the emphasis has been on the links between industry and the growth of cities at a broad level. However, our understanding of such relationships must rest on a more detailed examination of individual cities. The rise of large cities involves not only a consideration of the relative importance of different economic activities, but also the state of business initiatives. City growth during the nineteenth century owed as much to the imagination of individual entrepreneurs, as to the natural advantages of particular locations. The economic prospects of city development depended on the vigour of entrepreneurs who could engender a new set of economic attitudes amongst their fellow citizens. The importance of such skills and the successful images they created is well illustrated by Lampard's account of the growth and transformation of New York's economy. According to Lampard (1986), the city's merchants initiated, as well as responded to, opportunities in their wider economic environment, a fact borne out by the scale of transport improvements and company developments in the early nineteenth century: for example, in New York State there were some 250 legislative incorporations of turnpike roads between 1799 and 1819, whilst between 1811 and 1818 129 manufacturing companies were launched.

In English provincial cities the role of individual entrepreneurs is perhaps more readily identified in the formative years of industrial development. Thus, in Leeds Connell and Ward (1980) claim to trace the start of rapid industrial growth from the 'endless enterprise' of Richard Paley who introduced the factory system to the city in 1790. Paley's two mills at Bank, Leeds, were followed by the large Park Mills development of Benjamin Gott on a sixteen-acre site in 1797. It was the skill and enterprise of the early textile pioneers, together with engineers such as James Fowler, that laid the basis for Leeds's nineteenth-century industrial prosperity. In many respects the early nineteenth century was dominated by the regional businessman with a compulsion to sustain his city: thus, the term 'Manchester Man' became part of popular speech and, by the 1820s, referred to a cotton manufacturer or merchant who had won the respect of his fellow townspeople – often by membership of the Manchester Exchange where much of the city's business was transacted.

The economic commitment of many nineteenth-century entrepreneurs to their region often took the practical form of the development of local trade associations, such as the Manchester Commercial Society, active between 1794 and 1801, and the Manchester Chamber of Commerce established in 1820. These attempted to bring some semblance of order to the city's economy and in the absence of effective local government machinery during the first half of the nineteenth century, often acted as the city's mouthpiece to central government.

The city economy: crises and showpiece developments

Regional metropolises, such as Manchester, epitomized the strong bonds between industrialization and urbanization during the nineteenth century, and can serve as a template for further explorations of the urban economy. At the beginning of the nineteenth century Manchester was already the commercial centre of a regional system of textile towns within a ten-mile radius of the city. Vigier has described this urban system as the 'Manchester cluster', and shown how the development of the city occurred in a series of phases, each of which reflected the technological and economic restructuring of the textile industry. In the early phases of the mid and late eighteenth century Manchester was a collecting and commercial centre for the surrounding textile manufacturing centres. The combined built-up area of Manchester and Salford was just less than one-quarter of a square mile, although growth was taking place rapidly to the south to take advantage of new docking facilities on the improved navigation of the River Irwell and along the Bridgewater Canal.

The second phase of urbanization in the early nineteenth century was associated with Manchester becoming a finishing centre for the cluster's cotton textiles. This additional function, together with Manchester's existing role as a mercantile centre, made two significant impacts on the city's structure. The first was the introduction of textile manufacturing and finishing activities into what had previously been mainly a mercantile centre, which also had the effect of producing a relatively undifferentiated combination of manufacturing, commercial and retail functions within the central area of the city. Secondly, manufacturing activities attracted greater numbers of workers to the city, thereby increasing pressure on residential land use and leading to the development of working-class suburbs. Widespread use of steam power and the development of the factory system were responsible for initiating and sustaining this second phase of urbanization, which not only witnessed greater levels of manufacturing development and increased population growth, but also an extension in the physical size of the city. By 1800, for example, there were at least 52 spinning mills at work in Manchester, many of which occupied imposing buildings of at least four storeys (Farnie, 1956).

Within early nineteenth-century Manchester most of the industrial land occupied a broad band along the river Medlock, with a series of relatively isolated works around which urban growth had not fully encroached (Laxton, 1986). There was also an important area of factory development adjacent to and intruding into the central area. To a large extent these industrial areas formed the major focal points of growth during the first half of the nineteenth century.

The city's physical structure was also shaped by the expansion of the warehouse quarter. This reflected Manchester's continuing and increasing importance as a major mercantile centre for the region's cotton industry, which was focused on the Royal Exchange. Farnie argues that the city's warehouse region expanded in 'an eccentric rather than a concentric manner' during the early part of the century. This may have been the case, but the essential fact is that the demand for more space forced merchants to expand on the western edges of the commercial core where Farnie was estimated that the number of warehouses increased from 89 in 1820 to 279 in 1829. Whilst many of these were new firms, others had migrated the short distance from the area just to the north of the Exchange.

The rise of Manchester was not achieved without economic crises during the nineteenth century, largely because of boom and depression in the textile industry, often related to problems of cotton supply. The minute books of the Manchester Chamber of Commerce give a detailed insight into depressions in the cotton trade and their implications for the local economy (Redford, 1940). The shock waves from these problems were felt throughout the economy, especially in the city's service and retail trades, though they did little to dampen the entrepreneurial spirit of the city. No sooner had one crisis passed than plans were being laid for

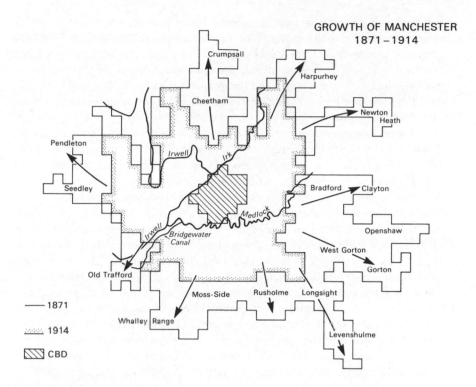

GROWTH OF MANCHESTER 1871–1914

— 1871

⋯⋯ 1914

▨ CBD

Figure 5.5 The growth of Manchester 1871–1914. The growth zones are based on 1cm grid squares with built-up areas of over 25 percent.

future expansions. For example, the stagnation of trade between 1827 and 1833, so clearly illustrated by Kay's account of distress in 1833 for the newly-founded Manchester Statistical Society, was quickly followed by a period of rapid growth. Thus, by 1836 – itself a year of financial crises – some 23 joint stock schemes were proposed in Manchester, together with a further 14 linked with Liverpool, involving in all some £9 million of new capital.

By 1837 yet another depression had commenced which was to reach its point of greatest severity between 1841–2. When William Cooke Taylor visited Manchester in 1842 he found the population 'labouring under severe and unprecedented stress' (Taylor, 1847, p. 8). Yet in 1843 the economy began to show signs of recovery which was completed by 1845: the gloom noted by Cooke Taylor in the Manchester Exchange during 1842 had given way to what Williams (1976) describes as 'feverish speculation' as the city became the 'diligent spider' in the words of Faucher (1844). Such activity was curtailed yet again during a further economic depression in 1847 when the scale of short-time working and unemployment became especially high in the cotton mills and dyeworks (table 5.5).

Physically, the city's entrepreneurial spirit was manifest in the rise of clear functional districts and the creation of a strong central core. It is difficult to be precise about when a recognizable central business district emerged. As Bowden (1975) points out we have no theory of central-district growth, though his work on North American cities indicates that the modern central business district is the functional and morphological expression of two processes which are in turn 'synchronous with the rise of the metropolis'. The first involves the concentration of establishments in an area of high accessibility; the second concerns the separation of place of work from home.

By the mid-nineteenth century Manchester had a central area that had become closer to the mono-nuclear form of modern central business districts. The speculative nature of economic progress associated with the cotton industry had produced a rapid rise in land values, and a clear land market was operating in the central core. Contemporary commentators were in no doubt about the importance of site variations: in central Manchester a site on Piccadilly had increased its value sixtyfold between 1790 and 1840 due to the demand for commercial land. From the 1840s railways were also exerting a potent influence on the internal structure of central areas. Apart from increasing accessibility to city centres, railways had two other significant controls. First, they forced up land values through differentiating site accessibility and what Kellett (1969) terms 'railway land hunger': for example, as much as 9 per cent of land in central Liverpool was occupied by railway companies. Their second control was through the physical constraint of the spatial expansion of many city centres by railway lines. In Manchester this situation had arisen by the 1880s when the central core was ringed by a series of railway lines, owned by companies that had fought bitterly to obtain access to the city centre in the 1840s and 1850s.

From 1850 to 1870 Manchester's commercial core expanded quite rapidly, by approximately 150 acres, in a southerly direction (see Figure 5.5). This increase was brought about by the continued expansion of certain retail and wholesale functions, together with the growing importance of financial institutions. Many firms were associated with the cotton textile industry and sought locations close to the Royal Exchange, whose membership more than doubled between 1852 and 1874 (Barker, 1881).

It was the accumulation of retailing and office functions that led to the restructuring of the centres of nineteenth-century cities. The early transformations were related to the growth in the number of shops and the physical expansion and reorganization of central markets. A closer examination of legislation concerned with markets shows that many local acts of parliament were associated with general town improvement schemes which usually involved the widening and realignment of congested streets around the market. These developments represented substantial investments either by local authorities or joint stock companies. The full impact of these schemes has been described at a city level for Sheffield, Leeds and Manchester by Blackman (1962), Grady (1970) and Scola (1975) respectively, whilst Shaw (1985) has examined national trends.

Such planning initiated important improvements in city centres, but it was the growth of the main shopping streets and large stores that carried through the full force of change. The attempts, at first by clothing retailers, to obtain scale

Table 5.5   Operating characteristics of textile mills in Manchester during 1847

| | Total mills | Percentage of mills | | | |
		working fully	working fully but with reduced employment	working short-time	not working
Cotton	91	48	11	23	18
Silk	8	25	-	75	-
Smallware	18	61	17	17	5
Dyeworks	20	15	-	85	-

| | Total number | Percentage of operatives | | |
		full-time	short-time	unemployed
Cotton	28033	54	21	25
Silk	3009	21	71	8
Smallware	1937	64	31	5
Dyeworks	1674	28	48	24

Source: 'Return showing the state of employment . . . in cotton factories and other large works within the City of Manchester', Town Hall Manchester, 26th November, 1847 (Manchester Local Archives, MSC 318)

economies by increasing the number and range of articles sold resulted in the demand for larger shop premises. One early means of achieving such increases in floorspace was through the amalgamation of adjoining shop premises. In London these processes came early, but in most provincial towns it became important during the 1850s and remained so until the early years of the twentieth century (Shaw, 1988). The development of larger shops led ultimately to the growth of department stores, a trend that can be first recognized in London's West End but which quickly spread to provincial cities.

Indeed, it was in the regional metropolises, such as Manchester and Birmingham, that department stores became linked with prestige city-centre developments during the 1880s. For example, Lewis's department store in Liverpool had six floors in 1886, whilst in Manchester the same organization had plans in 1885 to build a sixteen-storey 180–foot high tower as part of a new expansion scheme (Briggs, 1956). Although in the end only seven floors were constructed, such a development was part of the regional image-building. It is perhaps in Birmingham, however, that the importance of such stores is best articulated. In this case the local authority was

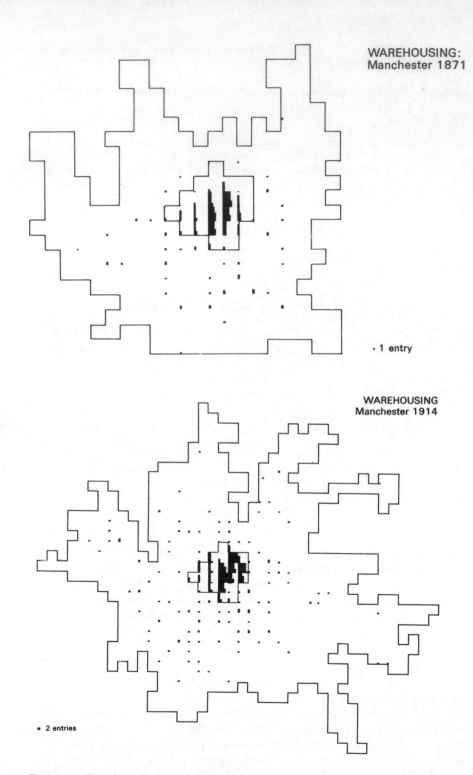

Figure 5.6 Distribution of warehousing in Manchester in 1871 (top) & 1914 (bottom).
Source: local directories.

involved in major city centre redevelopments under the imaginative leadership of Joseph Chamberlain. The main part of the scheme was the development of a large new street, Corporation Street, which was to form the focus of a new shopping area. Chamberlain recognized early on the importance of such a showpiece creation when he declared, 'only a new shopping street . . . would permit the city to become the retail shop of the whole Midland counties of England' (Briggs, 1956, p. 80).

While the years from the 1880s witnessed the final transformation and dominance of city centres by major retail facilities, another important stimulus in the economic and spatial restructuring of central areas was the growth in office functions during the second half of the nineteenth century. In a major city like Manchester, office growth was related to a number of economic sectors (table 5.6). Thus, despite the fact that the number of banking, insurance and accountancy firms increased by 41 per cent between 1871 and 1914, offices related to factories continued to dominate the city's non-retail commercial functions. As Varley (1968) has shown, many of these functions held similar locations within the city centre over long periods of time. Similarly, one of the dominant users of land in the outer parts of the central area was warehousing, concentrations of which occupied the eastern parts of Manchester's core with only limited growth outside of this area between 1871 and 1914 (figure 5.6).

The dominance of manufacturing, especially cotton textiles, made itself felt in all areas of the city's economy: in 1871 textiles and clothing employed some 1,886,820 people or 58 per cent of all employees in manufacturing (table 5.7); by 1911 the textile trades had lost ground relative to newer activities, but they remained the major employer. Indeed, employment increased in both clothing and cotton and it was only in the smaller sectors of woollen and other textiles that the labour force declined. Manchester's other major staple industry, engineering, increased its total labour force by over 250,000 between 1871 and 1911, and played an important role in creating new industrial areas towards the east of the city. Changes in industrial organization provided a further stimulus to economic growth as horizontal integration in the textile industry led to the development of large industrial combines.

Nevertheless, during the 1860s and 1870s industrial and commercial development in Manchester went through further series of economic crises. Economic problems on a large scale appeared in the early 1860s with the onset of the 'cotton famine' following the American civil war when the restriction of cotton supplies temporarily checked Manchester's prosperity. By 1862 some 90,000 people in Manchester and Salford were receiving poor relief, due to loss of employment. The situation was exacerbated by local and national trade depressions in the 1870s. One great difference, compared to the economic crises encountered during the first half of the nineteenth century, was that Manchester's local government attempted to intervene in a positive way. For example, under the provisions of the Public Works Manufacturing Districts Act of 1863, the Treasury was authorized to make loans to local authorities to develop works of public utility. Manchester quickly took up the scheme and used the loans to develop a number of public works in the city (Brady, 1963). Whilst such schemes may not have solved the

Table 5.6   Major commercial functions (non-retail) in Manchester and Salford, 1871–1914

Functions	1871 Number of firms	percentage	1914 Number of firms	percentage	Percentage change 1871–1914
Banking, insurance accountancy	365	8.8	514	8.8	+41
Office functions related to manufacturing	1712	41.3	2928	50.1	+71
Agents and merchants	1696	40.9	1848	31.7	+ 9
Warehousing	377	9.1	548	9.4	+45
Total	4150	100.0	5838	100.0	

Source: local directories

problems of unemployment, they illustrate the growing importance of local government in the city economy.

The opening of the Manchester ship canal in 1894 was another response to the depressions of the 1870s and 1880s, as well as to the trade rivalry with Liverpool. This development, along with the industrial estate of Trafford Park had a significant impact on the industrial geography of the city. In 1871 the city's manufacturing industries were still relatively concentrated in the traditional locations along the rivers Irwell, Irk, Medlock and the canals, giving a strong northeast–southwest orientation (figure 5.7). However, by the eve of the First World War, when Manchester had probably reached its economic zenith, manufacturing industry had broken away from its nineteenth-century locations. New sites in the east of the city were taken up by the expanding engineering trades, whilst the ship canal and Trafford Park provided new attractions in the west. As a consequence of new sites, and to some extent new industries, the pattern of manufacturing in 1914 was less concentrated, and most parts of the city had some industry (figure 5.7).

Conclusion

This chapter has drawn attention to the relatively neglected issue of the urban economy, and the problems in attempting to construct a picture of the economic geography of nineteenth-century cities. The rise of large cities was tied to the expansion of the capitalist modes of business organization and production, the thrust of industrial and commercial innovations, and the growth of regional economies. This last aspect has been neglected, particularly in Britain, yet the rise

ALL MANUFACTURING INDUSTRY
Manchester 1871

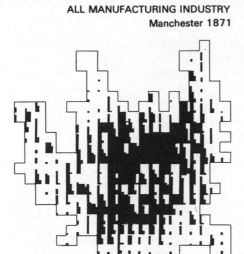

ALL MANUFACTURING INDUSTRY
Manchester 1914

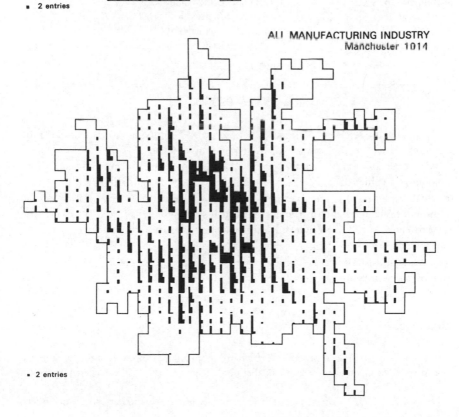

Figure 5.7 Distribution of all manufacturing industry in Manchester in 1871 (top) & 1914 (bottom).

Table 5.7   The changing structure of manufacturing employment in Manchester and Salford, 1871–1911

	1871			1911	
Activities (ranked)	Total	percentage	Activities (ranked)	Total	percentage
Clothing	919,181	(28.2)	Clothing	1,210,979	(23.6)
Cotton	597,627	(18.3)	Cotton	704,595	(13.7)
Metals	444,849	(13.6)	Engineering	695,973	(13.5)
Engineering	279,500	(8.6)	Metals	669,480	(13.0)
Woollens	253,775	(7.8)	Food, drink, tobacco	371,209	(7.2)
Food, drink, tobacco	160,819	(4.9)	Paper and printing	272,790	(5.3)
Wood and furniture	153,045	(4.7)	Woollens	251,895	(4.9)
Other textiles	116,237	(3.6)	Wood and furniture	229,204	(4.5)
Paper and printing	91,937	(2.8)	Vehicles	206,036	(4.0)
Vehicles	78,333	(2.4)	Natural products	129,635	(2.5)
Natural products	69,765	(2.1)	Gas and chemicals	126,952	(2.5)
Earthenware	65,418	(2.0)	Other textiles	102,889	(2.0)
Gas and chemicals	35,022	(1.1)	Earthenware	100,866	(1.9)
Electricity		(0.0)	Electricity	66,120	(1.3)
		100.0			100.0

Source: Censuses of England and Wales, 1871 and 1911

of large provincial cities, such as Manchester and Birmingham, can only be fully understood within the context of their regional systems.

Moreover, in large industrial centres like Manchester, economic and structural change was achieved in a very turbulent fashion, boom and depression being a normal sequence of events. Perhaps most noticeable in these economies was the rapidity of change: belief in the capitalist industrial system appeared to overcome all problems, yet it left powerful imprints on the economic structure and morphology of cities – in strongly centralized business districts and distinctive wholesaling and industrial areas – which have become progressively out of phase with twentieth-century needs (see chapters 2 and 4).

References

Barker, H. (1881), 'On the growth of Manchester population, extension of the commercial centre of the city and provision of habitation', *Transactions of the Manchester Statistical Society*, 9, 1–27.

Biggs, W.W. (1895), 'Cotton corners', *Transactions of the Manchester Statistical Society*, 123–34.

Blackman, J. (1962), 'The food supply of an industrial town', *Business History*, 5–6, 83–97.

Bowden, M.J. (1975), 'Growth of the central districts in large cities', in L.F. Schnore (ed.), *The New Urban History*, Princeton University Press.

Brady, E.A. (1963), 'A reconsideration of the Lancashire "cotton famine" ', *Agricultural History*, 3, 156–62.

Briggs, A. (1956), *Friends of the People: The Centenary History of Lewis's*, Batsford.

Carter, M. and Wheatley, S. (1982), *Merthyr Tydfil in 1851: A Study of the Spatial Structure of a Welsh Industrial Town*, University of Wales, Cardiff.

Chapman, S.D. (1972), *The Cotton Industry in the Industrial Revolution*, Manchester University Press.

Checkland, S.G. (1964), 'The British industrial city as history: the Glasgow case', *Urban Studies*, 1, 34–54.

Connell, E.J. and Ward, M. (1980), 'Industrial development, 1780–1914', in D. Fraser (ed.), *A History of Modern Leeds*, Manchester University Press.

Conzen, M.P. (1987), 'The progress of American urbanism, 1860–1930', in R.D.Mitchell and P.A. Groves (ed) *North America: The Historical Geography of a Changing Continent*, Hutchinson.

Ewers, H–J., Goddard, J.B. and Matzerath, H. (eds) (1986), *The Future of the Metropolis: Berlin, London, Paris and New York*, Walter de Gruyter, Berlin.

Farnie, D.A. (1956), 'The commercial development of Manchester in the late nineteenth century', *Manchester Review*, 7, 327–37.

Farnie, D.A. (1979), *The English Cotton Industry and the World Market, 1815–1896*, Clarendon Press, Oxford.

Faucher, M.L. (1844), *Manchester in 1844: Its Present Condition and Future Prospects* (reprint 1969, Simkin, Manchester and London).

Forsyth, W. (1982), 'Urban economic morphology in nineteenth century Glasgow', in A. Slaven and D.H. Aldcroft (eds) *Business, Banking and Urban History*, University of Glasgow Press, Edinburgh.

Gordon, G. (ed.) (1986), *Regional Cities in the U.K., 1890 1980*, Harper and Row.

Grady, K. (1970), 'The provision of markets and commercial amenities in Leeds, 1822–1829', *Publications of the Thoresby Society*, 59, part 3, no. 122, 122–95.

Groves, P.A. (1987), 'The northeast and regional integration', in R.D. Mitchell and P.A. Groves (eds) *North America: The Historical Geography of a Changing Continent*, Hutchinson.

Hall, P.G. (1962), *The Industries of London since 1861*, Hutchinson.

Hall, P. (1986), 'National capitals, world cities and the new division of labour', in H–J. Ewers, J.B. Goddard and H. Matzerath (eds), *The Future of the Metropolis*, Walter de Gruyter, Berlin.

Jacobs, J. (1969), *The Economy of Cities*, Random House, New York.

Kellett, J.R. (1969), *The Impact of Railways on Victorian Cities*, Routledge.

Kenny, S. (1982), 'The location and organisation of the early Lancashire cotton industry; a systems approach', *The Manchester Geographer*, N.S. 3, 5–27.

Kondratieff, N.D. (1935), 'The long waves in economic life', *The Review of Economic Statistics*, 17, 105–15.

Kuznets, S. (1953), *Economic Change*, Norton, New York.

Lampard, E.E. (1955), 'The history of cities in the economically advanced areas', *Economic Development and Cultures Change*, 3, 81–136.

Lampard, E.E. (1986), 'The New York metropolis in transformation: history and prospect. A study in historical particularity', in H–J. Ewers, J. B. Goddard, and H. Matzerath (eds),

The Future of the Metropolis, Walter de Gruyter, Berlin.

Laxton, P. (1986), 'Textiles', in J. Langton and R.J. Morris (eds) *Atlas of Industrializing Britain, 1780–1914*, Methuen.

Lee, C.H. (1984), 'The service sector, regional specialization, and economic growth in the Victorian economy', *Journal of Historical Geography*, 10, 139–55.

Lindstrom, D. (1978), *Economic Development in the Philadelphia Region, 1810–1850*, Columbia University Press, New York.

Martin, J.E. (1964), 'The industrial geography of Greater London', in R. Clayton (ed.), *The Geography of Greater London*, University of London.

Mayer, H.M. and Wade, R.C. (1969), *Chicago: Growth of a Metropolis*, University of Chicago Press.

Mensch, G. (1979), *Stalemate in Technology: Innovations Overcome the Depression*, Harvard University Press, Cambridge, Mass.

Meyer, D.R. (1983), 'Emergence of the American manufacturing belt: an interpretation', *Journal of Historical Geography*, 9, 145–74.

Meyer, D.R. (1987), 'The national integration of regional economies', in R.D. Mitchell and P.A. Groves (eds) *North America: The Historical Geography of a Continent*, Hutchinson.

Miller, R.B. (1979), *City and Hinterland: A Case Study of Urban Growth and Regional Development*, Greenwood Press, Westport.

Muller, E.K. (1977), 'Regional urbanization and the selective growth of towns in North American regions', *Journal of Historical Geography*, 3, 21–39.

Musson, A.E. and Robinson, E. (1959), 'The early growth of steam power', *Economic History Review*, 2nd series, 6, 418–39.

North, D.C. (1961), *The Economic Growth of the United States, 1790–1860*, Prentice-Hall, Englewood Cliffs.

Olson, S.H. (1981), *Baltimore: The Building of an American City*, Johns Hopkins Press, Baltimore.

Persky, J. and Moses, R. (1984), 'Specialized industrial cities in the United States, 1860–1930', *Journal of Historical Geography*, 10, 37–51.

Pred, A. (1966), *The Spatial Dynamics of U.S. Urban-industrial Growth, 1800–1914*, Harvard University Press, Cambridge, Mass.

Redford, A. (1940), *The History of Local Government in Manchester*, Longman & Co.

Robson, B.T. (1973), *Urban Growth: An Approach*, Methuen.

Rodgers, A.L. (1957), 'Some aspects of industrial diversification in the United States', *Economic Geography*, 33, 16–30.

Schumpeter, J.A. (1939), *Business Cycles*, Harvard University Press, Cambridge, Mass.

Scola, R. (1975), 'Food markets and shops in Manchester, 1770–1870', *Journal of Historical Geography*, 1, 153–68.

Shaw, G. (1985), 'Changes in consumer demand and food supply in nineteenth-century British cities', *Journal of Historical Geography*, 1, 280–96.

Shaw, G. (1988), 'Recent research on the commercial structure of nineteenth-century British cities', in D. Denecke and G. Shaw (eds), *Urban Historical Geography: Recent Progress in Britain and Germany*, Cambridge University Press.

Sutcliffe, A. (1986), 'Historical dimensions of the modern metropolitan problem', in H-J. Ewers, J.B. Goddard and H. Matzerath (eds), *The Future of the Metropolis*, Walter de Gruyter, Berlin.

Taylor, W.C. (1847), *Notes on a Tour in the Manufacturing Districts of Manchester*, Longman & Co., 2nd edn.

Varley, R. (1968), 'Land use analysis in the city centre with special reference to Manchester', unpublished Ph.D. thesis, University of Wales.

Vigier, F. (1970), *Change and Apathy: Liverpool and Manchester during the Industrial Revolution*, Harvard University Press, Cambridge, Mass.

Waller, P.J. (1983), *Town, City and Nation: England, 1850–1914*, Oxford University Press.

Williams, B. (1976), *The Making of Manchester Jewry, 1740–1875*, Manchester University Press.

6 What would one need to know to solve the 'natural decrease in early modern cities' problem?

Robert Woods

There certainly seems to be something in great towns, and even in moderate towns, peculiarly unfavourable to the very early stages of life: and the part of the community on which the mortality principally falls, seems to indicate that it arises more from the closeness and foulness of the air, which may be supposed to be unfavourable to the tender lungs of children, and the greater from the superior degree of luxury and debauchery usually and justly attributed to towns [Malthus, 1973, p. 242].

Thus Thomas Robert Malthus characterized the phenomenon now known as the 'urban graveyard effect' and in his own meticulous fashion proceeded to document his point. In London, half of those born died before reaching their third birthday; in Vienna and Stockholm, their second birthday; in Manchester and Norwich, their fifth; in Northampton, their tenth; but in the country villages at least half survived until their thirtieth and in certain circumstances even to their fiftieth birthday. In the great towns mortality was 2.16 times higher and in the moderate towns some 1.74 times higher than in the villages of late eighteenth-century England. Let us set aside for the time being the validity of these statistics and concentrate on the implications to be drawn.

To fill up the void occasioned by this mortality in towns, and to answer all further demands for population, it is evident that a constant supply of recruits from the country is necessary; and this supply appears in fact to be always flowing in from the redundant births of the country. Even in those towns where the births exceeded the deaths, this effect is produced by the marriages of persons not born in the place [Malthus, 1973, p. 243].

Malthus was certainly aware of two further and associated arguments. Great cities absorbed substantial amounts of the rural surplus population. London, for example, required a supply of 10,000 persons annually according to the estimates made by Dr Richard Price and quoted by Malthus. Further, large towns, as well as larger populations, were able to shrug off the effects of temporarily devastating crises within a relatively short period of time.

The traces of the most destructive famines in China, Indostan [India], Egypt, and other countries, are by all accounts very soon obliterated; and the most tremendous convulsions of nature, such as volcanic eruptions and earthquakes, if they do not happen so frequently as to drive away the inhabitants or destroy their spirit of industry, have been found to produce but a trifling effect on the average population of any state [Malthus, 1973, p. 307].

It is clear, even from these brief comments and quotations taken from *An Essay on the Principle of Population* (first published in 1803), that Malthus was echoing the opinions of contemporaries when he observed that towns had higher mortality rates than the surrounding rural areas; that they required for their survival an influx of rural emigrants; and that they were by this means able to withstand repeated crises just as long as they were not too frequent or the citizenry was not too demoralized by the excess of deaths. Since 1803 this has remained the orthodox interpretation, but in 1978 the journal *Past and Present* published an article by the American historian Allan Sharlin in which he challenged the conventional model of urban natural decrease. This essay takes up Sharlin's challenge by asking three questions. How, in theory, do cities grow? What do we know of the demography of early modern towns? The third, and most significant, question is given by the chapter's title.

How do cities grow?

Like all populations, those of urban places may grow in a variety of ways. Let us consider five possibilities using the following notation as a shorthand: d for deaths; b for births; e for emigrants; i for immigrants; and P for the total population of one or a number of urban places. Then, for example, during a unit of time (a year, a decade)

$$(1) \qquad (d > b) > (e > i) \Rightarrow P^-$$

would stand for the case in which population declines because the excess of deaths over births is greater even than the excess of emigrants over immigrants. No city could survive for long in these circumstances, but the possibility that (1) holds for short periods during crises is entirely plausible. A slower rate of decline might be expected in the following:

$$(2) \qquad (d > b) > (e < i) \Rightarrow P^-$$

where there is positive net migration, but at a level insufficient to cope with the surplus of deaths. In the third case

$$(3) \qquad (d > b) < (e < i) \Rightarrow P^+$$

the population is capable of growing since the gain from net migration outweighs the loss from an excess of deaths over births. This, in essence, is the model of urban natural decrease. In the fourth case there is likely to be rapid urban growth

(4) $$(d < b) < (e < i) \Rightarrow P^+$$

with positive net migration supplementing natural increase (a variant on (4) would have the symbol between the brackets reversed (4a)). Finally, the fifth case

(5) $$(d = b) < (e > i) \Rightarrow P^-$$

has population decline due to excess emigration and zero natural growth. It is also worth noting that the rural equivalent of (3) would be

$$(d < b) > (e > i) \Rightarrow P^+$$

and of (4)

$$(d < b) < (e > i) \Rightarrow P^-$$

giving rural depopulation.

These cases may also be used to characterize the pre-industrial (3), the industrial (4) and the post-industrial, counter-urbanizing city (5). It is also likely that (4), or its variant, represents many contemporary Third World cities.

Keyfitz (1980) has asked a related question: do cities grow by natural increase or by migration? When rates of natural growth in urban and rural places are similar he concludes that 'in-migration ceases to dominate urban increase at a point where the urban population is still much less than rural' (Keyfitz, 1980, p. 146). But when differential rates of natural increase are assumed, then the permutations increase substantially. For example, 'The assertion that in contemporary less-developed countries migration is a smaller element than the natural increase of the cities rests on the conditions (1) that urban and rural natural increases are both high and not very different from one another, and (2) that the cities have attained at least 30 per cent of the national population. These conditions apply in most of the contemporary world. They did not apply in the earlier history of urbanization' (Keyfitz, 1980, p. 150). That is at some point case (4) gave way to its variant as the potential pool of rural migrants began to dry up. Keyfitz's (1980, p. 156) concluding point is also relevant here: 'demographic/economic linkages make the question of whether the cities grow by in-migration or by natural increase answerable in terms of where investment mostly takes place: the more it is concentrated in the cities the more these will grow by in-migration; the more it takes place in the country-side, the more the growth of cities will be limited to their own natural increase.'

Since we know that, at least in medieval and early modern Europe, cities did maintain themselves in demographic terms even if urbanization was at a low level by modern standards, it should follow that either relationship (3) or (4) must have held for considerable periods of time to allow urban populations to grow. If we look more closely at (3) several other aspects need to be distinguished. First, it is widely assumed that in those urban places where $(d > b)$ mortality was particularly high both because the background level of endemic mortality was higher than in rural areas, but also – and here it is common to place even greater emphasis despite Malthus's observation to the contrary – because urban populations were especially prone to the ravages of epidemic diseases. Although the chances of survival were far less in urban than rural places, it remains an open question whether there were also substantial differences in fertility and if so whether these were dictated by variations in marital fertility or by the timing, duration and extent of marriage, especially among women. These are unresolved issues to which we shall return frequently. Secondly, for (3) to work there must be a surplus rural population with $(d < b)$ or the attractions of urban life must outweigh those of the village *and* the rural population must be both free and able to move to the city.

Relationship (4) contains similar ambiguities when compared with (3). For example, one may move from (3) to (4) in two distinct ways: via mortality decline or fertility increase. If it is the former that is largely responsible, then on which component of the mortality pattern should emphasis be placed? The disappearance of bubonic plague and the fall of infant mortality would both affect the level of mortality, but would result from rather different circumstances. Similarly, the components of fertility will respond to very different influences. If the sex ratio of unmarried and eligible young people equalizes or changes in favour of women, then the level of celibacy may decline, marriages may not need to be postponed and will thus occur at an earlier age and remarriage after widowhood may be more likely. The period spent in marriage will thus increase for the average individual as will the total number of married years experienced by a population. In combination, the effect would be to raise the birth rate, even if mortality stayed high, as long as marital fertility remained unplanned. It is also possible to imagine circumstances in which, quite independently, infant mortality declines and the sex ratio of eligibles equalises. Nuptiality would increase and with it the birth rate, but a larger proportion of children would survive to marry and have children themselves. In this case the reasons for the move from relationship (3) to (4) would be complicated since they relate neither to mortality nor fertility changes alone.

Some of these relationships can be traced via figure 6.1 in which the closed systems models developed by Schofield (1976) and Wrigley and Schofield (1981), pp. 457–66) have been adapted to the circumstances of an urban population (see also de Vries, 1985). If one begins by considering the consequences of a sustained increase in urban population, then the first effect might be to raise the price of food sold in urban markets so stimulating imports from the surrounding agricultural area. Persistent food price increases would reduce the level of urban real wages, but gross wages would largely be determined by the health of the urban economy in both its commercial and manufacturing sectors. An expanding urban economy would draw in and retain many economically active young people as apprentices, servants, vagrants or opportunists looking for work, thereby increasing the level of net migration $(e < i)$ and the size of the urban population. Such a buoyant economy would also encourage early marriage among natives and migrants alike, assuming a balanced sex ratio. Increased nuptiality would also raise the level of overall fertility and thus, again, the size of the urban population. Both nuptiality and net migration provide instruments by which the urban economy influences its population size and structure in ways that may generate cumulative expansion as long as the rural economy can provide the food and the people. If urban food prices do increase, real wages will be adversely affected, nuptiality will be restricted and at the extreme mortality will increase. However, it is also obvious that if the rural economy was unable to provide agricultural surpluses in the long term then not only would the level of urbanization be restricted, but the very existence of a non-agricultural population brought into question. In order for a substantial urban sector to exist the positive link between urban population and food price in figure 6.1 must be weak or non-existent; increased urban demand must be met by rural supply.

Figure 6.1 may also be used to consider the impact of an increase in mortality associated with epidemic disease, for example. The size of the urban population will obviously decrease, but high adult mortality might also serve to encourage those who survive to marry sooner or to remarry. Increased infant and childhood mortality would reduce the level of effective fertility, but it might also hasten conception among those women whose infant had died. The normally high level of mortality associated with urban conditions would tend to create a highly mobile society in which the problems of succession for the élite were perilous and the opportunities for advancement among the migrants considerable. (Davis (1962) and Yamamura (1985) provide interesting examples for, respectively, the Venetian élite and the forcibly urbanized Japanese samurai.)

The fortunes of the urban population are thus tied to the ability of the agricultural sector to feed it; the success of its own economy to generate wealth and employment, to maintain a viable market; and its good fortune in avoiding excessive crisis mortality on top of the normally high background level. With a buoyant economy a city would be able to buy food for itself and replace if not reproduce itself, and thereby fend off the effects of high death rates. But once the economy faltered, the migrants diverted elsewhere, then the urban population would be left a victim of its own internal demography at the mercy of disease and political disorder.

What do we know about the demography of early modern towns?

It will be apparent that even a brief theoretical discussion of the question 'how do cities grow?' raises a number of difficult issues which will not be resolved until it is possible to trace in detail the demographic history of a substantial number of urban places over the course of several centuries. Jan de Vries's important work on European urbanization makes the point most forcefully. 'The demographic characteristics or urban populations in the early modern period are not well known. In fact, the impressive advances made in historical demography during the last twenty years have only made more acute our sense of ignorance about fertility, mortality and nuptiality among city-dwellers' (de Vries, 1984, p. 180). It is not that there is no evidence, rather that what there is may be at worst unreliable and at best contradictory and difficult to interpret.

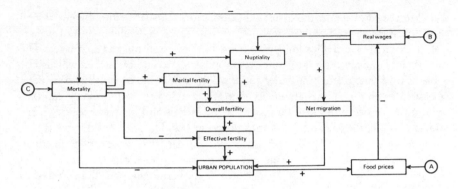

Figure 6.1 A closed-system model of urban population dynamics
Source: based on E.A. Wrigley and R.S. Schofield, 1981, pp. 457–66

Despite these rather gloomy statements it does seem that there existed among early modern urban places a clear positive relationship between the likelihood of a death surplus and the size of the centre's population. Cities like London and Paris suffered a continuous excess of burials over baptisms (see Dupaquier, 1988, on French towns). Large villages may have experienced certain crisis years, but in general their populations were capable of growing naturally. In between, the small towns were often able to grow by a surplus of births, but natural increase was by no means continuous. Indeed, there is good reason to believe that many small towns in England (York, Chester, Norwich, for example) and Japan experienced stagnation and that for middle-ranking centres in general de-urbanization characterized the late seventeenth and eighteenth centuries. The implication is that potential rural out-migrants were drawn either to first-rank cities, like London and Edo, or they were retained in non-agricultural occupations located in industrial villages (many of which ultimately grew into larger industrial towns) or were engaged in by-employment while remaining part of the agricultural community (Wrigley, 1987; Smith, 1988).

The mechanism behind this positive relationship is thought to be the strong association between level of mortality and population density. The first-ranking cities had a particularly high level of mortality which was bound to exceed even the highest birth rates. In the nineteenth century this association was dignified with the status of a law by the eminent social statistician Dr William Farr, but what could be demonstrated precisely in Victorian England must be left to plausible supposition for earlier centuries (Farr, 1885; Weber, 1899; Woods and Woodward, 1984, p. 50; Kearns, 1988; Williamson, 1988, 1989). It has also been assumed, perhaps too hastily, that the essence of Farr's law applied to urban systems outside Europe. However, the huge size and low-density construction of many Chinese and Japanese cities, together with the high population density of agricultural areas, should lead one to pause before transferring any such Western model in its entirety (Skinner, 1977; Hanley, 1987).

The many attempts to describe the demography of early modern towns are to some degree thwarted by the quality of population statistics before the era of vital registration. Most studies use parish registers or some equivalent form of household register that provides information on burials, baptisms and marriages. The burials and baptisms series bear some relation to deaths and births, but will also be subject to varying degrees of under-registration, only some of which is systematic in nature. Even the most rudimentary demographic indices require some approximation of the size of population in which the burials and baptisms are occurring and, if possible, the age and sex of those most at risk. Despite considerable recent advances in the use of family reconstitution and partial reconstitution on urban parish registers, it is still the estimation of at risk populations that is the most important drawback for the calculation of conventional period measures of mortality and fertility. Even when some approximation can be made of the crude or age-specific rates these measures are not sufficient to solve the problems raised by Sharlin's challenge as we shall see in the following section.

London provides an interesting instance of what can be achieved with inadequate demographic sources and is used here to illustrate the ingenuity required and the limitations encountered. More comprehensive accounts of the technical issues involved are to be found in the work of Finlay (1981), Landers (1986, 1987) and Landers and Mouzas (1988). Table 6.1 estimates crude birth and death rates for London by twenty-five year periods from 1551–1575 to 1776–1800 using the population estimates provided by de Vries (1984, p. 270) and the estimates of London baptisms and burials given by Wrigley and Schofield (1981, p. 167, table 6.4). The figures in brackets are linear interpolations. Finlay and Shearer (1986, p. 39) provide alternative estimates of London's population (1550–120,000; 1600–200,000; 1650–375,000; 1700–490,000; 1750–675,000; 1800–950,000). The mean populations of the ten 25–year periods provide denominators for calculating the crude rates. It seems likely that the true population of London in 1801 was closer to 900,000, the figure given by Wrigley (1987, p. 133), and may have been as high as 960,000 judging by the 1801 census. If Wrigley's figure for 1801 had been used in table 6.1, then for 1751–1775 CBR would be 25.14 and CDR, 33.45 and for 1776–1800 CBR would be 26.32 and CDR, 28.51. The estimates for provincial England have been found by inflating the ratios of baptisms and burials to total population for provincial England (England minus London) by a factor derived from the ratio of Wrigley and Schofield's own CBR and CDR estimates for England with the baptism and burial ratios again for England as a whole. By this means London may be distinguished from provincial England while rates for the latter are adjusted upwards to allow for the known discrepancy between births and baptisms, deaths and burials. Figure 6.2 plots the ten-point time paths for CBR and CDR in London and provincial England.

The last two columns in table 6.1 reveal some of the problems created by this simple method of estimation. The level of annual net migration to London required to overcome the birth deficit implied by the discrepancy between CBR and CDR whilst achieving actual growth is given in the penultimate column. The numbers involved are very substantial averaging nearly 4,800 a year over two and a half centuries. But what of the ability of provincial England to produce rural-urban

Table 6.1 Estimates of the population of London and crude birth (CBR) and crude death rates (CDR) for London and provincial England by twenty-five year periods, 1551–75 to 1775–1800

Twenty-five year periods	Years	London population (000s)		London		Provincial England		Annual net migration required by London	Annual birth surplus in provincial England
		de Vries	Period means	CBR	CDR	CBR	CDR		
	1551	80							
1			110	16.91	40.57	35.12	27.84	3160	8532
	1576	(140)							
2			170	30.22	36.55	33.29	23.62	2760	13229
	1601	200							
3			250	35.31	38.28	32.52	24.03	4240	13278
	1626	(300)							
4			350	33.40	43.05	31.24	24.97	5160	11012
	1651	400							
5			443	26.51	46.99	28.60	26.48	6680	4096
	1676	(485)							
6			530	27.54	41.23	31.77	28.72	6240	5691
	1701	575							
7			600	30.81	39.59	31.45	26.13	4000	9544
	1726	(625)							
8			650	29.24	41.84	33.79	28.58	5160	9993
	1751	675							
9			718	25.63	34.10	34.63	25.83	5680	17934
	1776	(760)							
10			813	27.33	29.60	35.73	23.49	4880	31628
	1801	865							

Note: see text for explanation

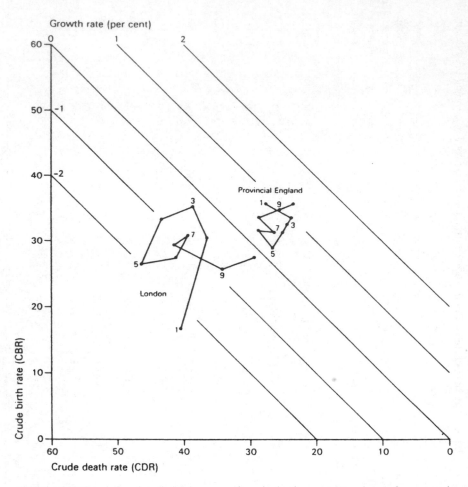

Figure 6.2 Time paths of crude birth rates and crude death rates in London and provincial England, 1551–1880. *Source*: calculated from estimates based on de Vries 1984; Wrigley and Schofield 1981; and Finlay and Shearer, 1986: see pp. 86–89 for a fuller explanation

migrants in such numbers? The final column in table 6.1 suggests that provincial England generated a natural surplus of perhaps 12,500 a year over the same period, of which London would have required up to 40 per cent and this even before one takes into account the probability of survival from birth to the mean age of migrating to London.

Obviously, none of the estimates in table 6.1 can be taken at its face value. Yet important points for emphasis are signified and critical issues revealed. Let us select two for closer examination. First, assuming that Wrigley and Schofield's national estimates of CBR and CDR are of the correct order of magnitude then so too will be the figures for provincial England in table 6.1. During the late seventeenth century the pace of English population growth slackened to such an extent that the surplus of births over deaths was unlikely to have exceeded 6,000 per annum despite London's apparent need for more than that number of net migrants in order to ensure the momentum of its growth. How was the population of London able to grow when that of England could not? Should London's baptism, burial or population series be questioned? Secondly, while, as we would have expected, the crude death rates for London were always higher than the ones for provincial England, the crude birth rates were usually lower, but not always substantially so. Over the 250–year period London's CBR was 13 per cent lower than that for provincial England while its CDR was 50 per cent higher. In these two percentages we probably have the essential features of the demographic problem facing all early modern cities. Malthus and Dr Richard Price were thus not too far from the mark.

Despite the queries that must attend the estimates in table 6.1 or equivalent reconstructions for other large towns of the period, parish register data widely available for European cities do at least provide the basis for simple calculations. But even at their best such sources alone cannot adequately resolve all outstanding issues since the period measures to which they give rise do not capture the complex interplay between migration history, marriage, employment, childbearing and death. Only cohort studies based on collective biographies are likely to achieve the required precision by integrating the details of time, place, demography and economy.

The full extent of the problem may be judged when we turn to ask the third and final question which will be introduced via Allan Sharlin's (1978) iconoclastic paper.

What would one need to know to solve the 'natural decrease in early modern cities' problem?

The model of urban natural decrease represented by equation (3), above, has been described in very simple terms – deaths exceed births so, for population growth to occur, net migration must exceed natural decrease – but one particular point has been overlooked: namely the interaction produced by age- and sex-selective migration which is likely to influence nuptiality and thus both overall fertility levels and also the pattern of age at death. This, Sharlin's principal argument, he presents as a model of urban migration the essential feature of which is that a distinction must be made between permanent residents for whom $(d < b)$ and temporary migrants $(d > b)$: 'The temporary migrants substantially increased the urban population subject to the risk of death, but they had little effect on the size of the population actually having children. Thus, the counts of births and deaths do not suffice as conclusive evidence that a decline in urban population would have taken place without migration' (Sharlin, 1978, p. 127). The temporary migrants, mainly artisans, journeymen, apprentices or servants, were prevented from marrying by the terms of their employment. They could therefore contribute to the tally of deaths, but not to the number of births. In this scenario one of the contributors to the high death rate in urban centres is the presence there of temporary migrants. Without such migrants, according to Sharlin, cities would be able to grow naturally.

In order to confirm Sharlin's argument it would be necessary to establish the following: first to distinguish permanent residents (A) from temporary migrants (B) and to separate the latter from those who, whilst migrants, settle permanently, marry and have children before dying in the city (C); secondly, the relative proportions of (A), (B) and (C) and the ratio of (B) to (C) should be high; thirdly, the precise demographic characteristics of each of these three groups (see Clark and Souden, 1987, on migration patterns).

Figure 6.3, based on the Lexis diagram, demonstrates the impossibility of attaining any of these goals. Imagine fifteenth-century Florence (see Herlihy and Klapisch–Zuber, 1985) with a total population of between 37,000 and 40,000 but a substantial decline since 1338 from a likely population of 120,000, with the plague of 1400 accounting for the loss of at least 12,000. Figure 6.3 picks out the life lines of fourteen individuals who spent some of their years in Florence. All but four, three of whom died in childhood (E, F, I) and B, were in the city in 1427 when the great Florentine *catasto* or fiscal survey was carried out. All of the life lines are for women and only their periods of residence in the city are charted. Most of the women display quite conventional lives. They are born in the city, marry between the age of 15 to 20 a man some ten years older than themselves; they have children in a regular progression – perhaps four, five or six – into their late thirties; they are widowed and die in their forties to seventies, again in the city (A, B, D). Woman C married aged 17, has one daughter (D) when aged 20, is widowed at 22, remarries at 24, bears no children for her much older second husband and is widowed for the second time aged 35 shortly after becoming a grandmother. Woman D goes on to have six children, five of whom are daughters (E, F, G, H, I) and three die in infancy or childhood. Daughter H leaves Florence on marrying and only G stays on in the city, survives her mother, but dies young after the birth of her second child. In 1427 C, a widow of 52, is living with her married daughter (D) and her three surviving unmarried grandchildren (including granddaughters G and H).

These are the straightforward cases for urban historical demography. But consider cases J, K, L and M. Woman J is born in Florence, is married and moves to join her husband out of the city (as did H), she is widowed and childless at 30 and returns to the city to live – perhaps as a servant, cook, or housekeeper – until she dies aged 60. Strictly, woman J becomes a return migrant, but it is easy to see how her case could be confused with that of L who is a new migrant to the city arriving at age 15, she does not marry and have children, and dies at 30. Woman L is the temporary migrant of whom Sharlin was thinking. Migrant M is a different case. She arrives in Florence as a young servant, marries (later than normal) has four children, is widowed and probably dies in the city out of observation. Woman K presents the most difficult case for historical demographers. She was not born in Florence, nor married, bore children or died there, but as a resident for some twenty years may have appeared in the *catasto*.

In the preceding scenario, each of these women (A to M) is fictitious, but that is

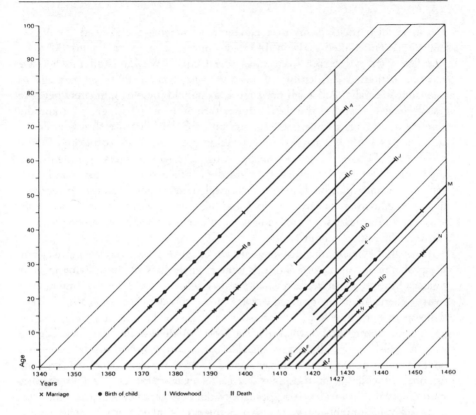

Figure 6.3 Life lines and vital experience of selected women in fifteenth-century Florence
Source: based on the 1427 *Castato* for Florence; D. Herlihy and C. Klapisch-Zuber, 1985

the very point at issue in figure 6.3. In order to answer urban historical demography's most pressing questions we require precise data on individual urban residents that can be treated in both a cross-sectional and a longitudinal fashion. It is not sufficient to know details of residence at a particular, or even a number of points in time as is provided by the *catasti* even if this is in combination with details of the number of vital events – births, marriages and deaths – in any one period. It will always remain difficult if not impossible to trace women like K, L, even J and M, yet it is on their contribution to the urban population, their ability to marry and have children that competing interpretations rely. Although genealogical studies permit an approach to these issues for members of ruling families, mobility wreaks havoc in the family reconstitution studies of lesser mortals.

Even the life of a well-documented commoner like Lusanna, the daughter of Benedetto di Girolamo (represented as woman N in figure 6.3), poses considerable problems. Born in Florence in 1420, Lusanna married in 1436, when aged 17, a man named Andrea Nucci, twelve years her senior, who died in 1453 when Lusanna was 33. Four months after being widowed she attempted to contract a marriage with the man who had been her lover for ten years, Giovanni della Casa, a man of high social position, a banker and merchant, also aged 33. When Giovanni's father died early in 1453 he contracted a marriage with Marietta Rucellai, a girl of 15, but Giovanni's social equal. We know all this because Lusanna contested the legality of his marriage claiming that her marriage to Giovanni was valid. Although her claim was upheld initially, ultimately her case was dismissed because of the clandestine nature of the marriage ceremony and the absence of a notary to officiate. Lusanna probably left Florence shortly after the court case of 1455; she may have remarried in the countryside (Bruckner, 1986).

The case of Giovanni and Lusanna, although it provides interesting insights into the form of Florence marriage rituals and the conflicts between church and state, serves ultimately only to tease the historical demographer because of its well-documented nature, its very notoriety, and, ultimately, because Lusanna was both sterile and disappeared without remark from Florence. We know much about N, but virtually nothing about K.

Through the lives of the characters shown in figure 6.3 we may see more clearly the problems involved for historical demography. Many of those living in early modern Europe – perhaps even a majority in England – were at some time in their lives residents of urban places. Likewise, many so-called permanent urban residents spent some time in the countryside on a seasonal basis, during times of crisis particularly of plague, and when they sent their children out to wet nurse beyond the city walls. These walls were permeable barriers, constructed for defensive and administrative purposes: they never served to create prisons. Here we have the essential difficulty facing those wishing to reconstruct the demography of early modern towns. Although urban populations did have certain distinctive characteristics, substantial numbers were neither permanently urban nor rural, with a constant flux of people living part of their lives in cities. For many of the young migrants there was an urban penalty – the city was a graveyard as one would expect it to have been for the old and destitute – but for many more the city was a means of escape, a source of wealth and vitality, a place of hope in which normal family lives could be lived albeit at higher risk of infants and children dying prematurely. Herlihy and Klapisch–Zuber (1985, p. 97) make the point clearly: 'Florence was thus a blazing sun of affluence, surrounded by dim planets of wealth in the smaller Tuscan cities – all of them set within a dark, nearly destitute rural space'. But this could be repeated for London, Paris, Peking, Edo and so forth. (Compare London (Wrigley, 1987, pp. 133–56), Madrid (Ringrose, 1973, 1981) and Edo (Rozman, 1974).)

Many questions; few answers

Lest the reader become disillusioned by the tone of resignation with which the inevitability of our ignorance in these matters has been described, it is worth repeating that very considerable advances have been made in the last few years in tackling the second of the questions – our knowledge of the demography of early modern towns – considered above. But, as far as the debate initiated by Sharlin's paper is concerned, we are still some way short of resolving the central issues. The most salient points now appear as follows.

First, despite the difficulty of constructing period demographic measures for early modern cities, the available evidence indicates that there were persistently higher levels of burials than baptisms, of deaths than births. Such places would have declined without a healthy balance of net migration. The model of urban natural decline (3) still retains its utility. However, there are two riders. One must be careful to distinguish the size and position of a town in the urban hierarchy, for many towns were apparently capable of natural growth at certain times even before the nineteenth century when even the largest of metropolitan centres grew naturally (4 or 4a). It is unwise to transfer models based on the population history of Europe's cities to Asia, in particular.

Secondly, Sharlin's model of urban migration is not discredited, merely not proven. It seems likely that the examples used in his 1978 paper tend to over-emphasize the restrictions placed on apprentices and servants marrying. If such restrictions delayed rather than prevented marriage then migrants certainly could make positive contributions to urban growth.

Thirdly, by focusing on the transience of urban residence and the circulatory nature of rural-urban movement. Sharlin has highlighted a point that should be taken further. Whilst it is important to distinguish between agricultural and non-agricultural populations and between rural and urban places, the early modern urban environment was home to a decreasing proportion of the non-agricultural population. The economic and demographic significance of the urban-rural dichotomy thus became blurred in ways that are often difficult to appreciate from a reading of urban history.

Fourthly, it seems that Malthus was entirely justified in emphasizing the prime importance of marriage and the preventive check over and above the positive check in north-west Europe as a whole while, at the same time, reversing the order of priority for England's towns. In order that urban and rural places appear demographically indistinguishable death rates in the former would be required to decline more than birth rates would need to rise. But this should not necessarily be taken to imply that the first stage in the movement from (3) to (4) was necessarily dominated by a decline in urban mortality alone. A fall in infant and childhood mortality and an increase in nuptiality associated with a balancing of the sex ratio among those in their early twenties, coupled with some economic encouragement to marry, would probably have been sufficient to take Georgian London from natural decline to Victorian growth.

Fifthly, it is a commonplace, none the less worth repeating, that the interactions between marriage, childbearing, migration, mortality, a population's age structure, its occupational specialization and social attitudes to, amongst other things, childbearing were highly complex matters which can only be analysed in full when demographers have the ability to trace the life course of individuals. Without such evidence we are left to speculate, approximate and theorize. The evidence appears more tantalizing because the often-asked questions remain unanswered.

References

Bruckner, G. (1986), *Giovanni and Lusanna: Love and Marriage in Renaissance Florence*, Weidenfeld and Nicolson.

Clark, P. and Souden, D. (eds) (1987), *Migration and Society in Early Modern England*, Hutchinson.

Davis, J.C. (1962), *The Decline of the Venetian Mobility as a Ruling Class*, Johns Hopkins University Press, Baltimore.

de Vries, J. (1984), *European Urbanization, 1500–1800*, Methuen.

de Vries, J. (1985), 'The population and economy of the preindustrial Netherlands', *Journal of Interdisciplinary History*, 15, 661–82.

Dupâquier, J. (ed.) (1988), *Histoire de la Population Française 2. De la Renaissance à 1789*, Presses Universitaires de France, Paris.

Farr, W. (1885), *Vital Statistics*, Sanitary Institute of Great Britain.

Finlay, R.A.P. (1981), *Population and Metropolis: The Demography of London, 1580–1650*, Cambridge University Press.

Finlay, R.A.P. and Shearer, B. (1986), 'Population growth and suburban expansion', in A.L. Beier and R. Finlay (eds), *The Making of the Metropolis: London 1500–1700*, Longman.

Hanley, S.B. (1987), 'Urban sanitation in preindustrial Japan', *Journal of Interdisciplinary History*, 18, 1–26.

Herlihy, D. and Klapisch-Zuber, C. (1985), *Tuscans and their Families: A Study of the Florentine Catasto of 1427*, Yale University Press, New Haven, Conn.

Kearns, G. (1988), 'The urban penalty and the population history of England', in A. Brandstrom and L-G. Tedebrand (eds), *Society, Health and Population during the Demographic Transition*, Almquist and Wiksell, Stockholm.

Keyfitz, N. (1980), 'Do cities grow by natural increase or by migration?', *Geographical Analysis*, 12, 143–56.

Landers, J.M. (1986), 'Mortality, climate and prices in London, 1675–1825: a study of short-run fluctuations', *Journal of Historical Geography*, 12, 347–63.

Landers, J.M. (1987) 'Mortality and metropolis: the case of London, 1675–1825', *Population Studies*, 41, 59–76.

Landers, J.M. and Mouzas, A. (1988), 'Burial seasonality and causes of death in London, 1670–1819', *Population Studies*, 42, 59–83.

Malthus, T.R. (1973), *An Essay on the Principle of Population* (reprint of the 7th edn, 1st edn published in 1803), Dent.

Ringrose, D.R. (1973), 'The impact of a new capital city: Madrid, Toledo and New Castile, 1560–1660', *Journal of Economic History*, 33, 761–91.

Ringrose, D.R. (1981), 'Madrid as an agent of economic stagnation in Spain', *Journal of European Economic History*, 10, 481–90.

Rozman, G. (1974), 'Edo's importance in changing Tokugawa society', *Journal of Japanese Studies*, 1, 91–112.

Schofield, R.S. (1976), 'The relationship between demographic structure and environment in pre-industrial Western Europe', in W. Conze (ed.), *Sozialgeschichte der Familie in der Neuzeit Europas*, Klett Verlag, Stuttgart.

Sharlin, A. (1978), 'Natural decrease in early modern cities: a reconsideration', *Past and Present*, 79, 126–38 and 92 (1981), 175–80.

Skinner, G.W. (ed.) (1977), *The City in Late Imperial China*, Stanford University Press, Stanford.

Smith, T.C. (1988), *Native Sources of Japanese Industrialization, 1750–1920*, University of California Press, Berkeley.

Weber, A.F. (1899), *The Growth of Cities in the Nineteenth Century*, Macmillan, New York.

Williamson, J.G. (1988), 'Migrant selectivity, urbanization, and industrial revolutions', *Population and Development Review*, 14. 287–314.

Williamson, J.G. (1989), *Coping with City Growth During the British Industrial Revolution*, Cambridge University Press.

Woods, R.I. and Woodward, J.H. (eds) (1984), *Urban Disease and Mortality in Nineteenth-Century England*, Batsford.

Wrigley, E.A. (1987), *People, Cities and Wealth*, Blackwell, Oxford.

Wrigley, E.A. and Schofield, R.A. (1981), *The Population History of England, 1541–1871: A Reconstruction*, Edward Arnold.

Yamamura, K. (1985), 'Samurai income and demographic change: the genealogies of Tokugawa bannermen', in S.B. Hanley and A.P. Wolf (eds), *Family and Population in East Asian History*, Stanford University Press.

7 Zivilis or Hygaeia: urban public health and the epidemiologic transition

Gerry Kearns

There have been striking changes in the way modern cities have been and are managed. Some of these concern collective responsibility for the health of citizens. In this regard, the nineteenth century sits athwart a transformation in the disease panorama of western cities. This shift is in part the result of the evolving techniques of urban health management. These techniques inevitably redefine the rights and responsibilities of citizens, the sick, property owners and medical professionals. Against the background of the changing nature of the urban public health problem, two distinct public health strategies are described and the question of how collective responsibilities compromise individual rights is considered. These are matters of continuing relevance.

The epidemiologic transition

Figure 7.1 shows the population history of Stockholm.[1] From some 45,000 at the start of the eighteenth century it had a population of 75,000 by the beginning of the nineteenth. This quadrupled over the next century and has more than doubled since 1900. Its crude birth rate shows the characteristic European pattern of relatively high fluctuating levels (over 30 live births each year per thousand people living) before a secular decline, in this case starting around the 1880s, with brief up-turns induced by economic booms and waves of young in-migrants. During the eighteenth century the crude death rate dipped below the birth rate for only nine out of the eighty years reported here, for 1801–58 the score was nil. The sixteen years 1859–75 had twelve in which there was an excess of births and thereafter there was a births surplus every year until 1927 when the two series merged

---

1. The sources are as follows: 1720–1916 – *Statistisk Årsbok för Stockholms Stad 1920* (Stockholm: Imprimerie K.L. Beckman; 1920), pp. 64–7; 1916–30 *Statistisk Årsbok för Stockholms Stad 1934* (Stockholm: K.L. Beckmans Boktryckeri; 1934), p. 32; 1931–46 – *Statistisk Årsbok för Stockholms Stad 1951* (Stockholm: K.L. Beckmans Boktryckeri; 1951), p. 39; 1947–66 – *Statistisk Årsbok för Stockholms Stad 1968* (Stockholm, K.L. Beckmans Tryckerier AB; 1968), p. 58; 1967–77 – *Statistisk Årsbok för Stockholm 1978* (Stockholm: Stockholms statistiska kontor; 1978), p. 83; 1976–86 – *Statistisk Årsbok för Stockholm 1988* (Stockholm: Stockholms utrednings- och statistikkontor; 1987), p. 82. There are death registers from 1720 and annual population counts from 1750; populations for the years 1720–49 were estimated by the Swedish authorities.

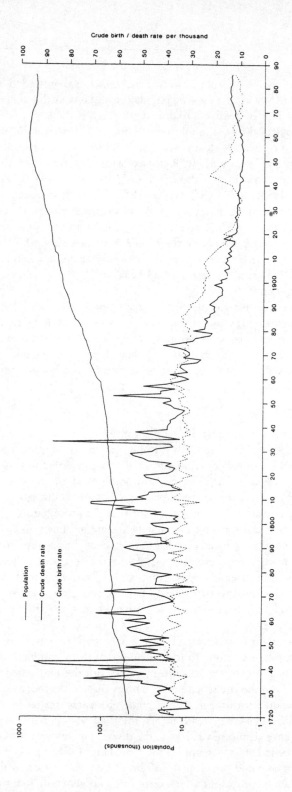

Figure 7.1 The population history of Stockholm 1721–1986. Total population (in thousands) and crude birth and death rates per thousand population are derived from the *sources* listed under note 1, p. 96.

before, in 1938, births took another upward swing which was grounded again in the 1960s. Since 1967 Stockholm's ageing population and low birth rate have produced a continual surfeit of deaths. Urban natural increase, then, was primarily a phenomenon of the period from the mid-nineteenth to mid-twentieth centuries.

Before 1850 the annual crude death rate in Stockholm was generally above 40 deaths per thousand persons living. It fluctuated widely from year to year with exceptional mortalities, over 60 per thousand, in 1736, 1740, 1742, 1743, 1763, 1772, 1806, 1808, 1809, 1834, and, finally, 1853. These sharp peaks on the mortality curve correspond to epidemics of diseases such as smallpox, dysentery, typhus and cholera. Over time the epidemics became less serious, a process we can date from at least the disappearance of the plague in the seventeenth century. A smallpox epidemic was the last event to push Stockholms's crude death rate over 40 per thousand (1874) and the last marked peak, in 1918, was caused by the Spanish influenza epidemic.

Similar mortality curves may be plotted for many European cities. They essentially show a change from high and erratic mortality to low, stable mortality. The former corresponds to the period of famines and epidemics in Omran's model of the epidemiologic transition and the latter to that of degenerating and artificial diseases with his second stage, that of receding pandemics, sandwiched somewhat indeterminately in between (Omran, 1982).

Famines and epidemics

Sieges, harvest failures or transport difficulties during bad weather could create food shortages for towns in early modern Europe. Because of the threat posed to public order, local and national governments were very concerned to mitigate the worst consequences of such hardship, requisitioning food in the countryside, holding stocks over from good years in public granaries and acting against speculators. Yet shortages created economic dislocation and the promiscuous migration of those short of work frequently brought epidemic disease to hungry and weakened city dwellers. Sometimes the reduced population was directly exposed to pestiferous troops billeted in town after these had wandered through and collected the diseases of other places. Epidemic disease could and did strike without the assistance of food shortages but the latter rarely had serious consequences for the mortality of early modern European towns without epidemic assistance; large-scale starvation was very rare.

Plague had been absent from Europe for over five centuries when, in 1348, it swept through killing between one-third and one-half of the population. There were epidemics of plague every six to thirteen years until the mid-sixteenth century and from then until the late seventeenth century plague was more exclusively an urban phenomenon with irregular sharp epidemics each apparently resulting from a fresh introduction of the disease. While the last great epidemic in western Europe was in Provence (France) in 1720–22, the disease ran amok in the Ottoman Empire about every twenty years until 1842 (Biraben, 1975, pp. 119–29). In individual years plague could occasionally kill up to one-third or one-half of the population of a town but such visitations were rare and generally followed long periods of relative respite (Panzac, 1985, p. 362). Taking the peaks with the troughs plague seems to have been equivalent to a constant annual rate of mortality of 10 per thousand and with a non-plague mortality generally around 40 per thousand in pre-industrial cities this ruled out any possibility of urban natural increase while periodically reducing cities to veritable death-traps (see chapter 6).

Waning pandemics

After 1535 plague visited the cities of western Europe less frequently and, although individual epidemics could still be very serious, its aggregate effect on total mortality may have been somewhat less than during the previous two centuries.[2] During the eighteenth century plague was practically absent from most of western Europe. Other epidemic diseases periodically disturbed European cities but they hardly ever carried off as much as a tenth of the population. Paradoxically, at this very time the increasing size of cities, the acceleration in transport and greater contact with tropical countries exposed Europeans more regularly and effectively to epidemic diseases. To some extent more frequent encounters may have moderated their severity (Kunitz, 1983). However, at least one disease ran its course so quickly in its host that poor communications had previously kept it confined near to its endemic reservoir: the cholera of Bengal. Only in the early nineteenth century did it reach Europe. The first epidemic wave of 1817–24 reached Astrakhan (S.W. Russia) but the second (1829–37) tyrannized most of the European peninsula. While cholera never attained the mortality levels of plague, from the start it was a specifically urban disease particularly of ports. Even at its worst it was only equivalent to a minor plague epidemic.[3] Cholera moved more quickly than plague had done, running its course in cities in weeks rather than months and in a month being transmitted over distances that had characteristically detained

---

2. London's last plague killed 68,596 people in 1665, perhaps a sixth of the population. Yet plague had been temporarily endemic in London during much of the 1640s and there had been a reasonably serious epidemic in1636 with 10,400 deaths (Biraben, 1975, pp. 186, 196). Other European cities which had enjoyed longer spells without plague and whose people had, therefore, built up less immunity suffered quite dreadfully during their last visitation: Lyons, 51 years since its previous plague, half the population died in 1628; Milan, 54 years, nine-twentieths of the population died in 1630; Verona, 54 years, eleven-twentieths in 1630; Venice, 54 years, a third in 1631; Barcelona, 62 years, nine-twentieths in 1651; Naples, 127 years, half in 1656; Genoa, 70 years, two-thirds in 1657; Marseilles, 71 years, half in 1720; Messina, 96 years, seven-tenths in 1743 (Panzac, 1985, p. 362). Very few cities have any demographic records going back to the start of the plague years but Biraben presents some data on Barcelona. The city had eight epidemics during the period 1348–1535, the worst being that of 1348 (a third of the population died). It had three thereafter, ending in 1653 with the most catastrophic in its history (nine out of every twenty people died). The plague epidemics were equivalent to an annual mortality of 10 per thousand for the whole period, 13 in the first and 7 in the second part (Biraben, 1975, pp. 216–17). Thus plague accounted for around one-sixth of all Barcelona's deaths during the second period, about the same as in London in 1600–80.

3. The cholera spread through the Ottoman Empire, northwards to the Baltic coast and from there infected most of the north-western Europe. Compared to the mortalities cited in note 2 these few from the first cholera epidemic in Europe show its relative mildness: Smyrna (1831), 50 per thousand; Alexandria (1831), 66; Cairo (1831), 128; Berlin (1831), 6; Paris (1832), 23; London (1832), 4; Stockholm (1834), 45. The first three rates are from Panzac (1985), p. 400; Berlin: Evans (1987), p. 260; Paris: Delaporte (1986), p. 5; London: Kearns (1985a), p. 148; Stockholm: Zacke (1971), p. 5.

plague for a year (Panzac, 1985, p. 418). It also reached out across the Atlantic to the Americas with the reduction by three-quarters in the duration of the crossing, courtesy of the steamships of the 1860s (Bourdelais and Raulot, 1987, p. 50).

By the last quarter of the nineteenth century urban epidemics were increasingly a matter of periodic surges in endemic childhood diseases such as measles, diphtheria and scarlet fever. The Spanish 'flu pandemic of 1918 was only a brief return to the earlier pattern of urban epidemics striking down adults and effectively marked the end of an era, the close of the period of waning pandemics.

Degenerative and artificial diseases

In the mid-nineteenth century a city with a crude mortality rate of 20 per thousand was considered healthy. By the end of the century many of the cities of western Europe met this criterion. Of the 23 European cities in table 7.1, 18 had crude death rates less than twenty per thousand in 1901–5; St Petersburg, Venice and Dublin persisted with such a high rate into the second decade of this century.[4] The causes of death were somewhat different in healthy and unhealthy cities.

Cities with lower mortalities (table 7.2) were less troubled by the diseases of dirt; typhus, cholera, typhoid, diarrhoea and dysentery. There was surprisingly little difference in the mortality associated with the infectious diseases of childhood; measles scarlet fever, scarlatina, whooping cough and diphtheria (table 7.3). Tuberculosis of the lungs was somewhat lower in the healthy cities, reflecting levels of overcrowding, patterns of in-migration and, perhaps, nutrition. Smallpox was absent from nearly all cities but was present in the worst six cities on the list; maybe this indicates the general state of the sanitary authorities in these places since the preventive measures (vaccination, the isolation of early cases) were well understood. The epidemic diseases which had caused so much concern in the mid-nineteenth century (cholera, typhus, smallpox) were virtually absent from the European and north American cities in this list. The age of waning pandemics was over in these places.

Indeed, if we examine the full range of cities in any country there is a suggestion that the improvements of the late nineteenth century came a little earlier in the largest cities. In French cities over the period 1886–98 (table 7.4) the contagious diseases of childhood, control of which showed little improvement at this time, were higher in large than in smaller towns and cities (measles, scarlet fever, scarlatina, whooping cough, diphtheria). Paris, however, had a better record on smallpox, typhoid, diarrhoea and dysentery which perhaps reflects better public health services in the capital. Maybe the relatively poor record in Paris with respect of respiratory tuberculosis indicates its continuing problems of overcrowding. Moreover, the Parisian lead over smaller places was especially marked among infants, a tribute to the reduced infant diarrhoea which greater cleanliness ensured (table 7.5).

4. Taken from successive volumes of *Statistisk Årsbok för Stockholms stad*. The figures for Philadelphia do not include any data for 1910, otherwise the series looks complete. This data set does not include any Chinese or Japanese cities and tends towards a more even coverage of countries rather than a strict listing of the world's largest cities. Nevertheless, it includes the top eight cities and fourteen of the top twenty cities of 1890; figures taken from Weber (1899), p. 450.

Table 7.1   Mortality in some world cities, 1908–13

City	Mean pop. 1908–13 (000s)	Crude death rate per 1,000			
		1908–13	1901–5	1906–10	1911–15
Cairo	704	37.7	35.4	39.0	42.4
Bombay	979	36.4	64.1	40.8	32.9
Alexandria	398	30.9	34.5	34.9	33.3
Calcutta	930	28.0	34.6	32.0	28.2
St Petersburg	1,626	23.5	23.5	25.4	21.8
Rio de Janeiro	867	22.0	26.5	22.6	21.7
Venice	170	20.8	24.1	21.4	20.6
Dublin	401	20.8	23.2	21.6	21.0
Budapest	873	18.9	19.8	19.3	19.1
Stettin	240	17.9	22.7	19.6	17.4
Prague	442	17.5	23.2	19.6	14.9
Rome	561	17.5	19.9	18.3	17.2
Hamburg	833	16.9	16.3	14.8	13.3
Paris	2,816	16.9	17.9	17.7	16.0
Glasgow	872	16.9	19.5	17.3	17.2
Vienna	2,057	16.3	19.1	17.6	15.4
Philadelphia	1,575	16.1	18.1	17.5	15.8
Hull	279	15.4	17.5	15.9	15.2
New York	4,887	15.2	18.9	17.0	14.4
Edinburgh	338	15.1	17.4	15.3	15.6
Lubeck	100	15.0	16.6	15.4	14.7
Berlin	2,084	14.8	16.8	15.3	15.8
Chicago	2,243	14.6	14.2	14.6	14.6
Copenhagen	462	14.6	16.1	15.1	14.0
Stockholm	349	14.1	16.1	14.8	13.4
London	4,677	13.9	16.1	14.0	14.7
Brussels	714	13.6	15.2	14.1	13.2
Gothenburg	168	13.4	16.1	14.5	12.6
Oslo	243	13.3	15.3	13.3	13.0
Helsinki	147	12.7	15.6	13.8	12.7
Amsterdam	576	12.3	14.7	13.1	11.6

Source: Statistisk Årsbok för Stockholms stad (1908–1920)

Table 7.2 Some causes of death in some world cities, 1908–13

Deaths per hundred thousand living

City	Measles	Scarlet fever/ scarlatina	Whooping cough	Diphtheria	Smallpox	Typhus	Cholera	Typhoid	Diarrhoea, dysentery	Respiratory TB	Bronchial pneumonia
Cairo	69	5	1	74	1	39	0	29	1014	165	0
Bombay	34	0	1	0	7	0	51	14	341	279	190
Alexandria	50	8	1	37	1	3	0	40	799	242	0
Calcutta	20	0	1	4	8	6	242	26	236	213	76
St Petersburg	82	40	22	32	1	2	76	52	223	303	219
Rio de Janeiro	27	0	12	6	14	0	0	6	321	394	38
Venice	18	8	12	18	0	0	9	25	173	197	116
Dublin	33	10	30	19	0	1	0	13	88	249	164
Budapest	24	44	6	19	0	2	0	15	137	316	134
Stettin	13	19	12	28	0	0	0	9	222	158	115
Prague	14	20	9	14	0	0	0	10	107	331	77
Rome	52	5	9	16	0	0	4	23	104	124	200
Hamburg	16	16	20	53	0	0	0	5	143	148	133
Paris	25	6	10	9	0	0	0	10	63	350	58
Glasgow	61	13	61	22	0	0	0	7	45	116	170
Vienna	26	12	9	15	0	0	0	3	106	257	150
Philadelphia	10	10	6	29	0	0	0	7	90	109	63
Hull	30	3	22	14	0	0	0	12	112	89	86
New York	16	17	7	30	0	0	0	10	112	178	158
Edinburgh	25	10	32	12	0	0	0	2	33	108	106
Lubeck	14	6	17	18	0	0	0	6	104	107	100
Berlin	13	18	15	32	0	0	0	3	75	171	102
Chicago	8	24	6	36	0	0	0	12	155	151	171
Copenhagen	10	15	27	8	0	0	0	3	78	130	84
Stockholm	13	13	12	14	0	0	0	2	37	225	117
London	42	6	23	12	0	0	0	3	63	130	82
Brussels	15	5	6	9	0	0	0	10	98	135	105
Gothenburg	19	5	21	26	0	0	0	10	47	227	91
Oslo	16	6	18	23	0	0	0	2	59	193	88
Helsinki	13	26	19	15	0	0	0	5	131	239	93
Amsterdam	28	2	20	7	0	0	0	6	47	130	107

Source: Statistisk Årsbok för Stockholms stad (1908–1920)

Table 7.3   The disease panorama in some large cities, 1908–13

Deaths per hundred thousand living

Mortality range (per thousand)	Measles, scarlet fever/ scarlatina, whooping cough, diphtheria	Smallpox	Typhus fever, cholera typhoid fever, diarrhoea, dysentery	Tuberculosis of the lungs	Total
over 30	85	4	718	233	3579
20–30	99	5	352	292	2381
15–20	72	0	108	213	1631
10–15	73	0	92	144	1397

These changes may be summarized by the decline of the contagious diseases in one particular city. Changes in cause-specific and age-specific death rates in Liverpool over the second half of the nineteenth century reveal the practical elimination of smallpox and the halving in the mortality from most of the contagious diseases (figure 7.2).[5] On the other hand, mortality from degenerative diseases showed no such decline and afflictions of the urinary, digestive, circulatory, respiratory and nervous systems remained about stable or even deteriorated. In terms of the different age-groups, these improvements show up most strongly among children, adolescents and young adults. The first half of this century has added infants to this roll-call of the very healthy and mortality and sickness are now more exclusively the preserve of the elderly. Table 7.6 shows the age-structure of this improvement in mortality. For each age group the age-specific mortality for 1980 is set at unity and the values for previous years register the deterioration in mortality as one goes back in time, clearly showing that the mortality of the elderly today is little better than in the middle of the last century but that almost all other groups have experienced substantial improvements.

5. The diagram is based on the Decennial Supplements of the Registrar General for 1851–60 and 1891–1900. The functional unit of Liverpool includes four registration districts, those of Liverpool, Toxteth, West Derby, and Birkenhead by the close of the century. At mid-century only Liverpool and West Derby need be included. Since we are comparing rates rather than absolute figures, it seems appropriate to accept these different definitions of Liverpool for the two dates; in fact it does not affect these results very much. This question of the mismatch between registration districts and functional cities is discussed in Kearns (1985a), pp. 171–3.

Table 7.4 Some causes of death in French cities, 1886-98

Group	Measles	Scarlet fever/ scarlatina	Whooping cough	Diphtheria	Smallpox	Typhus	Cholera	Typhoid	Diarrhoea, dysentery	Respiratory TB	Bronchial pneumonia	Stroke	Cancer	Heart
						Deaths per hundred thousand living								
I:1908–13	25	6	10	9	0	0	0	10	63	350	58	N.A.	N.A.	N.A.
I	41	8	16	46	5	0	0	26	150	408	180	96	114	126
II	36	5	14	48	27	0	0	46	249	284	239	140	99	150
III	31	6	12	36	17	0	0	44	192	229	195	122	81	136
IV	28	6	13	38	11	0	0	41	206	203	217	142	84	150
V	24	6	11	37	15	0	0	38	182	192	194	132	82	141
VI	20	5	16	28	5	0	0	29	168	168	166	111	71	127

Source: République Française. Ministère de l'Intérieur. Direction de l'Assistance à de l'hygiène publiques. Bureau de l'hygiène publique, *Statistique sanitaire des villes de France et d'Algérie pendant l'année 1898 et tableau récapulatifs des années 1886 à 1898* (Melun, Imprimerie Administrative; 1899)

N.A. – not available

Table 7.5   Age-specific mortality in French cities, 1886–98

Group	Total mean pop. ('000) 1886–98	Growth (%) p.a.	Crude Birth Rate (per 1,000)	Crude Death Rate (all)	(Deaths per 1,000) Age				
					<1	1–19	20–39	40–59	>60
I	2451	0.7	23.5	21.0	135.5	12.9	9.9	20.3	68.8
II	2213	2.0	24.2	24.2	187.4	13.3	9.9	20.6	82.4
III	2380	0.5	22.3	23.0	177.9	11.6	9.9	20.0	79.7
IV	1267	2.3	22.0	23.3	176.2	11.0	9.1	19.7	84.2
V	1821	0.8	23.3	24.3	171.8	10.8	9.7	20.7	88.1
VI	2282	0.4	23.8	22.5	171.7	8.9	8.7	17.4	81.6

Groups: I   Paris; II   Places of 100,001 to 467,000; III   30,001–100,000; IV   20,001–30,000; V   10,001–20,000; VI   5,001–10,000.

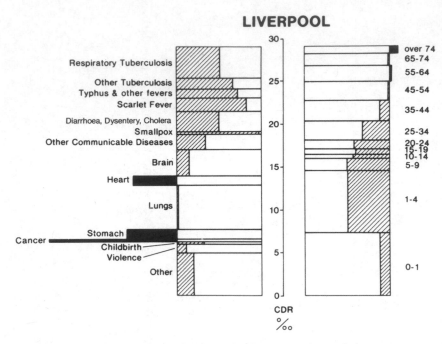

Figure 7.2 The changing mortality pattern of Liverpool 1851–60 to 1891–1900. For Liverpool and West Derby Registration Districts (1851–60) and Liverpool, Toxteth, West Derby and Birkenhead Registration Districts (1891–1900) the diagrams show first, on the vertical axis, the crude death rate for 1851–60 apportioned by cause and age; secondly, on the horizontal axis, the proportionate change in mortality in that age or due to that cause 1851–60 to 1891–1900 (shaded areas indicate decrease, black areas an increase). See p. 103 and for a full discussion Kearns, 1988b
Source: Registrar General's *Decennial Supplements*, 1851–60 and 1891–1900

On this evidence, then, the rise of the great cities might appear to be inexorable. Yet there are grounds for caution. These average figures conceal both spatial and social differences. The progressive improvement in the average has not been accompanied, at least more recently, by any comparable narrowing of this internal variation. Although shifting definitions of social class make the effort a brave one, there is some suggestion that inter-class differences now may be as wide as at any time this century. Table 7.7 gives the standardized mortality rates (SMRs) for males aged 20–64 for five socio-economic groups with the weighted mean being set at 100 for each date. The class gap appears to be widening. Clearly, many causes interact, stress and lifestyle are interdependent but Whitehead (1987, p. 68) reports that when one can control for lifestyle (such factors as smoking and exercise), the social-class gap for mortality from causes such as lung cancer and coronary heart disease is still wide. Whitehead shows that the gap between the social classes for overall standardized mortality is greatest in the regions with the highest mortality. Class and region are mutually reinforcing. In table 7.7 it can be seen that this result holds true also for those specific causes of death taken by

Table 7.6   Changes in age-specific mortality rates for England and Wales
1851/5-1970

	Under 1	5-9	Index values, 1980 = 1.0			65-74	85 and over
			15-19	25-34	45-54		
1851-5	13.0	34.6	12.5	14.0	3.4	1.8	1.5
1876-80	12.1	24.4	8.2	11.6	3.4	1.9	1.6
1901-05	11.5	15.0	5.2	7.6	2.9	1.7	1.3
1926-30	5.7	9.5	4.2	4.9	1.9	1.5	1.4
1951-5	2.3	1.9	1.1	1.7	1.2	1.2	1.2
1970	1.5	1.3	1.1	1.1	1.1	1.1	1.1

Note: Ratios relate age-specific death rates to those of 1980 (see p. 103)
Source: Adapted from OPCS (1986).

Whitehead to be indicative of lifestyle and stress factors (lung cancer, cerebrovascular disease, coronary heart disease) and adopting the definition of class-gap used in the national study (the ratio of the SMRs for classes IV and V to those of classes I and II). Perhaps the major control on mortality in Britain today is deprivation. Deprivation causes stress and induces changes in lifestyle. The human waste of unemployment has predictable and sad effects on individuals: sickness, depression, early death, suicide, as Smith (1987) chronicles with such appropriate bitterness. The most careful studies show that, even controlling for the effects of class, unemployment adds 20-30 per cent to the already unequal SMRs (Moser et al., 1986). Deprivation is deepest in areas of high unemployment; their housing, age-structure, infrastructure and job prospects all combine to make the position of the weak and poor desperate. In this sense, as shown by a recent study of the north of England (Townsend et al., 1988), geography and class reinforce one another and with unemployment and deprivation piling up in the cities of the north of England, the urban penalty rears up once again only now the causes of the fall of great cities are principally social rather than environmental. It remains to be seen whether the collectivist spirit of the period of the rise of great cities, the period of the epidemiologic transition, can meet the challenge of this new urban scenario, the city as the wasteland of the jobless.

Public Health strategies

Against this background, collective action to promote the public health became one of the primary responsibilities of urban authorities. Two strategies of this collective action were developed: quarantine and environmentalism. These two lie astride and basically drive the transitions between the stages of the epidemiologic transition. Quarantine involves separating the sick from the well to reduce the risk of contagion. Environmentalism concerns attempts to clean up the breeding grounds of disease within cities. These strategies highlight different

Table 7.7   The health divide by class and region, 1979/80–1982/3

Region	Ratio of SMRs for socio-economic groups IV and V to those of I and II (%)				
	All causes	Lung cancer	CHD	CVD	SDR
Central Clydeside	207	247	179	214	7.86
Strathclyde	177	224	172	160	7.14
North	188	264	158	217	6.43
North West	176	245	140	200	6.37
Rest of Scotland	164	208	148	182	6.13
Wales	182	241	170	166	5.86
Yorks, Humberside	169	225	146	178	5.83
West Midlands	170	239	139	190	5.72
East Midlands	165	221	151	167	5.28
South East	167	217	143	167	4.88
South West	156	214	135	189	4.82
East Anglia	144	185	132	154	4.37
Britain	175	235	151	190	5.57

Sources: Age-standardized death rates for men 20–64 (SDR) – Townsend *et al.* (1988); Ratio of SMRs for all causes of men 20–64 SEGs IV, V/I, II – Whitehead (1987); Ratio of SMRs for lung cancer, coronary heart disease, cardio-vascular disease – calculated from OPCS (1986)

aspects of urbanism. Quarantine draws attention to the urban system as a whole, cities as nodes in networks of goods, people and diseases. Environmentalism underlines the new ecological relations that big cities create among large groups of people and between them and their natural environment. We may identify a progression from quarantine to environmentalism over the period 1400–1900. The present stage of the epidemiologic transition, dominated by degenerative diseases, is perhaps characterized by a new strategy of hospitalization, a phase which lies outside the scope of this study.

Quarantine and cordons sanitaires

The separation of the sick from the healthy is the earliest collective public health strategy and was initially developed to deal with plague. The elements of the strategy were established at different times and in something like the following order: persons and goods from infected places would be required to submit to a quarantine and even disinfection before being admitted to a city; towns started issuing and expecting bills of health and they kept in contact with one another so that nations and city-states obliged their diplomats abroad to return regular reports on the presence or absence of plague; within towns the sick might be confined to their homes or, especially if they were poor, consigned to pesthouses, often beyond the city walls. The first and most comprehensive development of all these measures came in the republics and principalities of northern Italy and these practices were taken up later in France and Spain and later still in northern Europe and finally in eastern Europe and the Middle East.

For many cities in northern Italy the plague of 1630–1 was their last serious visitation (figure 7.3; Cipolla, 1981, p. 100; 1973, p. 22). This was true of Prato, a town of 6,000 people in the Grand Duchy of Tuscany of which the capital city was Florence. Cipolla's study of Prato offers us an opportunity for examining the highest development of the quarantine strategy. On October 21st 1629 the Florentine observer in the neighbouring State of Milan wrote saying that plague had been confirmed on the northern side of Lake Como (Cipolla, 1973, p. 37 *seq.*). The public health authorities, permanent Health Magistrates, of the Italian capital cities were in frequent contact on how things stood in relation to plague: 'Florence "corresponded" regularly with Genoa, Venice, Verona, Milan, Mantua, Parma, Modena, Ferrara, Bologna, Ancona and Lucca. The frequency of the correspondence with each of these places ranged from one letter every two weeks in periods of calm to several messages a week in times of emergency' (Cipolla, 1981, p. 21). By October 27th 1629, on instructions from Florence, four health officers had been appointed in Prato. Boards of health had been used in Italian cities almost from the start of the fourteenth-century plagues. Other countries followed later and it was not until 1666–70 that the French government, for example, made them obligatory in towns threatened by the plague (Biraben, 1976, p. 143).

With the news that plague had reached Bologna, once again on an order from Florence, Prato gave two people responsibility for issuing bills of health to all local people travelling from Prato. Bills of health were an established part of the quarantine strategy. The earliest example Biraben has found of a city requesting a bill of health from travellers is a French case in 1476 and the slow adoption of this measure can be seen from the fact that Russia made its first such request in its Baltic ports in 1665, Algiers in 1707 and Tunisia in 1720. The practice of issuing such *billets de santé* Biraben again traces to France, Baignoles in 1494, and its slow diffusion is clear from its tardy adoption by Paris in 1619 (ibid, pp. 86–8). On November 8th 1629, the Florentine authorities banned all intercourse with the infected districts of the State of Milan. On December 29th Florence followed a number of other Italian cities in extending the ban to more of Milan. On June 12th 1630, guard posts of Florentine troops were placed every three miles along the border with Bologna. June 16th saw the guards at the gates of Prato increased and on July 10th the most frequently used gates were barricaded. Nor were such measures new. During the Black Death of 1348–9 some towns banned visitors from infected places while, in 1377, Ragusa (Greece) imposed a quarantine of one month on travellers from plague cities and Venice followed suit that same year (ibid., p. 174). On the other hand, only in 1620 did the English authorities set in place an adequate system for quarantining ships from dangerous places (Slack, 1985, p. 203).

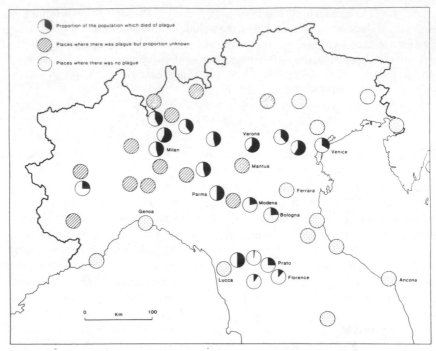

Figure 7.3 The incidence of plague in Northern Italy 1630–31. Symbols indicate for each place those which were free of plague (stippled) and those stricken by plague with either the proportion which died (black or, where this is unknown, shaded). The boundary is that of modern Italy. *Source:* based on Cipolla, 1973 and 1981

By July there were a number of suspicious cases in Prato and on September 19th the game was up. The following day the authorities in Florence acknowledged receipt of the terrifying news and sent instructions for managing a plague city, cut off from the rest of the world. The sick were to be removed to a pesthouse. Their families were to be walled up in their houses and maintained at public expense for a quarantine of 22 days. The bedding and carpets of the sick individuals were to be burned. If the plague victims recovered they were to go to a convalescent home for further quarantine and on leaving they were to get a new set of clothes, their old ones having been burned. Again, some of the measures were of long standing. At Avignon in 1348, Pope Clément VI built wooden cabins for the sick beyond the city walls. That same year at Rodez (France) an isolation hospital was built. In 1403 Venice did likewise. Yet for its first isolation hospital eastern Europe had to wait until 1738 (Ukraine) (Biraben, 1976, pp. 170–3). England had no pesthouse before 1630 and by and large the poor supply of hospitals meant that during plagues the sick were immured with the well inside their houses, their doors marked with a cross and guards posted there (Slack, 1985, p. 203). The use of fire to fight infection was also well supported: indeed, in 1348 Bordeaux burned the entire *quartier* of La Rousselle (Biraben, 1976, p. 176).

Despite these measures Prato lost a quarter of its population to the pestilence in about a year. Why? In the first place the instructions of the authorities in Florence were not followed in every particular. The rich refused to enter any pesthouse or to have their personal effects destroyed. The pesthouses had a poor reputation:

Cardinal Spada reporting on the condition of the pest-houses of Bologna during the plague of 1630 recorded that 'here you see people lament, others cry, others strip themselves to the skin, others die, others become black and deformed, others lose their minds. Here you are overwhelmed by intolerable smells. Here you cannot walk but among corpses. Here you feel naught but the constant horror of death. This is the faithful replica of hell since here there is no order and only horror prevails' (Cipolla, 1973, p. 27)

With respect to bedding, chronic shortages at the pesthouse led to suspect articles of bedding being requisitioned rather than destroyed (ibid., p. 91). The regulations restricting the movements of the people of the city were openly flouted by citizens going to the countryside to help harvest grapes while the inmates of the pesthouse appear to have come and gone almost at will during the early months of the epidemic (ibid., p. 60). The major source of irritation though was the local authority's chronic shortage of funds. This made it impossible to separate the contacts of the sick in a distinct pesthouse so they stayed with the rats and their fleas in their homes. The quarantine of the suspects and convalescents was sometimes untimely aborted because the town could not afford to feed them. Those fortunates who recovered were generally not given new clothes. As Cipolla concludes: 'Scarcity imposed choices and safety had to be sacrificed to economy' (ibid., p 174). Always during a plague, the wandering poor were detained and amid the economic catastrophe of a complete rupture in trade they had to be fed. In Pistoia 1630-1 (a modest epidemic killing 1.5 per cent of the population) the public health expenses were equivalent to 40 per cent of the normal annual expenditure of the city authority. This was met mainly by charity (45 per cent) and loans (52 per cent) while the bulk of the expenditure was on food (53 per cent) (Cipolla, 1981, pp. 67-75). Plague could bankrupt local governments leaving them in debt for many years thereafter. Quite simply, once plague took grip the main determinants of mortality were beyond the control of local government: the ecology of the rat and flea populations, the level of immunity among the human population, the season of the year.

The importance of the quarantine strategy lay not with the internal regulation of infected cities but with the regional control of the spread of disease. In particular the strict application of the strategy in port cities from the mid-seventeenth century was a watershed. It entailed international co-operation to hold the Mediterranean ring against the oriental affliction. Indeed, as both Biraben and Panzac argue, the clearest evidence for this lies in the quite different history of the Ottoman Empire. The plague disappeared from western Europe between the late seventeenth and early eighteenth centuries. It persisted in the Ottoman Empire until the 1840s. There, the inefficiency of local government was compounded by a genuine, fatalistic, Muslim belief that to avoid plague was to cheat God's clear intentions. Indeed plagues stimulated religious revivals and holy martyrdom. The flight of non-Muslims during plagues only increased the economic tragedy for the rest. By the late eighteenth century some local *pachas* had limited success by following European methods of quarantine urged on them by foreign consuls. Epidemics every 23 years or so, after each of which it may have taken 15 years of rural population supply to make good the deficiency, created demographic stagnation (Panzac, 1985, pp. 379–80). During the wars between Egypt and Turkey, strictly mercantilist arguments began to tell on central governments. In 1831–2, faced with a new disease, cholera, for which no fatalistic instructions could be found among the writings of the prophets, the states turned to Europeans for advice. By the 1840s dictatorial health regulations (especially quarantine) were in force against most epidemic diseases. After 1843 in Turkey and 1844 in Egypt, these measures succeeded in excluding plague although the pestilence periodically erupted in neighbouring Cyrene, Iraq, Iran and Arabia (ibid., p. 508).

The many legacies of the plague to western societies included: the engagement ring, a magical diamond to protect loved ones (Biraben, 1976, p. 185), a periodic commitment to provide the poor with the means of life, the building and equipping of isolation hospitals and measures of international collaboration to preserve the common health. In general, these factors have in common the *collective* responsibilities which follow from seriously trying to separate the sick from the well in time of plague. No longer were such matters left to private initiatives or charity: public health strategy must be underwritten by collective action.

Environmentalism

Whereas the health strategies of the seventeenth century emphasized the danger of contamination from without and thus sought to regulate intercourse with foreign parts, the predominant emphasis of the nineteenth century was on dangers from within, above all the need to clean up the cities. This is a real shift of attention and not simply a response to a changing disease panorama. When, in 1720, plague in Marseille caused alarm in most European countries, in England there was now strong medical opposition to the imposition of quarantine on the grounds that the disease was generated *in situ* and that quarantine was, therefore, ineffective and needlessly expensive (Slack, 1985, pp. 329–31). Richard Mead advised the government that 'nothing approaches so near to the first original of the plague as air pent up, loaded with dumps, and corrupted with the filthiness that proceeds from animal bodies' (Simon, 1897, p. 113). Similarly, in 1838 the British representative in Cairo broke with the other European consuls and tried to persuade the ruler, Muhammed Ali, to abandon quarantine and *cordons sanitaires* just as, in retrospect, they appear to have started bearing fruit (Panzac, 1985, p. 470). No other country went as far as England on this matter but all failed to exclude cholera by quarantine and all accepted that urban fevers, like gaol fevers, were nourished by poor sanitation.

Of the four cholera epidemics in England, the second was the most serious, nationally and in individual cities (table 7.8).[6] On each occasion, London

---

6. The cholera statistics come from Kearns (1985a), ch. 2. The population totals refer to the municipal limits of each city; Manchester includes Salford. The populations do not refer to precisely the same units for which the mortality rates were calculated. This table includes cities with a population of 100,000 or more in 1851.

accounted for at least one quarter of all cholera deaths in England and Wales and in 1854 it made up almost half of them. In 1832, London's recourse to quarantine and prayer had manifestly failed. By the time of the second epidemic, England had new centralized systems of poor relief (the New Poor Law of 1834) and of vital registration (the General Register Office, dating from 1838). It had also recently acquired a Public Health Act (1848), creating a central General Board of Health under which towns could set up local boards of health whose activities would come under the purview of the central agency, and a Nuisances Removal and Diseases Prevention Act (1848) which permitted the General Board to recommend and enforce health regulations during epidemic crises. London was excluded from the Public Health Act but its private sewerage companies had been taken under government direction through a Metropolitan Commission of Sewers (1847) while the sacred square mile of the City of London had secured its own sanitary powers (1848). In the eye of the storm stood Edwin Chadwick, the famous public health reformer. Secretary to the central Poor Law authority until 1847, dominant member of the Metropolitan Commission of Sewers and the General Board of Health and anxious to extend 'scientific' principles of local government and public health to the whole of London he hoped, despite his ill health, that: ' . . . I may be spared to see the accomplishment of some of our objects such as the expulsion of Typhus from the dwellings of the labouring classes, as complete as it has been from the prisons' (Finer, 1952, p. 338).

The General Board of Health's advice on cholera was as follows: 'Before the appearance of the disease in this country we warned the local authorities that the seats of the approaching pestilence in their respective districts would be the usual haunts of other epidemics' (Great Britain Parliamentary Papers, PP 1850 1273, p. 19). Early cholera cases in 1848 were reported from London (22nd September), Scotland (Edinburgh, 5th October; Glasgow, 16th November) and north-east England (Sunderland, 6th November; Tynemouth, 8th November) (ibid., p. 151). After issuing official Notifications of the presence of cholera, the Board published its Regulations on 3rd November 1848. The local poor law authorities, the Guardians of the Poor, were immediately to draw up lists of local environmental nuisances prejudicial to health, to have their medical officers report on them and then to have the nuisances cleaned up. Should cholera appear in a locality, the poor law authorities were to provide dispensaries for supplying constipative drugs and houses of refuge for the healthy caught in a house with cholera cases. Furthermore, they were to carry out house-to-house inspections in affected areas to identify people apparently in the early stages of the disease whom, it was believed, could be easily treated with laudanum and chalk thereby preventing them from going on to develop full-blown cholera (PP 1850 1275, pp. 189–92). All the measures of the General Board of Health were based on the idea that cholera was not spread from person to person and that it was generated from rotting organic matter in the environment: ' . . . it is propagated not by the contact of one infected person with another, but by a general influence operating on particular localities and persons, according to certain localising conditions and predisposing causes; (PP 1850 1273, p. 36). The Board had very little confidence that full cholera could be cured. Chadwick was quite explicit: 'I always doubt the success of mere medicine' (Finer,

Table 7.8 Cholera mortality in the largest cities of England and Wales, 1831/2–1866

	Deaths per 1000 from cholera				Total population in thousands 1851
	1831–2	1848–9	1853–4	1866	
London	3.8	6.2	4.3	1.9	2362
Liverpool	7.8	13.7	3.0	3.7	376
Manchester	6.1	3.7	1.5	2.4	367
Birmingham	0.1	0.2	0.1	0.05	233
Leeds	5.5	14.6	0.5	0.1	172
Bristol	6.6	8.2	1.1	0.2	137
Sheffield	6.8	1.1	1.1	0.1	135
Bradford	1.3	2.5	1.8	1.5	104
England and Wales	1.5	3.1	1.2	0.7	17,928

Source: Kearns (1985a), ch. 2

1952, p. 341). The emphasis, therefore, was placed on preventive measures to remove the accumulations of filth which were thought to be the cause of all epidemic disease. Yet, according to the General Board of Health, the Boards of Guardians did not use 'the powers intrusted to them for the prevention of disease' and although the Nuisances Removal and Diseases Prevention Act was presented to them as 'a special provision applicable not merely to one class but to all classes; for though in a season of pestilence some classes may be in greater danger than others yet none are exempt', they continued to deal with disease only as and when the sick poor applied for medical relief (PP 1850 1273, p. 137). Furthermore, preventive cleansing was frequently only adopted when cholera had appeared and then only applied to a few of the worst sites in each place 'but as *continued cleansing and inspection of fever districts* was the preventive measure really required, the simple abatement of a few nuisances, though praiseworthy in itself, and useful as far as it went, was by no means sufficient to protect the public health' (ibid., p. 83).

Cases of Asiatic cholera had been reported in London in late September 1848 and the Regulations of the General Board of Health were issued shortly after. In the eastern part of Southwark, the district of St Olave was the earliest affected part in 1848 and, after Rotherhithe, the most troubled in 1849 (figure 7.4).[7] As early as October 6th 1848, the local Registrar of Births and Deaths reported two cholera deaths from the same house adding that the family 'were cleanly in their habits, but . . . one or other of the family has been constantly ill since they lived in their

7. Based on statistics in PP 1850 1275. These statistics are evaluated in Kearns (1985b). The map is based on data for the 135 registration sub-districts of London. The inset map labels the 36 registration districts: 1. Kensington; 2. Chelsea; 3. St George Hanover Square; 4. Westminster; 5. St Martin in the Fields; 6. St James Westminster; 7. Marylebone; 8. Hampstead; 9. St Pancras; 10. Islington; 11. Hackney; 12. St Giles; 13. Strand; 14. Holborn; 15. Clerkenwell; 16. St Luke; 17. East London; 18. West London; 19. City of London; 20. Shoreditch; 21. Bethnal Green;

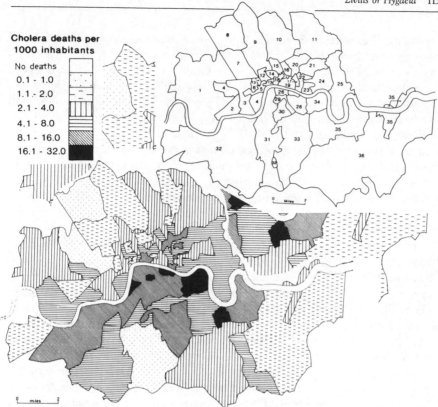

Cholera deaths per 1000 inhabitants

No deaths
0.1 - 1.0
1.1 - 2.0
2.1 - 4.0
4.1 - 8.0
8.1 - 16.0
16.1 - 32.0

Figure 7.4 The incidence of cholera in London 1848–49. Cholera deaths per 1000 inhabitants (top) are shown for the 135 registration sub-districts of the registration county of London (bottom). *Source: Parliamentary Papers 1850 (1275)*; for further details see Kearns, 1985b and pp. 114–17.

present residence There are, I believe, upwards of 20 houses within 4 or 5 feet of a filthy open sewer, and this fact has been constantly represented to me (as Registrar) by the inhabitants of those houses. The illness which is caused by so great a nuisance can hardly be wondered at, for in some places I do not think it is above 3 feet from their doors' (Registrar-General, 1852, p. xiv). Ten months later with the London epidemic at its height, with over 800 cholera deaths per week, the same local Register seemed in despair: ' . . . no less than 9 deaths have taken place this week in Surrey-buildings from cholera, and other persons are lying dangerously ill. The court contains about 14 houses which are constantly exposed to the effluvia of an open sewer; the water they drink is from a well, which is not protected from the drainage of the sewers' (ibid., p. 206). Yet, reflecting on the effect of their Regulation enjoining preventive inspection and cleansing, the General Board of Health's chief London officer complained that 'with some few

---

22. Whitechapel; 23. St George in the East; 24. Stepney/Mile-End Old Town; 25. Poplar; 26. St Saviour Southwark; 27. St Olave Southwark; 28. Bermondsey; 29. St George Southwark; 30. Newington; 31. Lambeth; 32. Wandsworth; 33. Camberwell; 34. Rotherhithe; 35. Greenwich; 36. Lewisham.

exceptions, they were disregarded. . . . In spite of these regulations and significant warnings much precious time was thus irrevocably lost; no systematic sanitary precautions were adopted; and I consequently found on visiting various localities on the reappearance of the disease in June and July 1849, as the medical visitors did subsequently in September, that foul and obstructed drains, filthy houses, and overflowing cesspools, were as rife as they were before Christmas, when the epidemic first broke out' (PP 1850 1275, p. 123). In fact, many local Boards of Guardians had not asked their medical officers to prepare the requisite reports on the insanitary parts of their Poor Law Unions. In Whitechapel, the local Medical Officers prepared a list of filthy localities in November 1848 only to have the Guardians explicitly tell them not to pay further visits there (Finer, 1952, p. 345). In the worst parts of London, the tenor of local politics was set by the involvement of petty landlords, for the implementation of sanitary measures would clearly 'interfere with private interests, and especially with interests which, in all parishes, but particularly in large and populous ones, are largely represented in Boards of Guardians (PP 1850 1275, p. 121). This reluctance was reinforced by the electoral popularity of local authorities careful not to spend overmuch of their clients' rates.

From September 1848 to September 1849 Chadwick directed that the London sewers be repeatedly flushed clean. Boards of Guardians were urged to appoint extra medical officers to seek out environmental nuisances. On the appearance of cholera, they were to institute a house-to-house visitation in affected areas so that early cholera cases might be treated and further nuisances cleaned up. As with the preventive cleansing, the General Board of Health complained about the response of the London local authorities: ' . . . in the great majority of instances, all the essential regulations and instructions of the General Board were disregarded or directly rejected' (ibid., p. 131). By the second half of August, with over one thousand cholera deaths each week in London, the Board went on the offensive. On 23rd August, a Principal Medical Inspector and four assistants were appointed and they went into the worst districts of London, taking with them orders for the enrolment of sufficient Medical Officers for a proper house-to-house visitation. By the second week of September, the weekly toll in London was 2,000 deaths. The Board, against Treasury advice about its legality, appointed a further four inspectors. They ordered some of the most overcrowded graveyards to be closed, a direction which was thrown out by a court of law (Finer, 1952, pp. 348–51). Certainly, Bethnal Green, St Pancras and Whitechapel were obstructive to the point of criminal negligence, but other Unions acted earlier and more conscientiously than the General Board allowed. Islington, for example, suffered a handful of cases in October 1848 before the outbreak of June to October 1849 and although this represented a relatively mild visitation, the parish took a number of preventive steps in good time (Kearns, 1989). In 1847, the parish had enlarged its medical complement from one to six. In June 1848, the Vestry undertook to clean and water all the roads of the parish, both private and public. In 1849, the parish Trustees began to use their nuisance powers to force the owners of private roads to have them paved. From late August to late October 1849, the Trustees paid for the medicines any medical practitioner in the parish supplied to the poor. From the start of the epidemic, the Trustees set up permanent district Sanitary Committees who, from 6th December, did indeed seek out nuisances and dealt with over a thousand in their first year; cajoling the owners of filthy houses, worrying pig-keepers and washing streets.

An environmentalist strategy lay behind both the recommendations of the General Board of Health and the measures undertaken by local authorities such as Islington. It was a component of most anti-cholera measures in western cities. For example, the preventive action urged by Brussels on the local authority at Leuven, a town of around 30,000, in the face of the threat of cholera, which brought a mortality of 19 per thousand in a total mortality of 45 per thousand, worse than most British cities, included monitoring the food supply, housing conditions and hygiene (van der Haegen and de Vos, 1980, p. 205). At St Louis, Missouri, the citizens' Committee of Public Health: appointed 140 block inspectors to survey sanitary conditions; supplied free water to the poor; imposed a quarantine on boats approaching the city; isolated the sick in temporary hospitals and provided medicine free to the poor (Brewer, 1975, p. 117). Yet, in many cases, the local authorities in other European and north American cities proved less willing than the British actually to implement an environmentalist strategy. Thus, in 1849, the New York Board of Health, despite being empowered 'to do or cause to be done *any thing* which in their opinion may be proper to preserve the health of the city' were in fact unable to force private street cleaners to fulfil the basic terms of their contracts; saw no response to their urging that householders clean up their tenements; and even seemed incapable of ensuring the decent burial of cholera's victims (Rosenberg, 1962, pp. 110–13). In St Louis, interventionism was so unacceptable that finally the local government resigned, ceding power to a Committee of citizens who belatedly undertook certain emergency measures but who, at the close of the epidemic, left St Louis as they had found it, without a sewerage system of any description, with unpaved streets, with a garbage removal system excluding three-quarters of the population and with some parts of the city even lacking piped water. Yet St Louis lost 4,577 of its population of 63,471 to cholera that year, a mortality of 72 per thousand and far above that of the worst European cities (Brewer, 1975, p. 102). It is clear that sanitary regulations rather than quarantine or medication became of increasing significance over time in most cities and it is also clear that the English model was held in high esteem. In 1853–4, preventive measures were given greater prominence in Paris than they had in 1832, chief among them house to house visitation to detect premonitory diarrhoea. Justifying this strategy, the head of the Cholera Commission of the Academy of Medicine, Jules Guérin, referred to its successful application in Newcastle in 1849 (Bourdelais and Raulot, 1987, p. 215). When Hamburg was replanned after the fire of 1842, William Lindley, an Englishman and a disciple of Edwin Chadwick, took a leading part. He discussed the city's sewerage system with Chadwick and, with letters of support from the world expert, proposed an integrated system along the lines Chadwick was advocating for London. Instead of carts, sewers driven by water supplied by a municipally-owned company would remove dung from houses and might, then, spread it on the land as fertilizer. All but the last part of the scheme was adopted (Evans, 1987, pp. 133–4).

In England, despite the removal of Chadwick from power in 1854, there was little let-up in the advance of the environmentalist strategy. Centralization went largely unchecked because central government would not trust local authorities to decide technical questions involving the expenditure of tens of thousands of pounds. Consequently, the approval of cheap loans from the Treasury to local authorities, secured by mortgaging the rates, continued to require the submission of plans to the central Local Government Board (from 1858) (Lambert, 1962). At the International Cholera Conference in Constantinople in 1866, the English delegates almost alone violently opposed all forms of quarantine against cholera in the Mediterranean, but William Farr, of the General Register Office, noted:

The influence of the English delegates is, however, evidently perceptible in the importance, unusual in such a body, attached to hygienic measures. The Conference 'demands for every man pure and abundant air, pure water, and a pure soil. The Conference believes that these elements should constitute the permanent privilege of populations', and should not be postponed until cholera epidemics threaten, or are in the midst of populations (PP 1867–8, p. lxxxix).

Spending by urban local authorities on sanitary works continued to rise and new water and sewerage systems were largely responsible for the improvements in mortality from contagious diseases in the 1860s, 1870s and 1880s (Wohl, 1983, pp. 114–16). Voluntarism died more slowly in the United States where, as late as 1909, 20 per cent of the population in places of 30,000 or more still lacked main sewers. Indeed smaller cities were the worst served. In places of over 300,000 only 15 per cent of the population was not served by sewers for places of 100–300,000 it was 23 per cent, 50–100,000 26 per cent and 30–50,000 32 per cent (Department of Commerce, 1913, p. 34).

As urban authorities took on wider responsibilities, the British began to speak of 'municipal socialism' and in 1900, at the instigation of the London Chamber of Commerce, a joint select committee of both houses of parliament was set up to enquire into the appropriate limits of municipal enterprise (PP 1900). Of 314 urban authorities in England and Wales and 205 in Scotland, 265 English or Welsh and 73 Scots were found to be engaged in some forms of municipal trading and the bulk of these enterprises were relatively new (see table 7.9; also, chapter 3). Water supply was the most common. It was relatively expensive, yielding only a moderate rate of profit on capital employed (ROP1 in table 7.9). Furthermore this modest return all but disappeared if account was taken of depreciation costs, interest payments and the repayment of principal (ROP2) and would almost certainly have completely disappeared if all municipalities had made proper provision in their accounts for depreciation or a sinking fund (almost half the water enterprises had no sinking fund at all).

Yet the Committee paid very little attention to the question of whether the supply of water came within the proper remit of local government for, despite

Table 7.9 Municipal trading in nineteenth-century Britain

| Undertaking | Established | | | | Average | ROP1 | ROP2 |
	no date	before 1836	1836– 67	1868– 98	capital outlay (£,000)	(per cent per annum)	
Waterworks	16	10	57	143	213	3.60	0.06
Gasworks	4	4	26	85	167	5.85	1.84
Tramways	1	0	0	32	95	4.15	1.06
Electric lighting	4	0	0	56	56	4.02	0.20
Baths, washhouses	0	3	26	85	13	0.33	−2.95
Cemeteries	0	0	33	33	16	1.24	−2.33
Housing	0	0	0	8	72	1.21	−1.83

Source: PP 1900, Appendix B, pp. 377–451

some of the more extreme remarks that, for example, local authorities should pro-vide 'nothing they could get anybody else to undertake' (q. 1383, p. 111), the gen-eral tone of the enquiry was captured in an invitation to Sir Thomas Hughes, alderman of the Council of the City of Liverpool, to give his evidence on water '. . . very briefly, because as a matter of fact, the supply of water by a corporation such as yours, within its own area at any rate, receives very little objection from anybody' (q. 2214, p. 176). The basis of this near unanimity was a recognition of the sanitary importance of water, the clear acceptance that no citizen was safe so long as any were dangerously dirty, as Hughes went on to say in his evidence, '. . . a good and unlimited supply of water should be the first thought of every com-munity, and I may say we lay great stress upon keeping up the purity of our water, so much so that we bought the watershed [where the supply originated] to regulate agriculture, the keeping of cattle, and anything that can possibly pollute the water, and even after that is done the water is all passed through filter beds before being distributed' (q. 2243, p. 178). The sanitary argument was used to justify house-building since the clearance of filthy sites and the provision of cheap enough replacements was beyond private enterprise, the running of trams since they encouraged a move to healthier suburbs while private enterprise would not supply the classes in greatest need of this escape, the supply of bathhouses so the poor might wash themselves and their clothes whereas private enterprise could not stoop to housing them at densities which allowed the luxury of indoor washing facilities and even the delivery of gas for street lighting since visibility was next to cleanliness and private enterprise found collecting adequate rents from the poor too troublesome. The sanitary argument was very flexible but it rested on the belief that cleaning-up the environment was in the general interest since it made cities healthy and on the further recognition that this matter was too important to leave to the market logic of private supply, it needed the collective responsibility of public enterprise.

In France, cholera gave rise to the St. Vincent de Paul Society and the Miraculous Medal but more generally its repeated visitations index the gradual secularization of responses to adversity (Bourdelais and Dodin, 1987, pp. 132 and 99). It was also associated with strategies for promoting the public health which directed attention to environmental factors. Increasingly, the major systems regulating society's ecological relations came to be placed under *collective* direction. In England, by the late nineteenth century, the fullest development of the environmentalist model was based on a recognition that public control of water supplies and sewerage systems was efficient, desirable and necessary. Environmentalism required interventionism.

Individual rights and collective responsibilities

The separation of the sick from the well is a collectivist act since, in the general interest, it seeks to restrict the movements and activities of people thought to be sick or under suspicion of being sick. At the same time this strategy might also entail extending to the sick the basic rights of food and shelter. The balance between collective interests and individual rights is weighted differently depending on time and place but must always be struck. This is a perennial issue, changing in response to moral as much as medical arguments. In this debate disease itself is frequently given a moral dimension, as having some meaning in the wider scheme of things. These meanings are at least as contentious as the strictly scientific aspects of epidemiology. In persuading the English belatedly to adopt a proper public health strategy against the plague, the belief that 'disorder and unrulyness of all kinds were commonly conceived to be both physical and moral sources of disease' (see Cardinal Spada's definition of hell quoted above) meant something very similar to the claim that plague was contagious (Slack, 1985, p. 304). Indeed notions of moral contagion and physical contagion were tightly bonded together: hence Felix Driver has traced the congruity of moral and physical environmentalism, '. . . the sanitary movement was never simply a medical enterprise narrowly defined. There were said to be moral miasmas corresponding to physical ones . . .' (Driver, 1988, p. 279). Along with poor law policies, then, 'public health policies were part and parcel of a general drive towards greater social control' (Slack, 1985, p. 305). Consequently, the aims of the English Plague Act of 1604 were 'the charitable relief and *ordering* of persons infected with the Plague' (ibid., p. 211).

This conjunction of medical and moral arguments is a common one and fears of contagion are still an important part of the way this link is experienced. Most recently, AIDS hysteria is only the most obvious of a range of examples including drug addiction, ethnic health, sexually transmitted diseases and cancer. In general these arguments might be described as 'victim blaming' and the victims themselves may even take part in it. For example, Randy Shilts reported a meeting between an American epidemiologist and an AIDS patient who was reflecting on the aspects of his lifestyle and attitudes which had brought him to such a pass:

The monologue was taking Brandy to a conclusion that irked the scientific side of Don Francis's mind. Brandy was trying to find a reason he was lying in Room 428A about to die.

The old moral teachings, Francis thought, die hard. 'I think this is a communicable disease and you got it', said Francis, matter-of-factly. 'You're not being punished. A virus has made you sick' (Shilts, 1987, p. 159).

Yet health care is not an appropriate area for policing morals because moralizing attitudes inevitably get in the way of treating, attracting to treatment or advising members of the target group. Health policy cannot be the unaccountable hand-maiden of the criminal law. Illegal practices should be pursued by the police quite separately from how the casualities of those practices are treated by the medical profession. Where no illegal practices are involved, moralizing is even less accept-able. This conjunction of moral and medical arguments, embedded in many notions of contagion and basic to the quarantine policies of the first stage of the epidemiologic transition, can only be countered with a well-developed commit-ment to the rights of the individual. In this regard, the American constitution appears to promise greater protection than the *ad hoc* case-law of the British. Ideas such as strict scrutiny could play a valuable part in British society particularly if they were tied to a more efficient way of enforcing rights than the individual appealing to a court of law. Strict scrutiny prevents legislation restricting the rights of large groups in society when only a portion of the group represents any sort of risk: 'Strict scrutiny requires the state to prove that the chosen action was the least restrictive alternative: the state must show that the legislation is drawn with precision, that it is closely tailored to serve the objective, and that there is no other reasonable way to achieve the goal with a lesser burden on constitutionally protected activity' (Anon., 1986, p. 1277). This sort of protection would outlaw unacceptable dis-crimination and might cover matters such as confidentiality and inappropriate prying by insurance companies. The main problems with this sort of protection is that it requires groups to have ready access to the law but the difficulties the under-privileged have in this regard might be mitigated by entrusting the enforcement of these rights to a public ombudsperson.

In making environment the focus of public health intervention, the English sanitary reformers explicitly rejected arguments that took the individual as their focus. Chadwick urged that in some cases ill health may cause poverty but that poverty was not the general cause of ill health. The general cause, picked out by the miasmatic theory of disease, was the accumulation of decomposing filth in the environment. In this Chadwick broke with the French hygienists who 'emphasised poverty as the underlying cause of disease and death' (la Berge, 1988, p. 36). The French social theory of epidemiology also appeared to commit the hygienists to very radical policies in the name of public health, policies which questioned the entire social structure and policies with which bourgeois reformers were uncomfortable. In a sense, then, the hygienists overreached themselves and swung erratically from major to minor key depending on whether the tune was theoretical or practical (Coleman, 1982). La Berge argues that, in contrast, the 'acceptance of poverty as the principal cause of disease could not lead to the kind of action Chadwick wanted' which included 'municipal reform, sanitary engineering and legislation' (la Berge, 1988, pp. 39–40). But in order to assert this collective interest over environmental matters, Chadwick had to contend with a countervailing set of individual rights, those of people holding relevant property titles. These included private companies providing inadequate water and sewerage services as well as landlords who rented out insanitary and overcrowded dwellings. Chadwick's line of argument was that the market could not operate properly with respect to the management of the urban environment (Kearns, 1987, 1988a). In water, sewerage and housing, market forces were continually compromised by 'natural' monopolies. Consequently, the socially most beneficial solution was not the one delivered by these imperfect markets. In contrast to the more ambitious programme of the French hygienists, Chadwick's sanitary idea came closer to being realized. At a time when the ideology of the enterprise culture has politicians reaching for a gun at the mere mention of social ownership, we should remember the impact of environmental systems on health and the reasons why public ownership was considered appropriate in the first place. We should also remember that the people who had experienced both forms of ownership in their own lifetimes were overwhelmingly satisfied with the performance of the municipalized utilities (Hassan, 1985).

The rise of great cities owed a good deal to the success of such collective action in mitigating the worst of the urban demographic penalty. These public health strategies redefined individual rights in asserting collective interests. Yet these benefits also carry with them some warnings. Health care cannot be allowed to run roughshod over civil liberties. Neither should the prospect of private profits be allowed to prejudice the gains made under social ownership of public utilities. Both of these concerns seem apposite at present with moralizing on one hand and privatization on the other as forces which could nudge the quality of life in cities into a decline if not a fall.

Acknowledgements

I would like to thank the following people for their assistance in preparing this chapter: for comments – John Rogers, Marie Clarke-Nelson, Naomi Williams, Paul Laxton, Robert Lee, Sally Dent; for data collection – Hannah Moore and Julie Holbrooke; and for drawing the diagrams – Sandra Mather and Paul Smith.

References

Anon. (1986), 'Note. The constitutional rights of AIDS carriers', *Harvard Law Review*, 99, 1274–92.

la Berge, A.F. (1988), 'Edwin Chadwick and the French Connection', *Bulletin of the History of Medicine*, 62, 23–42.

Biraben, J.N. (1975), *Les hommes et la peste en France et dans les pays européens et méditerranéans. I. La peste dans l'histoire*, Mouton, Paris.

Biraben, J.N. (1976), *Les hommes et la peste en France et dans les pay européens et méditerranéans. II. Les hommes face à la peste*, Mouton, Paris.

Bourdelais, P. and Raulot J-Y. (1987), *Une peur bleue: histoire du choléra en France, 1832–1854*, Payot, Paris.

Bourdelais, P. and Dodin, A. (1987), *Visages du choléra*, Belin, Paris.

Brewer, P. (1975), 'Voluntarism on trial: St Louis' response to the cholera epidemic of 1849', *Bulletin of the History of Medicine*, 49, 102–22.

Cipolla, C.M. (1973), *Christofano and the Plague. A Study in the History of Public Health in the Age of Galileo*, Collins.

Cipolla, C.M. (1981), *Fighting the Plague in Seventeenth-century Italy*, University of Wisconsin Press, Madison and London.

Coleman, W. (1982), *Death is a Social Disease. Public Health and Political Economy in Early Industrial France*, University of Wisconsin Press, Madison and London.

Delaporte, F. (1986), *Disease and Civilisation. The Cholera in Paris, 1832*, MIT Press, Cambridge, Mass. and London.

Department of Commerce, Bureau of the Census (1913), *Special Reports. General Statistics of Cities: 1909. Including statistics of sewers and sewage disposal, refuse collection and disposal, street cleansing, dust prevention, highways and the general highway service of cities having a population of over 30,000*, Government Printing Office, Washington.

Driver, F. (1988), 'Moral geographies: social science and the urban environment in mid-nineteenth century England', *Trans. Institute of British Geographers*, N.S. 13, 275–87.

Evans, R.J. (1987), *Death in Hamburg: Society and Politics in the Cholera Years 1830-1910*, Oxford University Press.

Finer, S.E. (1952), *The Life and Times of Sir Edwin Chadwick*, Methuen.

Great British Parliamentary Papers (1850) [1273] xxi, p. 3, 'Report from the General Board of Health on the Epidemic Cholera of 1848 and 1849'.

Great Britain Parliamentary Papers 1850 [1275] xxi, p. 365, 'Report from the General Board of Health on the Epidemic Cholera of 1848 and 1849. Appendix B. Sanitary Report on epidemic cholera as it prevailed in London. By R.D. Grainger'.

Great Britain Parliamentary Papers 1867-8 4072 xxxxvii, p. 1, 'Report on the cholera epidemic of 1866 in England, Supplement to the twenty-ninth annual report of the Registrar-General of Births, Deaths, and Marriages in England'.

Great Britain Parliamentary Papers 1900 303 vii, p. 183, 'Report from the Joint Select Committee of the House of Lords and the House of Commons on Municipal Trading, together with the proceedings of the committee, minutes of evidence and appendix'.

Hassan, J. (1985), 'The growth and impact of the British water industry in the nineteenth century', *Economic History Review*, 2nd series, 38, 531–47.

Kearns, G. (1985a), Aspects of cholera, society and space in nineteenth-century England and Wales, unpublished Ph.D. thesis, Cambridge.

Kearns, G. (1985b), *Urban Epidemics and Historical Geography: Cholera in London 1848-9*, Geobooks, Norwich.

Kearns, G. (1987), 'Private enterprise rains O.K.? London and its water supply', *London Journal*, 12, 180–86.

Kearns, G. (1988a), 'Private property and public health reform in England 1830–70', *Social Science and Medicine*, 26, 187–99.

Kearns, G. (1988b), 'The urban penalty and the population history of England', in A. Brändström and L.-G. Tedebrand (eds), *Society and Health during the Demographic Transition*, Almqvist and Wiksell, Stockholm.

Kearns, G. (1989), 'Cholera, nuisances and environmental management in Islington 1830–55', in W.F. Bynum (ed.), *Living and Dying in London 1500-1900*, Routledge.

Kunitz, S.J. (1983), 'Speculations on the European mortality decline', Economic History Review, 36, 349–64.

Lambert, R.J. (1962), 'Central and local relations in mid-Victorian England: the Local Government Act Office, 1858–71', Victorian Studies, 6, 121–50.

Moser, K.A., Fox, A.J., Jones, D.R. (1986), 'Unemployment and mortality in the OPCS longitudinal study', in R.G. Wilkinson (ed.), Class and Health. Research and Longitudinal Data, Tavistock.

Office of Population Censuses and Surveys (OPCS) (1986), Occupational Mortality: Decennial Supplement 1979–80, 1982–3, Great Britain, HMSO.

Omran, A.R. (1982), 'Epidemiologic transition', in J.A. Ross (ed.), International Encyclopaedia of Population, Free Press, New York.

Panzac, D. (1985), La peste dans l'Empire Ottoman 1700–1850, Editions Peeters, Louvain.

Registrar-General (1852), Report on the Mortality of Cholera in England, 1848–9, HMSO.

Rosenberg, C.E. (1962), The Cholera Years. The United States in 1832, 1849 and 1866, University of Chicago Press.

Shilts, R. (1987), And the Band Played On. Politics, People and the AIDS Epidemic, St. Martin's Press, New York.

Simon, J. (1897), English Sanitary Institutions, John Murray.

Slack, P. (1985), The Impact of Plague in Tudor and Stuart England, Routledge and Kegan Paul.

Smith, R. (1987), Unemployment and Health: A Disaster and a Challenge, Oxford University Press.

Townsend, P., Phillimore, P., and Beattie, A. (1988), Health and Deprivation: Inequality and the North, Croom Helm.

van der Haegen, H. and de Vos, R. (1980), 'L'épidemie du choléra à Louvain en 1849', Bulletin Trimestriel du crédit communal de Belgique, 133, 195–208.

Weber, A.F. (1899), The Growth of Cities in the Nineteenth Century. A Study in Statistics, Macmillan, New York.

Whitehead, M. (1987), The Health Divide: Inequalities in Health in the 1980s, Health Education Council.

Wohl, A. (1983), Endangered Lives. Public Health in Victorian Britain, Dent.

Zacke, B. (1971), Kolera epidemien i Stockholm 1834, Kungliga Boktryckeriet P.A. Norsedt and Söner, Stockholm.

8 Working-class housing in European cities since 1850

Colin G. Pooley

Introduction

The concept of the 'rise and fall' of great cities is inapplicable to the study of low-cost housing provision. Ever since the rise of industrial capitalism in Europe, there has been a persistent crisis in working-class housing: capitalist economies and societies have proved incapable of providing adequate supplies of good-quality housing in urban areas at prices that the majority of the working-class population can afford.

In Britain, the surveys of Henry Mayhew (1861), Charles Booth (1892–7) and others demonstrated the atrocious housing conditions experienced in nineteenth-century London, and similar problems were found in most large cities (Burnett 1978; Gauldie, 1974). In 1891 over 50 per cent of the population of inner London districts such as Whitechapel, Shoreditch, St. George's and Holborn lived in over-crowded housing according to Booth's criteria, and 37 per cent of the entire population of inner London was overcrowded (Stedman Jones, 1971, Part II). In late nineteenth-century Liverpool over 18,000 houses were declared unfit for habitation by the Medical Officer of Health (Annual Reports, various 1964) while Shimmin graphically illustrated the acute housing poverty of many inner-city residents of Liverpool. There have been variations in the nature and acuteness of the crisis over time, but the fundamental problem remains: even if the absolute quality of housing has improved in the twentieth century, the relative distance between the housing conditions of rich and poor has remained almost unchanged. Thus, the English House Condition Survey (Department of Environment, 1981) revealed that 4.3 million housing units required substantial repairs, including 1.1 million houses unfit for human habitation (see also Malpass, 1986), and Harrison's (1983) survey of inner-city housing need revealed conditions that had changed relatively little since the mid-nineteenth century.

The crisis in low-cost housing provision is not solely urban – acute housing stress also occurred in rural areas in both nineteenth- and twentieth-century Europe – but the concentration of population in towns made the problem more obvious and unacceptable, and progressive urbanization of Europe since the early nineteenth century exposed more and more people to sub-standard urban housing. The inadequacy of working-class housing is thus a fundamental and, seemingly, inevitable part of the society and economy of capitalist Europe in the nineteenth and twentieth centuries, and is not tied to specific locations and time periods.

This chapter briefly examines attempts in three European countries to improve the supply of low-cost housing and to lessen the impact of the housing crisis from circa 1850 to the 1980s. In each case it is suggested these attempts have failed because the solutions adopted have themselves been inextricably caught up in, and constrained by, the social and economic structures which produced the housing crisis in the first place.

Context

As a physical structure a house takes on real meaning only when it is related to the political, economic and social structures which produce it and to the occupants who convert it into a home. Individual occupants bring particular characteristics, beliefs, aspirations and behaviours which affect the ways in which a house is used, and also influence perceptions of the relative desirability of different types of housing. These characteristics are also interlinked with the social, economic and political structures which produce housing, and control the allocation of accommodation to different groups within society. There are many factors which affect the operation of the low-cost housing market (Bourne, 1981; Short, 1982; Harvey, 1985a, 1985b) of which three aspects are briefly considered here.

Economic controls

In a capitalist economy the production of housing, either new or second-hand, is clearly related to the money available for housing investment which depends on the relative attractiveness of predicted returns and on the level of interest rates. Those who provide new housing units (either for rent or for sale) or who provide finance to gain access to housing (building societies and banks) or who deal in the second-hand housing market, will seek to maximise returns from housing investment and loan finance. Inevitably this will tend to push up house prices and channel investment to those sectors of the housing market where the highest returns are possible.

From the perspective of housing consumption, the housing market is fundamentally linked to the labour market and the wage structure of the economy. Because all workers require accommodation, housing costs become a labour cost and high housing costs will tend to push up wage levels. Most capitalist economies depend upon a supply of low-cost wage labour to retain the profitability of industry and to allow capital accumulation and reinvestment. An inevitable consequence for the housing market is a reduction in housing quality as this is the only way in which the need to extract profits from housing production can be reconciled with the maintenance of wages (and hence housing costs) at a low level.

Aspirations

In addition to economic factors, the housing market is affected by the aspirations and perceptions of individual occupants and by the ways in which these aspirations relate to the dominant ideology of housing in a particular society. Perceptions of the relative desirability of suburban and inner-city homes will vary over time and space, but the dominant housing ideology within society is of critical importance. Where homeownership is dominant (and is also used to reinforce capitalist ideology and economic principles), the inevitable effect is to downgrade and stigmatize other forms of housing provision. Those on low incomes who cannot gain access to the owner-occupied sector find themselves in increasingly marginalized sections of the housing market.

Access

Although economic constraints are usually the main controls on access to housing, the availability of good-quality housing in convenient locations will be further affected by the policies of individual landlords and institutions which control housing provision and housing finance. If institutions and individuals restrict access to good-quality low-cost housing, this can further marginalize those households who fail to conform to preconceived notions of what constitutes a good occupier. The poor are thus further concentrated in low-quality, and often relatively high-cost, accommodation.

In capitalist countries, these three factors have interacted during and since the nineteenth century to affect the operation of the housing market regardless of the dominant tenure type since all are subject to similar constraints. In the 1980s there are considerable variations in housing tenure in Europe. Homeownership ranges from 74 per cent of households in the Republic of Ireland to about 30 per cent in Switzerland, but in most Western European countries more than 50 per cent of households are now owner-occupied and homeownership rates are increasing rapidly throughout Europe (table 8.1). For instance, homeownership has increased from 46 to 59 per cent in Italy 1961–81, and from 24 to 37 per cent in West Germany 1950–78 (Boleat, 1985a; Pugh, 1980; Wynn, 1984; McGuire, 1981; Headey, 1978). Conversely, most West European countries have fewer than 50 per cent of households in rented accommodation (the principal exceptions being West Germany, Switzerland and the Netherlands), but the division of this rented housing between the public and private sectors varies considerably. Countries such as Italy, Norway, Germany and Switzerland provide only minimal amounts of public-sector housing, while in Sweden, France and the United Kingdom more than 20 per cent of households live in units rented from the state.

There are very great problems involved in the detailed comparison of housing tenure between countries, not least because precise definitions vary from nation to nation, and data for the comprehensive comparison of historical trends are not readily available. However, all Western European countries have been subjected to the same general constraints affecting the provision of low-cost housing, even if individual housing markets have responded in different ways. The free market of the nineteenth century failed to provide adequate accommodation for workers locked into a casual and low-wage labour market, but there were contrasts in the attempts to improve the supply and quality of low-cost urban housing in different European Countries, as will be seen from the following case studies from Britain, Austria and Norway in the late nineteenth and twentieth centuries.

Table 8.1   Housing tenure in selected European countries c. 1980

	Percentage owner occupied	Percentage privately rented, including housing associations	Percentage state rented	Percentage other tenures
Belgium	61	28	7	4
Denmark	52	38	4	6
Eire	74	10	12	4
Finland	61	14	7	18
France	47	18	26	9
West Germany	37	61	2	-
Italy	59	35	1	5
Netherlands	44	47	9	-
Norway	67	22	1	10
Sweden	55	22	21	2
Switzerland	30	64	3	3
United Kingdom	59	12	29	-

Principal source: M. Boleat, *National Housing Finance Systems* (Croom Helm, 1985a).

State intervention in housing provision

Direct intervention by the state in housing provision has occurred to some degrees in almost all modern European countries as the following two episodes of state intervention, within rather different social and economic contexts, indicate.

Liverpool, 1890–1918

Britain was one of the first countries in Europe to experience large-scale state intervention in housing: the Housing Act of 1919 made it obligatory for local authorities to survey housing need and to provide state-subsidized housing. However, a number of large cities, notably London, Glasgow and Liverpool, built substantial numbers of local authority housing units before 1919 in a direct attempt to improve the supply and quality of low-cost working-class housing. In providing low-cost housing the declared aim of Liverpool City Council after 1895 was to provide 'housing for the poorest poor' (Pooley, 1985) and a total of 2,895 council-owned units was built in the city before 1919 (figure 8.1) (Pooley and Irish, 1984). This housing was not provided with state subsidies, but was financed through loans sanctioned by the Local Government Board and secured against the rates. The intention was to achieve a return of 4 per cent per annum on capital investment (excluding loan charges), but this was rarely achieved and by 1913 loan

Table 8.2   Standard rents for 'restricted'* corporation dwellings, Liverpool 1905

	Ground floor	*1st floor*	*2nd floor*	*3rd floor*
1 room	2s. 6d.	2s.	1s. 9d.	1s. 6d.
2 rooms	3s. 6d.	3s.	2s. 9d.	2s. 6d.
3 rooms	4s. 6d.	4s.	3s. 9d.	3s. 6d.
4 rooms	5s. 6d.	5s.	4s. 9d.	4s. 7d.

* 'restricted' dwellings were those reserved for tenants dispossessed from slum clearance schemes

1 new penny (p) = 2.4 old pence (d); 5p = 1s.

Source: Liverpool Council Proceedings, 1904–5, p. 426.

Table 8.3   Percentage of population rehoused from specific improvement schemes: Liverpool 1904–14

Improvement scheme	*Percentage of tenants rehoused*
Adlington Street, 1902–3	54.6
Hornby Street, 1904–7	64.4
Upper Mann Street, 1905–6	55.1
Burlington Street, 1910	78.5
Grafton Street, 1911	15.7
Bevington Street, 1912	72.2
Northumberland Street, 1913	58.3
St. Annes Street, 1914	20.9

Source: Annual Reports of Manager of Artizans and Labourers Dwellings (Liverpool), 1905–14

charges incurred by the corporation were the equivalent of 2d (1p) in the pound on rates. The dwellings constructed in Liverpool were restricted to those dispossessed by slum-clearance schemes and, although most units were small and spartan in construction (often sharing sanitary facilities and lacking hot water), rents were rather higher than those currently being charged for multi-occupied inner-city property. In the 1890s, a small court house in the inner city could be rented for 2s 6d to 3s (12.5p–15p) per week, and a single room in a sub-let court house for only 1s 3d to 1s 6d (6–7.5p) per week; whereas in 1905 corporation rents ranged from 1s 6d (7.5p) for one room on the top floor of a tenement block to 5s 6d (27.5p) for a ground-floor four-room dwelling (table 8.2).

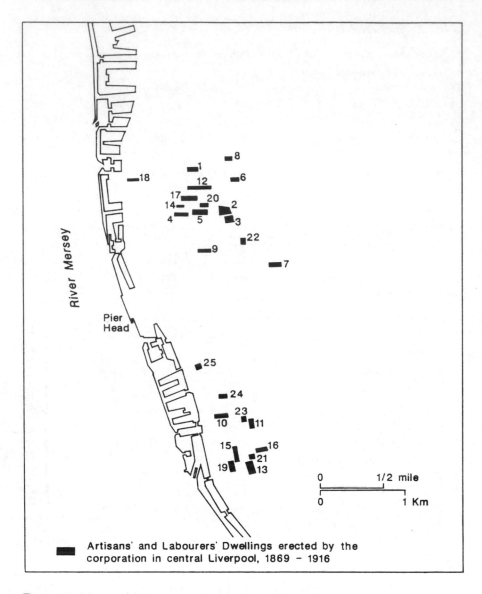

Artisans' and Labourers' Dwellings erected by the corporation in central Liverpool, 1869 – 1916

Figure 8.1 Municipal housing in central Liverpool 1869–1916. Dwellings erected by the Corporation in the following areas were opened in the year indicated

		Date opened	Number of units
1	St. Martins Cottages (Ashfield Street)	1869	124
2	Victoria Square (Nash Grove)	1885	270
3	Juvenal Dwellings	1891	101
4	Arley Street	1897/1902/03	46
5	Gildarts Gardens	1897/1904	229
6	Dryden Street	1901	182

7	Kempston Street	1902	79
8	Kew Street	1902/3	114
9	Adlington Street	1902/3	273
10	Stanhope Cottages	1904	60
11	Mill Street	1904	55
12	Hornby Street	1904/6/7	455
13	Clive Street/Shelley Street	1905	83
14	Eldon Street	1905	12
15	Upper Mann Street	1905/6	88
16	Combermere Street	1909	49
17	Burlington Street	1910	114
18	Saltney Street	1911	48
19	Grafton Street	1911	60
20	Bevington Street Area	1913	68
21	Northumberland Street Area	1913	68
22	St. Anne Street Area	1914	78
23	Gore Street	1916	24
24	Jordan Street	1916	31
25	Sparling Street	1916	16

Source: *Annual Reports*, Medical Officer of Health (Liverpool) 1890–1918: for further detail see Pooley, (1985)

Although the clear intention of Liverpool City Council was to provide decent accommodation for those most in housing need, the schemes failed to make any significant impact on working-class housing provision in the city for three principal reasons. First, the programme was underfunded and thus was too small to make any significant impact on the city's housing crisis. Between 1896 and 1915 no fewer than 11,308 houses were demolished in Liverpool, but only 2,387 corporation dwellings were constructed. As most new private development consisted of four-room cottages which were far beyond the means of most dispossessed families, there was no alternative but for them to crowd into multi-occupied property elsewhere in the city. Even within named Improved Areas, it was rare for more than two-thirds of tenants to be rehoused (table 8.3). Corporation housing schemes lagged well behind slum clearance, and only a minority of families could have been given the chance of improved accommodation in municipal housing.

Secondly, the corporation housing schemes were forced to operate on commercial economic principles; thus construction standards and amenities were poor and rents were relatively high in order to attempt to cover loan charges and achieve an acceptable return. A local newspaper, the *Liverpool Review* (25 April 1903, pp. 366–67), criticized the size, design and facilities in the new dwellings, calling them 'glorified courts' which were 'comfortless, ill-designed and inadequate'. Economic pressures had forced the corporation to provide dwellings which provided space and facilities little better than the schemes they were designed to replace.

Thirdly, the management of the dwellings operated in favour of those sections of the dispossessed population who were in the best position to gain access to decent quality private housing. As the Liverpool Medical Officer stated in his

Annual Report for 1907 (p. 2103) 'a selection of the better class of dispossessed is being made'. The allocation of tenancies was carefully controlled to ensure that only tenants who could pay the rent and who conformed to the standards of housekeeping demanded by the corporation were accommodated. Moreover, the turnover rate for tenants in new corporation tenements was also very high, with annual removals amounting to 60 per cent or more of the total stock in some blocks. This was caused by the council evicting families who either failed to conform to housekeeping and behaviour standards or who got into rent arrears, and by other families flitting because they realized the impossibility of meeting corporation demands for rent and behaviour. The corporation acted as a highly selective landlord and employed management and allocation policies designed to maximize economic returns and to protect the value of property.

The provision of state housing in Liverpool before 1919 took place within an economic and social context determined by market forces within a capitalist economy. Despite declared intentions to house the 'poorest poor', state provision had to provide an adequate return on investment. In order to achieve this the quality of housing was reduced, and the corporation managed its dwellings to secure the best return from selected tenants in much the same way that a private landlord might restrict access to property. Thus, in Liverpool, the vision of providing low-cost good quality housing for the poor was effectively constrained by the political and economic system.

Vienna, 1919–33

In May 1919 the Social Democratic Workers Party (SDAP) took control of the town council of Vienna, a city of over one million people. The period from 1919 to 1933 (when social democracy was destroyed by the Fascists) saw the development of housing and welfare policies in 'Red Vienna' which were quite unlike those in most of the rest of Europe (Hardy and Kuczynski, 1934; Maderthaner, 1985; Sieder, 1985). They provide a graphic illustration of the problems of developing a socialist approach to low-cost housing within a wider capitalist context. The housing policies developed were also influential in shaping state housing initiatives elsewhere in Europe, including policies and architectural styles adopted in other cities, for example, in Liverpool in the 1930s (Newbery, 1981).

The immediate aim of the Social Democrats was to intervene directly in the capitalist economy to improve the standard of housing and welfare. A longer-term aim was the overthrow of the capitalist system. The immediate programmes undertaken in Vienna involved tax reform, communal house-building, welfare and health-care systems, and the reform of public transport. All this was made possible by the financial independence which Vienna had gained after Austria became a Federal State. The Social Democrats levied direct taxes on luxury goods and a steeply graduated tax on the owners and tenants of large flats and businesses. This dwelling-house tax financed approximately 50 per cent of the council house building programme 1928–33, with the remainder of expenditure met from general revenue.

Vienna had an acute housing shortage before 1914. In 1910, 20 per cent of all dwellings in Vienna had more than two persons per room (including kitchens and halls as rooms); 58 per cent of one-room dwellings were overcrowded and 42 per cent of three-room dwellings were overcrowded. At the same date only 7 per cent of dwellings in the city had a bathroom and only 22 per cent had an integral toilet. The 1914 census showed that 72.8 per cent of housing units in the city consisted of only one or two rooms plus a small kitchen: overcrowding and insanitary conditions thus affected the majority of Vienna's working-class population (Hardy and Kuczynski, 1934, pp. 1–20).

These conditions were exacerbated by the effects of the First World War, the imposition of rent controls and the effects of rapid inflation and declining real wages. After 1919 rents were fixed at the level they had been in 1914 which, combined with massive inflation, reduced them to negligible amounts (in 1930–1 rents were effectively only 20 per cent of the pre-war level). Housing quality was very poor, since there was no financial incentive for new private building, and rates of residential mobility were very low as tenants clung to the flats they had. There was also a great deal of hostility between landlords and tenants.

In such conditions of acute housing shortage the Social Democrats began their massive programme of council house building in Vienna in 1919. The municipality was able to acquire land cheaply because private building was almost at a standstill and the council was the only buyer on the market. The programme was financed initially through loans but later through taxation and general revenue. Only 1,244 units were built 1920–2, but during 1923 some 25,000 units were planned for a five-year construction period and in 1927 an additional 30,000 dwellings were sanctioned (table 8.4). By 1934, 63,071 council units had been built and these accounted for 10 per cent of all dwellings in Vienna.

The dwellings provided by the state in 'Red Vienna' were undoubtedly an improvement on most low-cost private accommodation in the city, but they could scarcely be seen as providing high quality housing. They consisted mainly of massive blocks of four-, five- or six-storey flats in which most units were small. Under the 1923 programme 75 per cent of flats consisted only of an entrance hall, a main room, a kitchen and a WC., and each flat occupied only 38m². Under the 1927 programme some larger 'middle-class dwellings' were also provided, but these provided only 57m² of living space and accounted for less than 10 per cent of the planned building programme (Hardy and Kuczynski, 1934, pp. 60–6). Each dwelling had running water, a toilet, gas and electricity, but no individual bathroom. Most large tenements had public bathrooms and laundries, and this policy of encouraging communal living, in line with socialist principles, was also reflected in the large areas of communal open space with which the flats were provided. Many of the tenements were very large (the Karl Marx Hof contained 1,382 dwellings and extended for half a mile) and they were widely scattered across the city (figure 8.2). Rents were related to 1914 controlled rents and were designed to cover only operating costs, although slightly higher rents were charged in the more convenient inner-city locations. The administration of all tenements was in the hands of the

Table 8.4   Construction of municipal dwellings in Vienna, 1920–33

Year	Apartment buildings constructed	Dwellings in apartments	Suburban cottages	Total dwellings
1920–22	6	671	573	1244
1923	11	857	849	1706
1924	14	1503	975	2478
1925	26	6007	380	6387
1926	39	8548	486	9034
1927	32	6674	89	6763
1928	33	4126	458	4584
1929	49	4764	239	5003
1930	49	5974	601	6575
1931	34	5897	283	6180
1932	29	4821	277	5098
1933	13	3578	47	3625
Total	335	53420	5257	58667

Source: C. Hardy and R. Kuczynski, *The Housing Programme of the City of Vienna* The Brookings Institution, Washington D.C., 1934), p. 57

Housing Bureau established by the city council. In addition to the tenements, about 5,000 suburban cottages were also built by the municipality. These were larger than the tenements, they were provided with gardens, and were managed by tenants' co-operatives.

It is difficult to assess the success of this brief experiment in socialist housing. On the one hand rents were low (as they were in the private sector), and the comments of tenants at the time suggest a high level of satisfaction in relation to the private apartments which were the only alternative. On the other hand, many of the criticisms levelled at Liverpool's housing policy in the 1890s can also be applied to Vienna in the 1920s. The financial constraints imposed on a socialist council still operating within a capitalist economy meant that the supply of housing was limited, and the size and quality of units were restricted. The small size of most units meant that there was often acute overcrowding, with families housed in single-room flats, although this was no worse than in the private sector. Facilities were also frequently inadequate, with centralized bathing facilities providing only one tub for 165 people in some blocks. To try to overcome the overcrowding problem

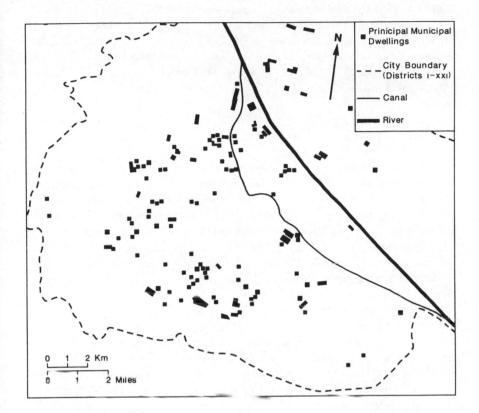

Figure 8.2 Municipal dwellings in Vienna 1920–33. The main areas of municipal housing built within the city (Districts I–XXI) are shown. *Source:* C.O. Hardy and R.R. Kuczynski, 1934

the council developed a points allocation system. Although they tried to allocate flats to those in most need, the system discriminated against families with large numbers of small children because the flats could not accommodate them. Financial constraints which forced the council to build small units as cheaply as possible thus prevented it from providing decent housing for large working-class families. The council also had a clear perception of the type of family it wished to house and the standards of behaviour it chose to encourage. Council inspectors regularly checked flats for cleanliness and good housekeeping. Children were strictly controlled and forbidden to play on the grass courtyards, and the whole system was geared towards a small, conformist nuclear family. Many potential tenants found the massive blocks and the management policies of the Housing Bureau oppressive and unacceptable: they were not accommodated in the new units either by choice or because the managers considered that they did not conform to the council's perception of a good tenant.

In May 1934 the Austro–Fascists began dismantling the socialist structures of Red Vienna. The tax system was altered, the building programme halted and council rents were raised by an average of 70 per cent. A brief period of socialist housing provision in Vienna was brought to an end by political change, but even before this happened it could be argued that the programme was still failing to provide good-quality housing for those in most housing need.

Housing co-operatives in Oslo

Like most other European cities, Oslo experienced an acute housing crisis in the late nineteenth and twentieth centuries. However, unlike British cities, there was both public sector investment and a co-operative housing movement which co-existed until a strong preference for the voluntary sector developed in the 1940s and most public rented housing was transferred to co-ownership and voluntary housing schemes. Examination of housing in Oslo allows some assessment of the effectiveness of co-operative schemes in the provision of low-cost housing. (Seip, 1984; Gulbrandsen and Torgersen, 1978a, 1978b; Gulbrandsen, 1983; Berg, 1983).

Nineteenth-century Norway was a predominantly rural society in which homeownership was common, even amongst the rural working classes. However, as the urban population grew, an increasing proportion of households became renters and in Oslo renting became the normal form of tenure in the late nineteenth century. For many urban tenants there was an acute housing crisis and Norwegians began to look elsewhere in Europe for ideas about housing provision and other social reform (Seip, 1984). In 1914 Oslo City Council began a public housing programme in response to the housing crisis, but by the 1920s there was a distinct movement away from renting towards various forms of homeownership in Oslo. This trend included the emergence of 'joint stock apartments' for the rich, and the development of housing co-operatives for the working classes. These began in the early 1920s as self-help housing movements, and were consolidated in 1929 with the formation of the Oslo Savings and Housing Society (OBOS). The OBOS adopted the Swedish model of housing co-operatives, and, with City Council representation on the OBOS Board from 1935, much of the public-sector housing in Oslo was transferred into co-operative tenure and management in the 1940s (Pugh, 1980; Gulbrandsen and Torgersen, 1978a and b).

Pugh (1980, pp. 28–29) suggests that the co-operative principle in housing has three requirements if it is to be successful: first, to achieve continuity of development and management; secondly, to overcome the desire of individuals and small groups to wind up the co-operative when their housing needs are met; and, thirdly, to apportion the risks of development so that they are acceptable to financiers. He argues that the co-operative principle used in Sweden and Norway seems to have managed to meet most of these requirements. The role of developer is separate from that of occupier, although each is organized on co-operative principles. Development co-operatives concentrate only on construction and acquisition; thus they build up expertise and can gain the confidence of financial institutions.

Occupiers take over estate management on co-operative principles after the development stage, although occupiers are also members of the development co-operative.

In Norway there has also been a long tradition of state involvement in housing finance (as opposed to the actual production of housing), and much of the finance for co-operative housing schemes has come from the state. In 1894 a Government Housing Loan Fund provided housing credit to low-income families; in 1903 the Workers' Agricultural Property and Housing Bank provided housing finance in rural areas; and in 1915 these arrangements were consolidated in the National Smallholding and Housing Bank. In 1946 a National Housing Bank was created, and by 1976 the state banks were providing finance for over 75 per cent of all new housing developments in Norway. In 1940 the Norwegian National Federation of Housing Societies was also formed (NBBL), and the National Housing Bank now provides most of the finance for its member co-operatives. Norway (and especially Oslo) has thus developed a system whereby working-class housing is provided through housing co-operatives which are largely dependent on state finance.

The advantages of this system over direct intervention (as practised in Liverpool and Vienna) are that the state is not required to carry out the onerous duties of management and maintenance, and that the voluntary self-help sector meets the self-fulfilment aspirations of the population in a capitalist society. Members of co-operatives are more likely to take pride in their homes and management problems are thus reduced. The political situation in early twentieth-century Norway was also well disposed towards the co-operative ideal. The Labour Party in Norway supported the demands of urban tenants for better accommodation and lower rents, but the high proportion of homeowners in rural areas and small towns meant that direct intervention in the housing market would have alienated many Labour supporters outside Oslo (Gulbrandsen and Torgersen, 1978a). An acceptable compromise was co-operative housing with state intervention in housing finance.

The co-operative movement in Oslo seems to have avoided some of the problems relating to finance and tenants' aspirations found in state housing schemes in Liverpool and Vienna, and the smaller scale on which apartment blocks were developed prevented the problems of alienation experienced by tenants in the massive blocks in Vienna. However, we must assess the extent to which co-operatives provided access to decent housing for the majority of genuinely low-income families in Oslo. Did they, like British council housing in the 1920s, cater mainly for the decent and relatively affluent working class?

It must be emphasized that, prior to the 1950s, the number of units constructed by OBOS was relatively small, and thus their impact on the city's total housing problem was limited. OBOS was the dominant co-operative in Oslo, yet in 1945 it managed only 2,935 dwellings, accounting for 2 per cent of the city's housing stock. Co-operative housing could not have been a solution to mass housing problems prior to the Second World War. From the 1950s the number of OBOS dwellings expanded rapidly (table 8.5): by 1975 they accounted for 22 per cent of Oslo's housing stock and OBOS had 131,070 members (Gulbrandsen and Torgersen, 1978b). In this period they had the potential to make a major impact on low-cost housing provision in Oslo.

Table 8.5   The growth of the Oslo Savings and Housing Society (OBOS), 1945–75

Year	Number of OBOS members	Number of OBOS dwellings	OBOS dwellings as % of total dwellings in Oslo
1945	6,194	2,935	2
1950	33,078	7,302	6
1955	49,566	16,628	11
1960	68,009	26,344	16
1965	90,000	34,611	18
1970	112,528	41,964	20
1975	131,070	50,134	22

Source: L. Gulbrandsen and U. Torgersen, (1978) 'Private sentiments in a public context: aspects of cooperative housing in Oslo', *Scandinavian Political Studies* (new series), 2, p. 264

However, this potential has been restricted by the changing characteristics of households in co-operative apartments. Recent research suggests that in their original form the relatively small number of OBOS dwellings built were available to families at the lower end of the social order, although the very poor were always excluded (Gulbrandsen, 1983; Berg, 1983). However, from the 1960s the Oslo co-operatives became more middle class and less radical in their membership at the same time as the number of housing units in the sector expanded. This is seen both in the occupation and income profile of members, and in the ways in which tenants' associations have ceased to function as effective pressure groups for direct action. These changes can be attributed to two factors: alterations in the rules for housing allocation in OBOS have led to membership of a co-operative being regarded as a housing investment, rather than the solution to a short-term crisis as in the 1920s; and broader structural shifts in the Norwegian economy have led to a generally high standard of living and a reduction of housing stress. Gulbrandsen and Torgersen (1978b, pp. 273–7) show that households joining OBOS in the 1970s have attained higher educational qualifications, have more middle-class occupations and are more likely to be non-labour voters than households that became members in the 1950s. Most new members are also young, and tend to see themselves as 'owners' rather than 'renters' within the co-operative sector. As most co-operative housing is relatively small (usually two- or three-room apartments) it is being used increasingly as the first step on the housing chain by upwardly-mobile, young middle-class families who aspire to homeownership, rather than fulfilling the original role of providing low-cost apartments for those most in housing need. Housing co-operatives seem to have worked for relatively affluent working-class families in the prosperous economy of Oslo, but the very poor have not been catered for and it is doubtful whether similar co-operative solutions would work in a low-wage casual economy.

Homeownership and housing finance in Britain

The housing market in twentieth-century Britain has been dominated by the expansion of both state housing and owner-occupancy. However, the state plays little direct role in financing homeownership: this is left almost entirely to private financial institutions, especially building societies, although mortgage tax relief has provided a large indirect subsidy to homeownership. In this final section the activities of building societies and the expansion of homeownership are examined, briefly, from two perspectives: first, the extent to which the expansion of homeownership has directly increased the supply of working-class housing in Britain; and, secondly, the effect of the expansion of homeownership on the low-cost rented sector.

Although permanent building societies have existed since the 1850s, it was not until the 1920s that they began to have a significant impact on homeownership. In the period 1851–4, for instance, only 16 per cent of mortgages granted by the Bingley, Morton and Shipley Building Society were for a private house, and 44 per cent of mortgages were on commercial and industrial property (table 8.6). In the nineteenth century building society finance was used primarily for commercial purposes, or for the purchase of several houses by property speculators who would then let them to tenants. Building societies were thus fuelling the dominant privately-rented sector. In contrast, the proportion of mortgages for housebuilding – especially of single homes – rose gradually from mid-Victorian times: by 1921 73 per cent of Bingley Building Society loans were on a single house and by 1941 this had risen to 86.8 per cent of loans. The 1920s and 1930s were a period of rapid expansion in owner-occupancy, as many rented houses were sold to sitting tenants and most new property was constructed for homeowners (Pooley and Harmer, forthcoming). Building society finance was increasingly directed away from renting towards homeownership (Daunton, 1987; Doughty, 1986).

However, the impact of such activity on the availability of housing for low-income families in the inter-war period was negligible. Although building societies did not operate rigorous income constraints when granting a mortgage, they did assess the suitability of a mortgage client carefully and were particularly concerned about the valuation of the property. Most mortgage clients were in regular employment, in skilled working-class work or lower white-collar employment, and few low-income families would have considered owner-occupancy (table 8.7). The effects of depression in the 1930s accentuated this divide, as those on good incomes progressed up the housing ladder while the low paid and unemployed were forced into low-quality rented accommodation (Pooley and Irish, 1987). There were also distinct geographical variations in the growth of homeownership, with suburban areas of southern England providing the best market for building society operations (Swennarton and Taylor, 1985). This is reflected in the expansion of northern building societies into southern markets and the regional transfer

Table 8.6   Percentage of mortgages on different types of property:
Bingley Building Society, 1851–1941

Property type	1851–4	1875–8	1890	1911	1921	1930	1941
One house	16.0	35.1	42.2	39.6	73.6	80.0	86.8
Two or more houses	40.0	40.3	35.0	37.2	12.0	10.8	3.6
Commercial or industrial property	44.0	24.6	10.0	18.4	12.4	9.2	5.2
Unclassified	-	-	12.8	4.8	2.0	-	4.4
Sample size (mortgages)	50	407	500	250	250	250	250

Source: Mortgage Registers, Bingley Building Society, 1851–1941

of funds. Most deposits into the Bradford Building Society and the Bingley Building Society came from branches in the West Riding, but a high proportion of mortgage loans went out in the midlands and southern England. In the short term, at least, this regional capital transfer could be seen as fuelling the expansion of good quality housing in the south-east at the expense of housing investment in the north.

Not only did the increase in homeownership in the 1930s fail to provide housing for those on low incomes, it also had a negative effect on the perception of alternative housing tenures, especially state housing. The building societies deliberately fostered homeownership as a dominant ideology which had a stabilizing influence on the country by encouraging thrift, thereby entangling borrowers in the capitalist system. This attitude is summed up by the statement made at the 1934 Annual General Meeting of the Bradford Building Society: 'the stability of England today was in no small measure due to the action of building societies in enabling the man with small capital to hold a stake in his country' (Bradford Second Equitable Building Society, 1936). State housing increasingly came to be perceived as a residual housing stock which catered only for the poor who had no other alternatives open to them. This marginalization of low-cost rented housing has in turn led to a low level of investment in council stock, the decline of the privately rented sector, and a further deterioration in the quality of accommodation available to low-income families.

Although the transition towards homeownership began in the 1920s when its dominance as an ideology became established, that expansion has been most rapid since the Second World War. In 1930 there were still only 720,000 mortgage borrowers in Britain: by 1950 this had approximately doubled to 1,508,000; but in 1985 the figure stood at 6,659,000 borrowers from building societies (Building Societies Association, 1986). The wider availability of mortgage finance, the contraction of other housing sectors, and the sale of council houses has pushed

**Table 8.7   Socio-economic group of successful mortgage applicants
(owner-occupied property), Liverpool 1920–30**

	Number	Percentage
Professional, managerial and intermediate	36	6.1
Skilled non-manual	216	36.6
Skilled manual	312	52.9
Semi-skilled	20	3.4
Unskilled	5	0.8
Other (e.g. retired, unemployed)	1	0.2
Total sample	590	100.0

Source: Sample from Mortgage Registers of the Liverpool Building Society and the
Liverpool Branch of the Huddersfield Building Society

homeownership in Britain to record levels. However, there is little evidence that
even this rate of expansion is achieving any significant improvement in the housing
quality of low-income families, and there is considerable support for the assertion
that homeownership in the 1980s is being pushed beyond levels that the labour
market and income structure of Britain can bear (Labour Housing Group, 1984;
Boleat, 1985b; Malpass, 1986; Karn et al, 1986). Thus it can be suggested that the
rise of homeownership in Britain in the twentieth century has had a negative effect
on low-cost housing provision. Finance has been channelled away from those in
most housing need, low-cost rented housing has been marginalized within the
housing system, and divisions between rich and poor have increased as
homeownership is perceived as a financial investment rather than simply a route
to a home.

Assessment

What conclusions can be drawn from this brief and partial review of low-cost
housing provision in modern Europe? First, it can be suggested that as long as low-
cost housing schemes are inextricably linked into the free-market policies of a
capitalist economy they are bound to be inadequate, especially in countries in
stages of economic development or with a predominantly low-wage, casual labour
force. Low-cost housing solutions are locked into the capitalist system through the
provision of housing finance, the structure of the labour market, the dominant
ideology of housing tenure, and management controls imposed on occupiers. The
different routes followed by individual European countries have each provided
good quality housing for more affluent working-class households, but have singu-
larly failed to provide a solution to the problem of housing provision for those on
genuinely low incomes.

Secondly, it is contended that adequate provision of low-cost housing can only be achieved through a system which does not marginalize certain groups or housing tenures. While homeownership and the promise of associated financial gain form the dominant ideology in the housing market, those who cannot gain access to the dominant tenure form, or who happen to live in a depressed region where house prices are stagnant or falling, will always be marginalized. State intervention in the housing market in the form of controls on house price inflation, limits to regional house price variations, restriction of financial gains from housing and regulation of housing finance, is one way through which the balance could be tipped in favour of those in most housing need.

Such policies should also be linked to a large-scale construction programme of good quality low-cost accommodation. It can be suggested that it is irrelevant whether this housing is provided directly by the state, through co-operative schemes, by housing associations, or through a regulated private sector. What is crucial is that the quality and convenience of such accommodation must be equal to those of other housing tenures, and it must be provided in such a way that those housed are not marginalized and perceived as occupying an inferior tenure form.

This brief and selective survey of low-cost housing provision in three European countries since the mid-nineteenth century has shown that each system has failed to solve the problem of housing provision for low-income families. State housing, co-operative housing and homeownership have all had limited short-term successes, but none has provided a long-term solution for those in the most acute housing need. If it is accepted that the right to a decent home is a fundamental human right, then it is imperative that solutions are found. Examination of past experiences in Europe suggest that radical change is necessary if significant improvements are to be achieved.

References

Annual Reports of the Medical Officer of Health, Liverpool (various).

Berg, E. (1983), 'Leieboerbevegelsen: fra kamporganisasjon til informasjonsorgan', Tidsskrift for Arbeiderbevegelsens Hist., 2, 57–78.

Boleat, M. (1985a), National Housing Finance Systems, Croom Helm.

Boleat, M. (1985b), Mortgage Repayment Difficulties. Building Societies Association.

Booth, C. (1892–97), Life and Labour of the People in London, Macmillan.

Bourne, L.S. (1981), The Geography of Housing, Arnold.

Bradford Second Equitable Building Society (1936), Minute Book.

Building Societies Association (1986), Building Societies Fact Book 1986.

Burnett, J. (1978), A Social History of Housing, Methuen.

Daunton, M.J. (1987), A Property Owning Democracy: Housing in Britain, Faber.

Department of Environment (1981), English National House Condition Survey, Part I, HMSO.

Doughty, M. (ed.) (1986), Building the Industrial City. Leicester University Press.

Gauldie, E. (1974), Cruel Habitations. A History of Working-class Housing, George Allen and Unwin.

Gulbrandsen, L. (1983), 'Popularitetens fordelings politiske pris: om endringer I den sosciale sammensteningen av medlemsmassen I OBOS I etterkrigstida', Tidsskrift for Arbeiderbevegelsens Hist., 2, 79–97.

Gulbrandsen, L. and Torgersen, U. (1978a), 'Concern with redistribution as an aspect of post-war Norwegian housing policy', Acta Sociologica, 21, 227–42.

Gulbrandsen, L. and Torgersen, U. (1978b), 'Private sentiments in a public context: aspects of cooperative housing in Oslo', Scandinavian Political Studies, 4, 255–83.

Hardy, C.O. and Kuczynski, R.R. (1934), The Housing Programme of the City of Vienna, The Brookings Institution, Washington DC.

Harrison, P. (1983), Inside the Inner City, Penguin, Harmondsworth.

Harvey, D. (1985a), Consciousness and the Urban Experience, Blackwell, Oxford.

Harvey, D. (1985b), The Urbanisation of Capital, Blackwell, Oxford.

Headey, B. (1978), Housing Policy in the Developed Economy, Croom Helm.

Karn, V.et al. (1986), Home Ownership in the Inner City: Salvation or despair, Gower.

Labour Housing Group (1984), Right to a Home, Spokesman, Nottingham.

Liverpool Review (25 April 1903), 366–7.

Maderthaner, W. (1985), 'Kommunalpolitik in "Rotenwien": ein Literaturbericht', Archiv für Sozialgeschichte, 25, 239–50.

Malpass, P. (ed.) (1986), The Housing Crisis, Croom Helm.

Mayhew, H. (1861), London Labour and the London Poor, Griffin Bohn.

McGuire, C.C. (1981), International Housing Policies. D.C. Heath, Lexington, Mass.

Newbery, F. (1981), 'Liverpool flats 1919–34', unpublished B.Arch. dissertation, University of Liverpool.

Pooley, C.G. and Harmer, M. (forthcoming), Property Ownership in Britain 1850–1965: The Role of the Bradford and Bingley Building Society in the Development of Homeownership, Bingley.

Pooley, C.G. and Harmer, M. (1989), Property Ownership in Britain 1850–1965: The Role of the Bradford and Bingley Building Society in the Development of Homeownership, Bingley, forthcoming.

Pooley, C.G. and Irish, S. (1984), The Development of Corporation Housing in Liverpool 1869–1945, Resource paper, Centre for N.W. Regional Studies, University of Lancaster.

Pooley, C.G. and Irish, S. (1987), 'Access to housing on Merseyside 1919–39', Transactions of the Institute of British Geographers, N.S. 12, 177–90.

Pugh, C. (1980), Housing in Capitalist Societies, Gower.

Seip, A.L. (1984), 'Motive forces behind the new social policy after 1870. Norway on the European scene', Scandinavian Journal of History, 9, 329–41.

Shimmin, H. (1864) The Courts and Alleys of Liverpool, Lee and Nightingale, Liverpool.

Short, J. (1982), Housing in Britain, Methuen.

Sieder, R. (1985), 'Housing policy , social welfare and family life in "Red Vienna", 1919–34', Oral History, 35–48.

Stedman Jones, G. (1971), Outcast London, Clarendon Press, Oxford.

Swennarton, M. and Taylor, S. (1985), 'The scale and nature of the growth of owner-occupation in Britain between the wars', Economic History Review, 38, 373–92.

Wynn, M. (ed.) (1984), Housing in Europe, Croom Helm.

9 Migration and the growth and decline of cities in Western Europe

Anthony J. Fielding

Introduction

Although complex in detail, the patterns and processes of population redistribution in post-war Western Europe show certain dominant characteristics. The first is the overwhelming importance of migration in effecting change in the population geography of the region. As spatial variations in fertility and mortality became less pronounced, the differences between places in their rates of population change were increasingly influenced by differing net migrational gains and losses and by the effects of the age, class and ethnic selectivity of the migration streams on rates of natural increase. The second characteristic of post-war population redistribution is the dominance of the trend towards an even greater concentration of population in the largest cities of Western Europe during the period up until the mid-1960s, followed by a marked trend towards deconcentration which peaked in the early 1970s, but which continued to some degree in most countries through the 1970s and into the 1980s.

In this chapter the term 'urbanization' is used to refer to the trend towards a spatial agglomeration of the population, and 'counter-urbanization' to the trend towards spatial deglomeration. Operationally, urbanization is said to exist when there is a positive relationship between net migration rate and settlement size (where size is measured in population terms and settlements are defined in terms of labour market areas). It follows that counter-urbanization (some would wish to call it 'decentralized urbanization') is thus equated with a negative or inverse relationship between net migration rate and settlement size.

How did migration bring about the rise of Western Europe's great cities during the urbanization period of the nineteenth and early twentieth centuries, continuing into the early post-war years? It did so in three ways. First, and most obviously, it did so through a continuation of rural depopulation and the migration of young men and women towards the largest cities where the biggest employment growth in manufacturing industry and in the services was occurring. At this time much inter-regional migration consisted of either a step-wise migration up the urban hierarchy or a direct move from an agricultural area towards a metropolitan city, often the administrative and/or financial capital of the country (Fielding, 1966). Secondly, migration contributed to the rise of the great cities through the international migrant labour system, which brought many millions of young men (sometimes accompanied, but often followed later, by members of their families) from the 'European periphery' and from former colonial territories to the core countries of Western Europe. These 'guestworker' migrants overwhelmingly settled in the largest metropolitan cities and in the major industrial conurbations. The peak period for such migration was rather later than that inter-regional migration: by the late 1960s and early 1970s when international migration was at its height, the decentralization tendencies within most of the core countries of Western Europe were already well developed (Fielding, 1975). Finally, and perhaps least obviously, the rise of the great cities of Western Europe was enhanced by the third main type of migration – residential mobility. This came about through rapid suburbanization which greatly expanded the built-up area of the major cities and resulted in the incorporation of formerly independent small towns and rural areas into the built forms and functional regions of those cities. Unlike other migrations the outward movement of the inhabitants of the major cities was selective of those whose employment was more secure and better-paid in both blue-collar and white-collar occupations and, above all, of those who were in the family formation stage of their life-cycle and were therefore rather older. The peak period of suburbanization was also the second half of the 1960s and the first few years of the 1970s.

While each of these forms of migration continued through the rest of the 1970s and into the mid-1980s, their effects on population redistribution were generally much reduced and, in many parts of Western Europe, were matched or overtaken by migration counterstreams. Thus the outward physical expansion of the city was checked by sharp decline in suburban house-building after 1973–4 and the trend towards a renovation (often in the form of a 'gentrification') of inner city areas, many of which prior to this date would probably have been demolished through redevelopment. At the same time, a sharp shock was inflicted upon the international migration system by the economic crisis of 1973–4 after which it became far more difficult for young people in the European periphery to gain legal access to the countries of Western Europe. Return migration (especially to Italy) had already become significant before this date: it was, from the mid-1970s, a major element of Western European migration and helped to reverse the previous population decline of many rural and peripheral regions (for example in western Ireland and large parts of southern Italy and northern Greece).

But by far the most important migration reversal in terms of its effects on the populations of the great cities was that of inter-regional migration. First in the core countries of north-western Europe in the late 1960s and then in most of the rest of Western Europe, urbanization, with its strong relationship between net internal migration and settlement size, came to be replaced by counter-urbanization. How may we explain the issues of fact and interpretation which are raised by this apparent replacement of urbanization by counter-urbanization? This is analysed first, by an examination of urban population trends and inter-regional migration in Western Europe since 1950. Secondly, the fact that each of the three counterstream migrations which turned metropolitan population growth into stagnation or decline differed in social composition from the migration streams which had earlier led to their growth is examined using recent data on migration flows to and from south-east England in the period 1971–81.

Inter-regional migration and urban development in Western Europe since 1950

In order to explain the emergence of counter-urbanization we must confront the complexities of the patterns and processes of inter-regional migration. Specifically, a satisfactory explanation might be expected to resolve three major paradoxes of contemporary inter-regional migration in western countries: first, that just at the time (around 1970) when western societies were supposed to be entering the high-mobility, 'post-industrial' era, migration rates, which had risen throughout the post-war period, began to decrease; secondly, that at about the same time, a situation emerged in which those who needed to migrate the most, that is the low paid and those with low job security, seemed to migrate the least, while those who least needed to migrate, that is those in secure, well-paid jobs, seemed to migrate the most; and finally, that despite the concentration in the great cities of favourable employment structures, higher-than-average incomes and lower-than-average unemployment levels, counter-urbanization came to replace urbanization as the dominant form of population redistribution. To resolve these paradoxes is a formidable task, but one of the paths towards an explanation of the third paradox provides some hints as to the reasons for the existence of the other two.

Before embarking on this problem, however, it is necessary to establish some of the facts about urbanization and counter-urbanization in Western Europe since 1950. The details are provided elsewhere (Fielding, 1982, 1986b, 1989a), but the main features can be summarized as follows:

(a) urbanization was dominant at all scales above the very local in almost every country in Western Europe during the 1950s and early 1960s;

(b) this began to change in the core countries of north-west Europe during the 1960s and elsewhere during the early 1970s so that in the decade 1970–80 in only one country, Spain, was urbanization still the main form of population redistribution;

(c) by the 1970s urbanization had declined but had not, as yet, been replaced by counter-urbanization in six Western European countries (Austria, Ireland, Italy, Norway, Portugal and Switzerland);

(d) counter-urbanization had become dominant by the 1970s in seven countries (Belgium, Denmark, France, Netherlands, Sweden, United Kingdom and West Germany;

(e) in the early to mid 1980s, of the eight countries for which migration statistics based upon registration data were available, only two (Italy and West Germany) showed a counter-urbanization form of population redistribution; in all other cases the relationship between net migration rate and settlement size (population density) was insignificant. This means that the counter-

urbanization trend of the 1970s had itself been superseded in at least four countries (Belgium, Denmark, Netherlands and Sweden);
(f) it follows from this that counter-urbanization as a form of population redistribution was dominant in Western Europe for quite a short period and that, whatever form redistribution is taking in the 1980s, it is not adequately captured in most countries by the statistical relationship between net migration rate and settlement size (population density).

The attempts to explain counter-urbanization have produced an interesting and lively debate (see Fielding, 1986a for a full discussion of the many arguments). Initially, it was argued that the decentralization of population growth was more apparent than real, and that it reflected little more than the well-known tendency for major cities to be statistically underbounded, so that their expanding outer edges were assigned to neighbouring rural areas. It soon became clear, however, that more than this was involved; many of the areas of net migration gain were far outside the commuting fields of the major cities. At the same time there was broad agreement that the rates of rural depopulation were decreasing due to the fact that by the late 1960s, in most countries of Western Europe, the long process of agricultural restructuring had reduced farm labour to such a low level that it could no longer be expected to fuel rural to urban migration in the way that it had in the early post-war years. It was also agreed that developments in transport and communications technology now permitted a spatial separation of functionally related activities which could not have been sustained at an earlier date and that the net effect of state provision of more effective transport and utilities infrastructures and of health, education and social welfare services was to create a spatial standardization of 'the general conditions of production', thus permitting a dispersal of private sector investment.

That, however, is where the agreement ended. Four contending lines of argument, each of them controversial, can be identified. The first concerns the issue of the importance of the place preferences of migrants in effecting the changeover from urbanization to counter-urbanization. While few would deny the significance of place preferences in the migration decisions of the well-off retired, it is a different matter when it comes to the bulk of the adult population, whose choices are severely constrained by the location of jobs requiring their particular skills and experience, and by family loyalties and commitments. Furthermore, it is unrealistic to suppose that there was a sudden mass shift in preferences about 1970 in favour of the rural over the urban; the 'village in the mind' has a longer history than this! (See chapter 4.)

The second controversial issue was the part that standard economic analysis should play in the explanation of counter-urbanization. Many commentators pointed out that expectations based upon economic theory were being flatly contradicted by the facts of migration: the great cities were losing by inter-regional migration when, due to their favourable employment structures, high wages and low unemployment rates, they should have been gaining; and gross out-migration rates were particularly low in declining industrial regions when they should have been particularly high (Fielding, 1971). In the face of these contradictions some writers were inclined to play down the importance of economic factors altogether; others sensibly contended that it was not that the key processes were non-economic but simply that standard economic analysis was poorly equipped to say what those processes were.

The third contentious issue was the importance that should be placed upon the role of the urban and regional policies of West European governments in bringing about a changed pattern of population redistribution. After all, some governments had developed policies designed to stem the growth of the main metropolitan cities (for example, Paris and London), while others were deeply involved in promoting the industrialization of peripheral rural regions (notably Italy and Ireland). Against this it was argued that the resources provided to back these policies were insignificant in relation to the forces at work, and that even within the operations of the state there were powerful influences upon the location of economic activity (for example, defence expenditure) which produced effects quite out of line with those sought through urban and regional policy.

Finally, there is increasing support for the argument that one cannot expect to explain the major shifts in inter-regional migration without considering their relationship to the fundamental changes in the geography of production consequent upon the restructuring of the economies of Western European countries. These ideas are to be found in the literature of political economy and, more specifically, in the concepts of spatial divisions of labour and régime of accumulation. These links are spelled out elsewhere (Fielding, 1985; 1986a), but the gist of the argument is as follows.

1. Population distribution and redistribution at the level of the inter-labour market area are largely determined by the geography of production, and by the manner in which that geography changes over time. Particularly important in this latter respect are the spatial changes which accompanied agricultural and industrial restructuring and the growth of producer and other 'basic' services (for example, tourism).

2. In 1950 the dominant geography of production could be characterized as regional sectoral specialization. This implies that population redistribution would result from the differential growth rates of the various branches of the national economy, through the impacts of such growth on single-sector towns and regions. This would explain both rural depopulation and out-migration from old industrial regions as well as the rapid population growth of metropolitan cities with their high concentrations of modern consumer goods industries on which much modern urbanization is based.

3. Most of the countries of Western Europe experienced a long period of economic growth from 1950 to the early 1970s. This growth was 'Fordist' in the sense that it was to a considerable extent based upon the mass production of standardized goods for mass markets (cars, clothes, television sets, furniture, records, washing machines, etc.). Such Fordist production required, and brought forth, large labour markets and mass suburbanization. Thereby it also enhanced the urbanization process.

4. The key to Fordist growth, however, was the link between higher incomes, improved living standards and a buoyant demand for modern consumer goods. The problem was that, in the context of keener international competition especially from Far Eastern producers, higher incomes meant lower profits. At the same time economic growth had resulted in labour shortages which were particularly severe in the major metropolitan cities. The responses to these problems were three-fold: a major concentration of ownership and control so that companies increasingly became multi-plant, multi-product and multi-national in character; the export of capital for production in cheap labour sites in third world countries; and the importation of labour from the European periphery in the form of 'guestworkers'. A further response was to disinvest in the major cities and seek out reserves of labour within national territories, partly among women in existing industrial regions but also among young people and other low-wage workers in free-standing cities, and in small and medium-sized towns in rural and peripheral regions. This response resulted in a spatially dispersed pattern of branch plant and back office developments during the 1960s and early 1970s.

5. These changes helped to bring about a new spatial division of labour. The hierarchical division of labour was characterized by the spatial separation of tasks within the production process which meant, in particular, the separation of command from execution and of white-collar employees from blue-collar, as well as a considerable separation of technical and professional workers from other white-collar workers and of skilled manual workers from the semi-skilled and unskilled. Typically, the higher-paid employees were located in the main metropolitan cities (such as London, Paris, Frankfurt and Milan) and in 'prestige environments' near to them, while those with lower status and pay were confined to the industrial conurbations and to the rural and peripheral regions. One of the effects of this change was to produce a marked shift towards regional sectoral diversification, and hence a reduced sensitivity in many towns and regions to sectoral change in the national economy. It also implied, however, the external control of most urban and regional economies, and a de-industrialization of the major cities.

6. The implications for migration of the emergence of this new spatial division of labour included a reduced need for manual worker mobility; an enhanced need for 'service class' mobility (to manage and to supply technical services to this spatially dispersed production); a major reduction in the migration of less skilled people to the great cities as those cities experienced disinvestment, especially in manufacturing industry; and a continued out-migration from the principal cities brought about by the major industrial and service sector investments into other towns, large and small, and rural areas within their regions. The product of these migration effects were reduced overall levels of mobility, an altered social composition of migration streams and counter-urbanization.

7. Finally, this concept of the new spatial division of labour also suggests that, while deindustrialization might affect all large cities, those which house the highest order functions of companies and public institutions may well con-

tinue to sustain employment levels through the further accretion of these kinds of activities. There are some signs that this is indeed the case, with capital cities and cities with major head office quarters maintaining their populations through migration, while other large industrial cities lose jobs and population. Paradoxically, however, this could increase the trend towards lower mobility overall and towards even lower levels of mobility for working-class households, since these major administrative and commercial cities will have increased costs of living (especially of housing) which reflect their increasing dominance by the new middle class (that is, their embourgeoisiement). They thus become problematic as destinations for all those excluded from this class.

Migration and social change in south-east England, 1971–81

Some of these speculations about the relationships between migration and the changing geography of production can be checked against the special data provided by the Office of Population Censuses and Surveys Longitudinal Study, 1971–81 which gives information on about half a million individuals in England and Wales for whom census returns for 1971 have been matched with those for 1981 (Fielding and Savage, 1987; Fielding, 1989b). By this means one can trace the changes in employment which they experienced and connect their migration behaviour to their social origins and to occupational change.

The first results from this analysis are intriguing. While the south-east region's labour market declined by about 25,000 as a result of migration exchanges with the rest of England and Wales, this loss was not distributed evenly over all social groups. The service class of professional, technical and managerial workers in the south-east gained over 60,000 jobs while the ranks of the unemployed increased by 16,000. Other social groups (the self-employed/small owners, junior white-collar employees and manual employees) all lost heavily. Those in service work who migrated into the south-east during this period and were still in the service class in 1981 were particularly mobile, with a migration rate of 134 per thousand persons employed in that class compared with the average figure of 65 per thousand for all workers. Those who went into blue-collar jobs were particularly immobile at 30 per thousand, and the migration rate for those in junior white-collar jobs was still below the average at 57 per thousand. The data allow these figures to be disaggregated to identify the balances and rates for those who were in the same class in the labour market in both 1971 and 1981. The picture which emerges is unexpected. The rapidly growing service class in the south-east region lost 27,000 more service class members than it gained during the decade. How can this be, given the overall gain of 60,000 persons mentioned above? The solution to the paradox lies principally in the way in which the south-east recruits a sizeable proportion of its service class from those born and educated in the other regions from which well-qualified young people migrate to London and the south-east. Promoted into and within the service class, a significant number of these young people then leave the region to take up service class jobs in other regions where they remain until they retire from the labour market.

These results are compatible with the conceptual framework outlined above. In 1971–81 the south-east region lost population not only through retirement migration but through net migration losses among the economically active. The migration exchanges, however, reinforced the middle-class character of the region, while at the same time permitting a net export of professional, technical and managerial workers to other regions. Finally, the migration rates show the strikingly high mobility of the service class in comparison with manual workers.

Conclusion: the relationships between the migrations which produced the rise and fall of the populations of great cities in Western Europe

In the period from 1945 to 1973 suburbanization was both an expression of the material gains made by ordinary working people through the expansion of the western economies, and also a major reason for that expansion, since it was the industries which fed suburban growth (the car, television and 'white goods' industries) which spearheaded economic growth. Rapid economic growth and high wages led, however, to a crisis for the producers of such products, because they found that their premises became obsolete and site-constricted, whilst the labour they needed to expand production and remain profitable was too scarce, too expensive and too unmanageable in the major cities in which they were then located. Since the *in situ* restructuring of production was costly, usually resisted and often difficult to effect, further expansion required either the use of immigrant workers – who thus came to occupy many of the semi- and unskilled factory, building site and other manual jobs in the major industrial cities from the early 1960s onwards – or, alternatively, the dispersal of the routine production of goods and services to regions (or countries) with reserves of 'green' labour. The latter represented a new element in the geography of production and helped to produce the migration turnround. In this way, the international migration and counter-urbanization trends of the late 1960s and early 1970s can be viewed as a complementary product of the further development of Fordist forms of production and consumption and of the rapid suburbanization with which these were associated.

After the mid-1970s, when this post-war expansion came to an end, there began a period of reorganization of what, how and where goods and services were to be produced. Slower growth in household incomes, the increase in the number of jobless people and intensified competition from low-cost producers in the Far East and elsewhere led to a sharp check to the mass production in western countries of standardized goods for mass markets and to its built-form equivalent, the suburb. To a considerable extent international migrant workers had not benefited from the suburbanization process, though it was their labour on the building sites and in the factories which had made that process possible. Hence the fortunes of these two migrations, the intra-regional and the international, were closely connected. Economic restructuring also brought about major changes in inter-regional migration: the counter-urbanization of the late 1960s and early 1970s had been as dependent as foreign worker migration and suburbanization on a continuation of the form and pace of post-war economic growth.

After 1973, new forms of production, now popularly characterized as 'flexible specialization' and associated with 'productive decentralization', became more important. This change sometimes sustained counter-urbanization, since the urban contexts favourable to such activities were not the large industrial cities of mass production but the small and medium-sized towns found in prestige environments and in non-peripheral and/or near-metropolitan rural regions. It is not surprising, therefore, that there has not been a simple return to the urbanization which formerly characterized the relationship between net migration and settlement size (see chapter 2).

We might, therefore, conceive of two phases of counter-urbanization (or decentralized urbanization) which overlap in time and space. In the first phase, which reached a peak in the late 1960s and early 1970s, the decentralization of employment and population was spearheaded by branch plant and back office developments: it favoured smaller labour markets over larger ones and free-standing cities over large industrial conurbations. In the second phase, which developed during the late 1970s and 1980s, decentralization was led by the growth of small firms and high technology industry and services: it was far more selective spatially, and its distribution tended to reflect the location of the key agents of the emergent entrepreneurial culture, that is the private sector segment of the service class of professional, technical and managerial workers (see chapters 10 and 11).

References

This chapter draws substantially on material presented in the following publications:

Fielding, A.J. (1966), 'Internal migration and regional economic growth: a case study of France', *Urban Studies*, 3, 200–14.
Fielding, A.J. (1971), Internal Migration in England and Wales, Centre for Environmental Studies, University of Sussex, Working paper 14.
Fielding, A.J. (1975), 'Internal migration in Western Europe', in L.A. Kosinski and R. Mansell Prothero (eds), *People on the Move*, Methuen.
Fielding, A.J. (1982), 'Counterurbanisation in Western Europe', *Progress in Planning*, 17, 1–52.
Fielding, A.J. (1985), 'Migration and the new spatial division of labour', in P.E. White and G.A. van der Knaap (eds), *Contemporary Studies of Migration*, Geo Books, Norwich.
Fielding, A.J. (1986a), 'Counterurbanization', in M. Pacione (ed.), *Population Geography: Progress and Prospect*, Croom Helm.
Fielding, A.J. (1986b), 'Counterurbanization in Western Europe', in A. Findlay and P. White, (eds), *West European Population Change*, Croom Helm.
Fielding, A.J. (1989a), 'Migration and urbanization in Western Europe since 1950', *Geographical Journal*, 155, 60–69.
Fielding, A.J. (1989b), 'Interregional migration and social change: a study of South East England based upon the Longitudinal Study', *Transactions of the Institute of British Geographers*, N.S., 14, 24–36.

Fielding, A.J. and Savage, M. (1987), *Social Mobility and the Changing Class Composition of South East England*, Centre for Urban and Regional Studies, University of Sussex, Working paper 60.

10 The city in the global information economy

John B. Goddard

Introduction

To entitle a volume of essays 'The Rise and Fall of Great Cities' inevitably leads to many challenging questions: Will great cities rise again? What could be the basis for such a revival? Would any revival be uniform or would it be confined to certain types of cities? In the late 1980s prognostications for great cities are certainly not as gloomy as they might have been ten years ago. After decades of suburbanization progressing to counter-urbanization or the urban/rural shift and, more recently, wholesale de-industrialization (see Fielding, chapter 9), many commentators are now more bullish about cities. In the United States, New York has staved off financial collapse and several cities in the industrial heartland – such as Pittsburgh, Baltimore and Boston – have experienced major reversals in their economic fortunes (see chapter 2). In Britain London has witnessed a reversal of its long-term population decline and confidence, if not population and employment, is rising in northern industrial cities which are experiencing urban regeneration programmes (see chapter 4).

This apparent revival of fortunes has been paralleled by a significant reawakening of academic interests in the city as an object to study, particularly as concepts of place and space have become increasingly central to the concerns of social scientists from a range of disciplines. Notwithstanding their past decline, great cities still contain the lion's share of population and employment in most countries of the OECD group. They are clearly the dominant arenas within which the latest phase in the restructuring of the capitalist system is being worked out. However, the contemporary changes are conceptualized: as a shift from industrial to a post-industrial society, from Fordism to post-Fordism or modernism to post-modernism, the significance of the city cannot be ignored; it is not simply a passive stage on which events are worked out but rather is central to the restructuring process itself. As will be argued below, many features of structural change are ensuring that cities are perhaps more important as the locus for industrial and social processes than was the case in the 1950s and 1960s. After decades of decentralization the forces for agglomeration would appear to be reasserting themselves.

This chapter considers one facet of this restructuring agenda, namely the rapid growth of the so called 'information economy' and discusses what this might imply for two particular categories of city; the largest city within a national settlement system: and the industrial city which grew to pre-eminence in the nineteenth century not only as a place of production in its own right but as a service centre for regionally-organized industrial sectors. As a starting point four interrelated developments that underpin the information economy can be proposed.

First, that information is coming to occupy centre stage as the key strategic resource on which the effective production and delivery of goods and services in all sectors of the world economy is dependent. Far from a transformation from an industrial to a post-industrial society where the emphasis is placed upon a shift from manufacturing to services, an information economy perspective would suggest that manufacturing and service activities are becoming equally dependent on effective information management. The city is – and always has been – the focus for information processing and exchange functions; as information becomes more important in both production and distribution, so the pivotal role of the city is reinforced as Jean Gottmann stresses in his conclusion (chapter 11).

The second proposition is that this economic transformation is being underpinned by a technical transformation in the way in which information can be processed and distributed. The key technical development is the convergence of the information processing capacity of computers (essentially a within-workplace technology) with digital telecommunications (essentially a technology linking workplaces). The resultant technology of computer networking is emerging as a key spatial component in the technical infra-structure of the information economy. Because of their historic role cities are becoming the nodes or switching centres of this network-based economy.

The third proposition is that the widespread use of information and communications technologies (ICT) is facilitating the growth of the so called 'tradeable information sector' in the economy. The transformation embraces traditional information activities like the media – press, broadcasting and advertising – and the creation of new industries like online information systems. Moreover, many information activities previously undertaken within firms can now be purchased from external sources at lower cost in the 'information marker-place': the growth of the advanced producer service sector can in part be accounted for by the externalization of information functions from manufacturing and other firms. While the use of ICT permits an increasing volume of inter-organizational transactions, it suggested that inter-personal contact remain sufficiently important, particularly in relation to the development of new services and relationships, that the role of cities is further enhanced (see Gottmann, chapter 11).

The final proposition is that the growing 'informatization' of the economy is making possible the global integration of national and regional economies. As the arena widens within which this highly competitive process of structural change is worked out, so the pattern of winners and losers amongst cities is likely to become more sharply differentiated. Far from eliminating differences between cities, the use of information and communications technology can permit the exploitation of differences between cities, for example in terms of local labour market conditions, the nature of cultural facilities and of institutional structures. It is therefore very important to see contemporary changes in a longer-term historical perspective and in the context of the specificities of particular national urban systems. For this reason the next section of the chapter provides some comments on the UK situation.

Information and communications technology and the evolution of an urban system

Any analysis of the evolution of great cities cannot fail to highlight the role of communications and innovations in communications technology in the emergence of dominant metropolitan centres in a national settlement system. In the United States Alan Pred (1973) has clearly demonstrated the importance of the control of information circulation in the emergence of New York, Philadelphia, Boston and Baltimore in the eastern seaboard of the United States. From a different perspective, the writings of Harold Innis in Canada have drawn attention to the interrelationship between communications and the control of territory by governments and enterprises (for example, Innis, 1972).

Within Britain the key issue relates to the dominance of London over the rest of the urban system. During the middle years of the nineteenth century such cities as Newcastle upon Tyne, Birmingham, Manchester, Sheffield and Liverpool emerged to challenge briefly the hegemony of London. Such cities became not only centres of production but foci for information-based activities like finance, legal services, education and the media. Many leading British banks had their origins outside London – the Midland in Birmingham, the District in Manchester and Martins in Liverpool. Universities were endowed by provincial industrialists to support local research and training needs. The period from 1890 to 1914, however, saw London reassert its dominance (Robson, 1986). London financial institutions were able to find a ready market for the profits of northern industry in the expanding empire. In this process London drew provincial institutions into the City; there was a spate of mergers between banks leading to the emergence of the big five by 1918. The roots of the future decline of provincial cities can thus be traced back to the particular form of British financial capital with its preference for portfolio investment overseas (cf. Massey, 1986). A further key factor facilitating this centralization was the emergence of the national railway system which made possible the easy transfer of information in the form of people and the mail: this system radiated from London.

The inter-war period saw further centralization, this time in the form of the control of industrial companies. The financial crisis of the depression led to a major restructuring of such companies to eliminate excess capacity. National companies like ICI emerged to replace regionally-organized companies, the majority with corporate headquarters in London and production spread around a number of cities. The key feature of this period was the widespread introduction of the telephone into larger companies. This communications innovation, like the railways earlier, assisted the inter-regional separation of production and administration, a division which had previously only taken place on an intra-regional basis to the advantage of provincial cities.

Developments in another important part of the information economy, the mass media, further accentuated these tendencies. The establishment of the BBC as a national broadcasting organization eventually led to the emphasis on national news and views (Hagerstrand, 1986). By 1939 the number of provincial daily newspapers had fallen to thirty, half of which were controlled from London (Robson, op. cit.).

The post-1945 period not only witnessed the continuation of these tendencies towards administrative centralization but also saw the emergence for the first time of a strong process of production decentralization and a resultant net decline in the overall economic base of London and all other major cities. This new process strengthened after the mid-1960s with the spatial scale widening to embrace first the peripheral regions of Britain and then the developing world. In this period of relatively stable products and production technologies, the main emphasis was on the search for economies of scale in manufacturing through the use of capital and space-intensive assembly line methods using low-cost and less skilled labour than was available in the cities. The consequence of this shift was widespread de-industrialization of British cities (see Hall, chapter 2).

In contrast to manufacturing, very few economies of scale were being reaped in the information or control sector of the economy. While computers were being introduced to assist information processing within office functions, there were few technical innovations in the ability to communicate information between sites – the telephone remained the dominant technology and it merely diffused more widely through the economic system. Because growth in productivity was so low, the increasing scale of organization necessitated the employment of more and more co-ordination staff. And because of the limitations in the essentially paper- and personal-based intra-organizational communications systems, hierarchical structures were required to connect production and distribution sites via inter-mediate levels to higher decision-making centres; in this process provincial cities became relays in the intra-organizational information system, housing regional or divisional office functions. It was thus possible to point to the isomorphism between the corporate hierarchy and the urban hierarchy at the national and indeed international scales (Goddard, 1978).

Such developments need to be seen in the light of fundamental changes in the regulation of the British economy that emerged in the post-war period, particularly the growing role for the local and national state. Increased state ownership of enterprises in many sectors resulted in a centralization of headquarters control in London. With the increasing indirect role of the state through public purchasing, through support for research and development (R&D) and through grants and loans, private sector companies found it increasingly desirable to transfer their headquarters to London which was the focus for state regulatory activities. The growth of collective wage bargaining through national sector-based unions was a further centralizing influence. In the sphere of personal services, local government and health services grew in provincial cities, often administering centrally-deter-mined policies. The hierarchical ordering of national space around provincial cities as administrative centres for the public sphere thus paralleled developments in the private sector.

It is now widely recognized that this mode of industrial organization and regulation of production and consumption, loosely referred to as 'Fordism', ran out of steam in the mid-1970s with profound implications for the development of cities in Britain and elsewhere. In keeping with the information perspective being adopted here these problems can most fruitfully be conceptualized as a 'crisis of control' in which the scale and rigidities of many organizations had *inter alia* outgrown the capacity to handle the large volumes of information necessary to maintain effective control (Roobeek, 1987). For example, major problems of structural overcapacity appeared in many sectors with excessive inventories produced by rigid production technologies (the so-called 'hard' automation). Contrary to the needs of the market, these technologies allowed little flexibility in production volumes. Economies of scale needed to give way to economies of scope but this required new production technology, new forms of organization and new labour processes. Similarly the national and international dispersal of production inevitably meant more 'travelling' capital and less contact with the market. Rigid bureaucratic corporate structures were not well placed to respond to the requirements of rapid market change.

The past ten years have seen a struggle to reassert control through more flexible forms of organization. The integration of computers and telecommunications technology (ICT) has been central to this struggle. As a result of the use of ICT many of the old hierarchical structures of organizations and related territorial management have been subject to challenge and the dominant position of global information cities over provincial industrial cities has been firmly reasserted. These changes have been intimately related to significant shifts in political and institutional structures which have given greater emphasis to flexible patterns of employment and a revised role for the state as a regulator of markets rather than the provider of services, changes which have had profound implications for the management of territory and the urban hierarchy.

The next section of the chapter discusses six types of organizational innovation based upon the use of ICT which are being utilized to overcome the crisis of control in Fordism (Gillespie and Williams, 1988); while many of the innovation types are not mutually exclusive, the categorization should help in the exposition. Because the innovations are applicable in a wide range of situations, examples are drawn from a variety of national contexts.

Production process innovations

A central objective in the introduction of production process innovations like a computer-integrated manufacture (CIM) has been to achieve production which is more responsive to rapidly-changing market conditions. The key note is integration – between marketing, research and production – an integration which necessitates close contact between the functions rather than the geographical separation that has come to characterize the Fordist era. Whilst this suggests powerful centralizing forces, a countervailing influence has been inflexible labour relations in many traditional centres of production. So while new production technologies have enabled the industrialized countries to regain competitive advantage from the Third World, this has not necessarily benefited those older industrial cities which lack the flexible working practices and information-rich environments necessary to support this form of production. High-technology industries which were at the forefront of the introduction of new production technologies have characteristically developed outside but adjacent to the largest cities as, for example, in Silicon Valley, California and the M4 corridor west of London (see Hall, chapter 2). Nevertheless, many traditional urban industries, which are poorly unionized, such as clothing, have been revived in urban locations through the adoption of new production technologies like laser cutting.

Transaction innovations

The adoption of flexible production is often associated with new divisions of labour between firms as various functions are externalized; physical components or information inputs are purchased externally as and when required by the dictates of the market. This requires a rapid transfer of information down backward and forward linkage chains, a transfer which is facilitated by the introduction of computer-based 'Just In Time' inventory control systems. In their various writings Scott and Storper suggest that this externalization of the transactional structure of production can act as a powerful agglomeration force (e.g. Storper and Scott, 1989). Agglomeration is further enhanced by the shared pool of labour; the transfer of information via inter-firm mobility of personnel; and through institutional networks such as trade associations which regulate business behaviour. Through collaboration between firms in an industrial district, as documented for the Italian case by Sable and Piore (1984), smaller enterprises may be able to compete effectively with great corporations with their inflexible hierarchical structures and inter-urban spatial divisions of labour. While such transactional innovations do not necessarily imply geographical agglomeration – Just-In-Time systems can equally support long-distance linkages and a Fordist division of labour – the possibility remains for a revitalization of industrial districts within an urban context.

Distribution innovations

While large cities may be able to reassert their role as centres for manufacturing production, the most significant developments can be seen in the service sector, particularly in terms of the way in which urban services can be delivered to distant markets. The information-intensive newspaper industry provides many examples of production process innovations (for example, computerized typesetting) but is also notable for innovations in distribution which enable copy to be transmitted electronically and printed in remote locations. For example, Hepworth (1986) has shown how the *Toronto Globe and Mail* has used satellite links to enable it to print local editions in all of the provincial cities of Canada using laser scanners: the result has been increased sales in these cities at the expense of provincial papers. While these developments may have led to more production jobs in the provinces, the additional editorial or information jobs have been created in Toronto. Computer links have also been used to arrange local advertising in the provincial editions, by-passing local agencies. The computerized version of the newspaper has also formed the basis of product innovations in the form of online databases, again provided from Toronto. In this example it is clear how information can be captured in one city, value added in another and the information sold back to the original source. In this way a leading city is able to reinforce its dominance in the information economy.

Process innovation in information activities

A major cost-limitation in many Fordist organizations was the labour-intensive back-office function which previous communications constraints in the telephone era suggested had to be located relatively close to corporate headquarters in expensive downtown sites. However, recent developments in computer networking have facilitated the separation of information capital in the form of central computers and information labour in the form of clerical staff. Information-intensive activities in metropolitan centres can therefore expand unconstrained by problems of access to low-cost labour; this can now be provided from other cities or indeed other countries. Thus the Caribbean, with its advantage of a low-paid English-speaking population, is able to function as a back office for data preparation for activities like online booking and data services controlled from world cities such as London and New York.

Computer networking is clearly central to such organizational innovations and evidence on the spread of computer networking confirms the dominance of metropolitan cities as nodes on such networks. Networking arose in the 1970s because of the need to achieve economies of scale in the use of expensive computer equipment and in order to translate the productivity gains associated with computerization throughout the organization by embracing different locations (Hepworth, 1987). Central computing resources in headquarters were therefore made available to other cities. This was essentially a Fordist view. The 1980s have seen the emergence of distributed processing; star networks running a limited number of applications in batch mode are being replaced by multi-function, multi-layer systems supporting a wide range of applications. However, these developments have usually been introduced *after* the initial centralized pattern which focused on the capital cities had been established. Thus, within the UK London is the hub of computer networking, with 36 per cent of main frame computers there being networked compared with only 19 per cent in the northern region of England (Goddard, 1988).

Managerial innovations

The use of information and communications technology in the management of large organizations is beginning to have profound implications for the national and international urban hierarchy. Two processes of organizational change can be observed: centralization of strategic information and related functions; and the decentralization of routine decision-making to local units. Thus Management Information Systems are now beginning to embody in computer software the interpretative skills of middle management; these skills are now being made directly available to branch offices. Such offices can now make decisions within well-codified parameters and these decisions can be readily monitored from a distant headquarters without recourse to a middle management layer in provincial cities. This form of development is particularly apparent in the financial services sector but is also beginning to emerge in public services. In both instances, regulatory changes and related competitive pressures have been forcing the pace of innovation. In the public sector, notably in local government and in the education and health services within the UK, demands for autonomy in the management of schools, hospitals and general practices are also dependent for their realization on effective computerized decision support systems and on network links for information transaction between the unit in question and higher authority. As a consequence of such developments, the relationship between the provincial cities as a central place and their contiguous territory is being challenged; the outcome could be more spatial discontinuities within the urban system.

Product innovations in information activities

Metropolitan cities have always been the focus for information-based activities like financial and legal services and other business services like advertising and the media, as Gottmann notes in chapter 11. Because information is the principal product of these activities they have been challenged and revolutionized by the spread of information and communications technology but in a way that has reinforced the dominance of the largest global cities.

Innovation in information products has occurred in a variety of ways. In many instances it has emerged in the opposite direction from that characteristic of manufacturing, with new products arising through the computerization of established processes (Barras, 1986). The driving force from process to product innovation rather than vice versa has often been the desire to obtain a more accurate assessment of the true cost of in-house information services: this can be achieved through externalization of the service in a way that enables market costs to be more readily calculated. Examples of such developments could be the marketing of a company's own customer information on an online database to third parties or the establishment of an in-house computer service operations as a subsidiary operation. Because the externalization usually emanates from corporate headquarters, the effect is to reinforce linkages within a metropolitan centre.

Innovation in information-based services can also arise from new entrants to a sector and through the forging of strategic alliances between organizations in previously separate sectors. Howells (1988) has identified newspaper and publishing companies, large industrial corporations, telecommunication companies, information technology goods manufacturers, new and small information services niche companies, institutions and professional societies and government agencies as key participants in the electronic information services markets. These can come together as information providers, publishers of software packages, host computer organizers, network operators and information brokers. In theory the technology enables such services to be provided from any location on a telecommunications network; but, in practice, because the innovation process is forged through linkages between very diverse actors, it is not surprising to find that most online and

VANS (Value Added Network Services) are provided out of large cities. For example over three-quarters of VANS registered in the UK are based in London and the south east. Moreover, because of the large costs of developing such services, a primary objective is to develop a global client base and this is again most effectively done from a major metropolitan centre.

Hepworth (1986) has provided a clear example of the processes involved. I.P. Sharp, based in Toronto, has used telecommunications to create a global market for its services sold over the network through sixty branch offices. IPSANET, Sharp's private package switched network, provides customer access to computer time, systems and applications software, public databases, private data storage and electronic mail. Systems software is marketed on a time share basis, and public and private data are processed to carry out management-related applications; the communication network adds to processed data by making it accessible and timely for dispersed users. Within Canada over half the traffic on the network is generated within Toronto, reflecting the concentration of corporate users in that city. There is also a significant usage generated in the USA and the UK. Indeed, over half Sharp's staff work outside Canada, in face-to-face collaboration with customers and gathering data using computer links to Toronto. Hepworth suggests that there are strong pressures to switch the computer centre to New York, not only because of the customer pull but because of its more favourable telecommunications infrastructure and environment for trade in information services, an issue that will be considered later in the chapter.

Metropolitan dominance is also being reinforced in another information-intensive sector, the audio-visual industries, as a result of technological changes which are driving product and process innovation and the de-regulation of the industry. For example, the diffusion of video technology has significantly lowered barriers to entry in the TV and film industry, allowing more flexible forms of production; a significant amount of work can now be sub-contracted to independent producers. The technology has also stimulated new products such as corporate videos. This vertical disintegration has inevitably increased the importance of linkages between producers and consumers and the role of metropolitan agglomeration (Storper and Christopherson, 1987). At the same time the growth of global entertainment businesses has also focused on a limit number of world cities. Within the UK, the de-regulation of broadcasting, supposedly driven by technological change, is likely to further undermine the position of independent regional television companies based in provincial cities as smaller franchises are acquired by major players (Cultural Industries Research Unit, 1989).

Finally, no discussion of innovation in the information economy and its impact on urban development would be complete without some reference to the well-documented financial services sector, an information industry *par excellence*. Here product innovation, technological change and market de-regulation have proceeded hand in hand to underpin the dominant position of a limited number of financial centres (Thrift et al, 1987). Tokyo, London and New York, each located within different time zones, have become the 'three legged stool' of global financial information markets bound together by electronic dealing systems (Hepworth,

1988). These systems have been used to create a widening array of financial products (for example, options, swops and bonds) which compete with traditional securities as debt instruments. These products are supported by an expanding range of online financial data services, trading-related data (such as share prices), company-related data (for example, annual reports), financial data (interest rate changes) and economic and political information. De-regulation of national financial markets has facilitated the internationalization process and has also contributed to the erosion of barriers between previously separate domestic financial activities. Within the UK this latter process has also favoured metropolitan concentration as London financial institutions have entered local provincial markets: for example, to acquire estate agencies as a route to the sale of other financial services like insurance. Metropolitan synergy has clearly assisted this diversification but at the expense of similar less powerful and less technology-intensive networks in provincial cities.

Telecommunications and world cities

The preceding examples illustrate the role of innovation in the application of information and communications technology in reinforcing the position of large metropolitan centres. Underpinning these developments in the use of what are largely private computer networks are massive investments in public telecommunications infra-structures in the Central Business Districts (CBDs) of such world cities as London and New York. The New York case has been particularly well documented by Mitchell Moss (Moss, 1987).

New York is the focal point of US international telecommunications, accounting for 24 per cent of all overseas business calls prior to divestiture of American Telephone and Telegraph Company (AT & T); two-thirds of this traffic was directed to only ten other countries and over one-third to one country, the UK. The concentration of business has justified investment in major facilities like the New York teleport on Staten Island which provides satellite links for large business users in Manhattan; users are connected to the teleport by a fibre optic ring around the CBD which by-passes the publicly switched network. These networks link with those developed by large private users like Citicorp which has its own fibre cables connecting five central offices. A number of office buildings are also under construction which are designed to provide advanced telecommunications infra-structure for integrated video, voice and data services – so called 'smart buildings'. Consortia of telecommunications companies and computer manufacturers are combining with property developers to provide services to such buildings, all in downtown locations.

Moss has suggested that the fact that only a few world cities can offer such a range of communications facilities has served to reinforce a tendency for multinational services to concentrate their overseas offices in a few locations. Thus he demonstrates how American legal offices in Europe are concentrated in London and Paris and, on the Pacific rim, in Hong Kong, Singapore and Tokyo. Likewise foreign banks in the USA are concentrated in New York.

National telecommunications networks and urban hierarchies

The preceding analysis suggests that, far from leading to a dispersal of communi-
cations-intensive activities from major metropolitan centres, the provision of
advanced telecommunications services, especially in a de-regulated environment,
is serving to reinforce existing nodes. Langdale (1983) has, for example, demonstrated how traffic between the sixteen largest metropolitan areas in the USA
accounted for one-third of the revenues of AT & T before divestiture. Furthermore this traffic was dominated by large corporate customers – those with
accounts of over two hundred thousand dollars per annum – representing less
than 4 per cent of the customer base but 62 per cent of the long-distance revenues. Such customers were the heaviest users of low-rate tariffs (private lines and
Wide Area Toll Services) and therefore paid the lowest unit cost for their communications. Such long-distance inter-city traffic generated by the largest users is
the focus of competition in the de-regulated telecommunications environment.
This competition has resulted in the lowering of long-distance inter-city tariffs and
in the increase of local charges, basically through the elimination of cross-subsidies
from trunk to local traffic.

Similar developments are apparent in the UK where Mercury is competing with
British Telecom (BT), initially through a fibre optic, figure-of-eight route follow-
ing the main railway lines from London through Birmingham to Manchester and
Leeds but with extensions to Edinburgh and Glasgow (Gillespie and Goddard,
1986). Significantly, Mercury is providing its own fibre optic loop in the City of
London. Customers outside a thirty-kilometre radius from the main arteries of the
Mercury system will have to pay higher charges and will have to depend on BT
and low-speed copper cable for interconnection.

In this competitive environment tariffs are falling rapidly for long-distance traffic
but rising for local calls which use the publicly switched telephone network. Yet in
smaller towns and peripheral regions, as compared with London and the south-
east, local traffic represents a higher proportion of total call billing, thus further
reinforcing the comparative advantage of the metropolis.

The reason for the falling costs of inter-city communications relate not only to
technological advance but also to competition for the large-volume corporate
business; in the case of BT around 300 companies account for about two-thirds of
profits. At present these companies are obliged to use either BT or Mercury for
communications within the UK; they cannot by-pass the public network. But,
given that this may be possible when the telecommunications licence is re-nego-
tiated, BT is looking to become an international telecommunications carrier
through the provision of telecommunications services to a number of other
countries. Even under the present licence it is not obliged to provide anything
other than basic telephony on a uniform basis throughout the UK and may, in the
future, have to withdraw from the provision of advanced services outside the
London metropolitan region, basically in situations where demand probably does
not justify maintaining existing investment.

Conclusion

This chapter has suggested that the extension of the information economy and the related spread of information and communications technologies are central to the revival of the once-flagging fortunes of certain great cities. Far from eliminating the so-called 'friction of distance' and thus undermining cities, these technologies are supporting more and more concentration of economic power in a limited number of global cities. This reference to technology should not be read as a technological determinist position: the use of technology on its own has not created existing differences between cities nor will the promotion of technology as an act of policy eliminate differences. Phrases like the 'distance-shrinking power of telecommunications' overlook the fact that technology is not being used by cities but by organizations whose objectives have very little to do with urban development. Similarly, the concept of 'electronic highways' connecting cities is misleading; although the key technology of computer networks may incorporate parts of the public telecommunications infra-structure, many computer networks are essentially private and proprietory (Gillespie and Hepworth, 1988).

Notwithstanding these caveats, information and communications technologies clearly pose challenges for the way in which urban economic development is conceptualized. Possibilities are opened up for informational labour power to be readily transmitted over space, breaking the connection between the location of investment and related productivity gains. While some of the structural changes that have been discussed favour urban agglomeration with respect to certain inter-organizational linkages, agglomeration diseconomies may not set in because intra-organizational linkages can be maintained at a distance. Moreover, these technologies permit the globalization of competitive forces with enterprises in particular cities finding it difficult to shelter behind the barriers of distance. Since many of the key players in the information economy are transnational companies, international relationships may be forged independently of national urban hierarchies. The possibility of global integration and national disintegration may be realized as the gap between leading cities with a strong stake in the information economy and the rest of the national urban system widens.

Such a scenario is extremely depressing from the perspective of the traditional industrial or provincial city within a national setting. However, many of the threats that have been described contain within them developmental opportunities for provincial cities. Clearly, in a period of very rapid economic, organizational and political change, more opportunities arise than in a period of stability or stagnation. For example, at the intra-organizational level, the widespread adoption of computer networking in conjunction with rapid changes in ownership structures may mean that there is considerable scope to re-configure the geography of information activities between cities. Similarly, at the inter-organizational level, the externalization of functions as large firms seek to reduce their overheads may increase the opportunities for small businesses and raise the significance of linkages within provincial cities. As information becomes the key strategic resource for businesses of all sizes, the expertise available in higher education institutions in provincial cities may provide a more significant locational pull. At the same time cultural facilities may also emerge as an important asset of provincial cities (as Robson argues in chapter 4), with technological change and de-regulation facilitating the development of cultural industries outside the largest metropolitan areas. But whether *all* provincial cities can make the transformation to post-industrial cities on the basis of the same mix of information-based activities remains an open question.

References

Barras, R. (1986), 'Towards a theory of innovation in services', *Research Policy*, 15, 161–73.

Cultural Industries Research Unit (1989), *Regional Development and the Future of Broadcasting*, Centre for Urban and Regional Development Studies, University of Newcastle upon Tyne (mimeo).

Gillespie, A.E. and Goddard, J.B. (1986), 'Advanced telecommunications and regional economic development', *Geographical Journal*, 132, 383–97.

Gillespie, A.E. and Hepworth, M. (1988), 'Telecommunications and regional development in the information economy: a policy perspective', *PICT Policy Research Paper*, 1, ESRC, London.

Gillespie, A.E. and Williams, H. (1988), 'Telecommunications and the reconstruction of regional comparative advantage', *Environment and Planning A*, 20, 1311–21.

Goddard, J.B. (1978), 'Urban and regional systems', *Progress in Human Geography*, 1, 309–17.

Goddard, J.B. (1988), 'Can new technology bridge the divide,' *Town and Country Planning*, 56, 326–8.

Hagerstrand, T. (1986), 'Decentralisation and radio broadcasting: on the "possibility space" of communications technology', *European Journal of Communication*, 1, 7–26.

Hepworth, M.E. (1986), 'The geography of technological change in the information economy', *Regional Studies*, 20, 407–24.

Hepworth, M.E. (1987), 'Information technology as spatial systems', *Progress in Human Geography*, 11, 157–80.

Hepworth, M.E. (1988), 'Information technology and the global restructuring of capital markets', in T. Leinbach and S. Brunn (eds), *Collapsing Space and Time: Geographical aspects of communication and information*, Allen and Unwin, New York.

Howells, J. (1988), *Economic, Technological and Location Trends in European Services*, Avebury, Aldershot.

Innis, H.A. (1972), *Empire and Communications*, University of Toronto Press.

Langdale, J. (1983), 'Competition in the US long distance telecommunications industry', *Regional Studies*, 17, 393–409.

Massey, D. (1986), 'The legacy lingers on: the impact of Britain's international role on its internal geography', in R. Martin and B. Rowthorn (eds), *The Geography of De-industrialisation*, Macmillan, London.

Moss, M. (1987), 'Telecommunications, world cities and urban policy', *Urban Studies*, 24, 435–546.

Pred, A.R. (1973), *Urban Growth and the Circulation of Information: The United States system of cities 1790–1840*, Harvard University Press, Cambridge, Mass.

Robson, B.T. (1986), 'Coming full circle: London versus the rest 1890–1980', in G. Gordon (ed.), *Regional Cities in the UK 1890–1980*, Harper and Row.

Roobeek, A.J.M. (1987), 'The crisis of Fordism and the rise of a new technological paradigm', *Futures*, April.

Sable, M. and Piore, C., (1984), *The Second Industrial Divide*, Basic Books, New York.

Storper, M. and Christopherson, S. (1987), 'Flexible specialisation and regional agglomeration: the case of the US motion picture industry', *Annals, Association of American Geographers*, 77, 173-96.

Storper, M. and Scott, A.J. (1989), 'The geographical foundations and social regulation of production complexes', in J. Welch and M. Dear (eds), *The Power of Geography*, Unwin Hyman, Boston.

Thrift, N., Leyshon, A., and Daniels, P. (1987), *The Urban and Regional Consequences of the Restructuring of World Financial Markets: The case of the city of London*, Centre for the Study of Britain and the World Economy, University of Bristol (mimeo).

11 Past and present of the Western City

Jean Gottmann

The modern metropolis is the largest and most complex artifact that humankind has ever produced. Its complexity, especially for those who try to govern, plan or just comprehend it, has been compounded in the twentieth century by an accelerated pace of growth and by the instability of most of the characteristics of the society that makes up the urban agglomerations. Change has been so rapid, especially after 1950, that it has been difficult to follow and even more difficult to explain and to forecast where urban evolution is leading.

Projections based on recent statistical data have often proved to be misleading, and endeavours to understand modern trends have turned to comparisons over a longer term. The nineteenth century offered abundant and increasingly safe data, well analysed by various specialists. One should therefore not be surprised when reading the preceding chapters of this volume to find so much attention devoted to historical background. Many aspects of urban evolution are reviewed there. So multi-faceted is the modern city that more could easily have been listed.

In the conclusion one could have attempted an overview of some: the new form and scope that cities are acquiring; the consequences for community structure, population, traffic; the changes in urban society and in the functions of cities; the ensuing political problems; the unity and diversity of the newly emerging urban picture. Treating each of these aspects of urban life would have required another book rather than a chapter: however, some comments are in order. The importance of urban evolution can hardly be overestimated. The demographers' projections are that the majority of humankind will be urbanized by the year 2000 or soon afterwards (see chapter 1). In the Western countries a vast majority of the population is urbanized or suburbanized; therefore the Western city already expresses the problems and trends of the society that is making it.

Growth and mutation

Traditionally a city was a tightly organized, self-governing, densely settled community, clearly set aside, often by a defensive wall, from the surrounding 'open' country. The majority of the urban people derived their incomes from non-agricultural work, although farms could be located within city limits, *intra muros*. The Bible, mentioning the size of the population of Nineveh (in the prophecy of

Jonas) adds 'and as many cattle'. During the cultural revolution in Maoist China, the theory of the ideal city held that one-third of its people should work on tilling the land around it. But in the Western world rural and urban were gradually sep-arated, even though it was necessary to keep within the city horses for transport and cattle for the supply of fresh milk. With the advent of the motor-car and refrigeration these requirements faded away. Still, in the 1950s a few cows were found to be kept illegally in New York City by Italian immigrants and were duly expelled.

The developing technology of the twentieth century has brought about much greater changes: mechanization and rationalization of the processes of production, enhanced by automation and the progress of telecommunications, have gradually produced, first, enormous growth and, secondly, an actual mutation of Western cities. As machines and automatisms increasingly replace human physical labour, large numbers of people move from the rural countryside or from small industrial or market towns towards bigger cities. In a richer metropolis the newcomers hope to find better pay for lighter work, better educational and medical services, a more exciting life. These prospects make it worth accepting some other inconveniences, at least temporarily, such as crowded lodgings, noise and pollution, longer trips from home to work, etc. So large cities experienced accelerated expansion. By 1800 there were in the Western world only four urban agglomerations of half a million or more: London, Paris, Naples and Constantinople (Istanbul). Some others of such size doubtless existed in China and Japan, but few statistical data are avail-able for the Far East at that time. By 1900 a few million-size metropolises were listed, but the multi-million city was still considered an exceptional, extraordinary phenomenon. Yet in 1899, H.G. Wells, in *When the Sleeper Awakes*, predicted a huge London in the twenty-second century, capital of a united world, with a popu-lation of more than 30 million. As we look today at the urbanization of the south-east, we wonder if such a figure will not be reached before the year 2100.

It has been observed more and more frequently as the century has rolled on that the urban structure may cease being the compact agglomeration intra muros of the past and spread to create loosely-settled urban systems with a nebulous struc-ture covering entire regions around one or several dominant nuclei. By 1985 the US Bureau of the Census listed 85 urban agglomerations around the world of more than two million inhabitants each; about 300 had more than a million. Counting the residents alone of the large modern city leads to illusion.

Such an enormous and accelerated growth in population could not have occurred without a considerable expansion in the area covered by settlement. Here statistics become useless. The *de facto* cities have broken out of city-limits; suburbs that are gradually acquiring fully urban characteristics mushroom *extra muros*, invading the open countryside. Residences and industrial plants scatter around. The nebulous pattern of settlement that results creates in some urbanizing areas of the countries of advanced economy a new symbiosis of urban and rural, confusing to specialists attached to what they had learned about cities some time earlier.

This new pattern of land use was made possible by the provision of public transport by rail and road, by the generality of individual car-ownership, by the rise of the standard of living and by a credit system favouring homeownership. Thus it was the consequence not only of the technology at work but also of a multi-faceted evolution of society. Among technological developments none was more instrumental than the improvement of the means and networks of transport and communication. The motor-car helped people adapt to the scattering over large areas of residences, schools, retailing and entertainment establishments, places of work and meeting. The telephone and other techniques of transmitting messages by wire and waves linked together distant places so that production plants and management offices of the same firm could remain in close contact even if located in separate and distant sites. Similarly places of work could remain in easy touch with homes and other related locations, and much office work could be done at home or in places other than the office itself. John Goddard (chapter 10) rightly emphasizes the enormous impact of the progress of telecommunications; these are an important factor in the evolution of society but only one among many.

The dispersion of urban settlement had never been envisaged before the twentieth century. Experts of city planning have had to adapt their concepts of urban settlement and their vocabulary. First came the idea of the *city-region*, which appears in various works before 1915. It was very popular in the 1960s, when in the more advanced countries the concepts of conurbations and metropolitan areas became fashionable. Some spoke of the 'metropolitanization of the United States', as the population in metropolitan areas kept increasing. In the 1970s central cities lost much residential population and the main increase of residences developed beyond in non-metropolitan areas. The census data were easily misinterpreted, for they counted the population of every place according to residence. In an era of commuting and of constant movement of people between city and suburb, city and rural countryside, city and city, the modes of living and the old concepts of urban and rural must be revised.

In the 1970s and early 1980s the old central cities and their more crowded suburbs kept losing residents – those whom the censuses counted as their population – while the residents of areas considered to be rural, by perhaps outdated standards, kept increasing. Impressed by the idea that this was an irrepressible trend and projecting it into the future, many experts decided that we were entering a new world of 'counter-urbanization' and of the 'dissolution of the cities'. These views originated in the United States and Britain and seemed to apply mainly there, because those were the most advanced economies. Peter Hall (chapter 2) and Anthony Fielding (chapter 9), for instance, mention 'counter-urbanization' as an important trend. Still, in other, advanced areas of the world, especially more densely populated Western Europe and Japan, these ideas have not been equally accepted. Indeed, the expression, 'counter-urbanization', may have been somewhat confusing in describing an evolution rather than a disappearance of cities.

In the 1980s a movement emphasizing the renaissance of urban centres emerged on the continent of Europe, while in the United States the Bureau of the Census noted after 1985 a return of residential population towards the major, the 'command' centres. One could see evidence for this in the great business centres through the 1970s by observing the cityscape: much new building and renovation of old structures was taking place; skylines were rising and not only in London and Paris, New York, Chicago and San Francisco, Milan and Frankfurt, Brussels and Stockholm, but also, if on a modest scale, in many smaller cities. Prices of land and buildings have also been rising in central cities as well as in many suburban areas.

In every country these trends have been clearer and stronger in some regions than in others. Some areas have suffered greatly since 1970 and the cities in these regions show marked decline in many cases: the areas so affected are mainly the mining and old metallurgical regions, and also some great seaports such as Liverpool and the Tyne, or Baltimore on the other side of the Atlantic. England illustrates dramatically this dichotomy of divergent trends in the contrast between its north, based on coal and traditional heavy industries, and the booming, prosperous south-east with London in the centre. Many other countries offer similar contrasts if on a smaller scale: thus in Belgium Brussels and Antwerp are prosperous while Liège, Namur and others are depressed; or in France, where the industrial north, around Lille, contrasts with the booming cities of the Mediterranean, from Montpellier to Nice; and in the United States, where the maritime cities are doing so much better than the industrial centres of the middle west.

However, large American cities have demonstrated a remarkable elasticity since 1950, bouncing back from depression to obvious prosperity in an impressive and little-expected fashion: this was observed in an especially spectacular manner in the great centres of the megalopolitan north-east, including New York, Boston, Philadelphia and Washington. The last is spawning a number of 'new cities' in its suburbs, such as Bethesda and Columbia in Maryland or Tyson Corner in Virginia. Similar satellite cities are developing in the vicinity of other active large cities; in the suburbs of Houston, Texas, impressive office towers have risen, signalling new business districts. In Tokyo new business sub-centres have been built, of which Shinjuku is the most spectacular, and Paris is completing a huge complex on the outskirts of the city at La Défense.

In the last millenium the cases of disappearing or abandoned cities of some size are very few in the Western world, but periods of decline and rise have been recorded for most of them through history. The modern method of projecting mathematically the trends observed appears chancy in the long term for the behaviour of something as complex as modern urban society. Even more misleading are the census population figures, which count only residents who form the *night-time* population of a district. The lively modern city is above all a business, entertainment and information centre; it is usually surrounded by dormitory suburbs. The city's *daytime* population is therefore very much larger than that of the night-time. Daytime presence is of course difficult to ascertain, but employment figures provide valuable indications. They must be supplemented by an estimation of the crowds that come to the city to transact business, gather information, attend meetings, seek legal or medical advice, or just for entertainment (see Robson, chapter 4). The heart of a lively metropolis is a great crossroads.

We do not know what is actually the daytime population of the City of London on a weekday: surely several hundred thousand people. Its census population was around 7,000 in 1981. By day it swells by a coefficient of 40 to 60. It is probably an extreme case. But let us consider that this daytime population is the one that must be serviced – not only for transport in and out of the area but in many other ways as well.

The Japanese have figures for the daytime/night-time fluctuations in their Tokaido Megalopolis. Catharine Nagashima (1981) reported that adding the number of jobs to those of residents gave by 1978 a day:night ratio in Central Tokyo of 15 in some districts. It has surely risen since, and the transients should be added in daytime. The day/night contrasts are most striking in the greater cross-roads: London, Paris, Zurich, Brussels, Manhattan, the 'Loop' of Chicago, etc. The day:night occupancy ratio may be only around 2 or 3 in more ordinary central cities, but it is becoming a common phenomenon. These facts indicate how mis-leading as an actual population approximation the official population figures for most cities are. Even official censuses now prefer quoting figures for 'urban agglomerations'. And many other problems arise: how to govern the daytime cities in which only the night-time residents vote? What of the concept of the city as a community? And so on . . . To understand the present evolution of the cities, one should look at what is happening to urban society.

The mutation of urban society

Every city, as an artifact crafted by the local society, evolves with the needs and means of that society. The social and economic structure of that society has undergone many changes since the industrial revolution began, first in England and France in the eighteenth century, later in other Western countries; but change has accelerated since 1920 at a pace previously unknown, even more since 1950. The momentum may seem to abate at times in some places but it revives and accelerates unexpectedly at others. Forecasting these trends is risky and projecting seldom pays off, especially when demographic, political and international factors are modified. Who foresaw the post-Second World War baby boom or its fading away for a time? Who would have announced that the very conservative attitudes in France in the first half of this century would turn into enthusiasm for techno-logical applications such as nuclear energy, the telephone and the computer, including the pioneering success of the Minitel system? And who needs to be reminded of the extraordinarily rapid changes occurring in Japan?

One of the great factors of change that came gradually, but latterly very fast in the larger urban agglomerations of the West and Japan, has been the mechaniz-ation, automation and expansion of work that used to require human muscular effort. Today the most rapidly growing sector of employment has shifted from industrial production and distribution to the qualified, specialized white-collar occupations requiring skills, responsibility, brainwork. I heard this trend announced in my youth by a few acute analysts of society in the years 1928–35. This evolution on a huge scale became obvious in the north-eastern United States in the 1950s, as described in my book *Megalopolis* (Gottmann, 1961, especially chapter 11). The signs were emerging of the coming of an information and transactional society, which was working out new and rather 'bourgeois' modes of living for itself (Gottmann, 1983). Most of the educated public in the West, especially in Europe, resisted the acceptance of such ideas: they were termed 'visionary', or affecting just small numbers of people while already millions were in fact undergoing this transformation. But at meetings in Japan, held in 1967, I found a full realization of the trend, and the Japanese were openly preparing for an information, white-collar society.

The urban way of life has become gentrified *en masse*. Nevertheless many students in the universities of the West are not yet fully aware of this mass trend. It is taking a long time for even intellectual élites to realize the size and scope of the phenomenon, its impact on political attitudes and, of course, on the whole economic and daily life of urban populations. The cityscape must bear the mark of these changes. Many cities have had to be rebuilt, often to be redesigned. The gentrified manpower (which is also increasingly a womanpower) does not accept the housing standards, the same constraints, the same environment at work and at play that satisfied the generation of their parents. A striking illustration is provided by the evolution of the city and Duchy of Luxembourg in the last hundred years: in the period 1880–1910 the main taxpayer in Luxembourg was the iron and steel industry; in the 1970s the iron ore mines closed and the steel mills needed government subsidies in order to survive; the main taxpayer was then the banking industry; in the 1980s, in certain years when international banking was depressed, the main taxpayers were the mass media, especially the RTL radio and television system. Obviously the employees of RTL radio and international banks could not be satisfied with the living and working conditions of the iron-ore miners and steel mill personnel. Needs and means have changed.

Such change, barely credible in ages past, is probably easier to achieve at the scale of Luxembourg (total population 400,000) than for a much larger nation. However, the example gives an idea of what the mutation of local and national structures ought to be. A less striking change in the same direction is proceeding everywhere; the buildings of the Manufactura de Tabacos in Seville, where Carmen, heroine of Bizet's opera, worked, have become part of the local university. No wonder the modern city has problems, is in trouble; and that at the scale of dense agglomerations of more than a million people a considerable lag has developed in the changes to be achieved in the built-environment, the infra-structure, the legislation and even the knowledge that the responsible leadership may have of what is happening around them. It is less difficult to describe what happened in the industrial economy of Lancashire in the nineteenth century, as Dr Shaw has done (see chapter 5), than to outline the rapid shifts that have occurred in Manchester or Liverpool since 1950.

Still, past and present remain interlinked. The heritage bequeathed by previous centuries is with us and will not be easily erased or adopted; and much of it is good and must be preserved not only in the environment but even more so within ourselves. The culture and inner life of individuals and communities are their most treasured possessions. That inheritance from the past makes for a lag in evolution, but it also helps the adaptation to new circumstances. Brian Robson provides us with an excellent example of 'change or adaptation' (chapter 4), emphasizing the importance of old inherited ideas about the green, 'natural' countryside and the evils of urban centres. Luxembourg, if we may return to that case, used to be a Department of Forests in the Napoleonic empire about 1810; it is becoming one loosely-settled metropolitan area. The case is striking but it is not unique: the high Alpine *massifs*, extending from south-eastern France to Austria, have been trans-formed from a world of forests, pastures and frozen solitudes into a vast web of loosely-scattered settlements of urban or suburban character, designed mainly to satisfy the new needs of the modern urban masses of *homo ludens* at play. The ongoing expansion of tourism in all its forms is incorporating historical cities with small, picturesque tourist towns and villages, and curious natural sites in a sort of immense distant and dispersed suburbia of the growing urban networks.

These networks have become international, indeed a global system made possible by many factors: the evolution of employment from brawn to brain; the capability of present technology and organization to conquer distance; the extension of the duration of life and, within a life, of free time; and, last but not least, the rise of the standard of living owing to the greater financial means now available to a majority of contemporary town-dwellers. This last trend may well be what differentiates most past and present, and the 'Western' city from that of the other parts of the world.

An immense movement of people has developed around the world, essentially between distant urban agglomerations (Dogan and Kasarda, 1988). The aims of the travellers are varied; transactions of all kinds; professional meetings and con-sultations; straight tourism; health and medical services; recreation; search for jobs; and gathering of information of all sorts. Often several of these aims can be achieved simultaneously: the visit to a large centre of business offers the oppor-tunity for shopping and getting medical advice and some relaxation at the same place. A fairly isolated and specialized locality may develop in unexpected ways. Thus Davos, in Switzerland, a high altitude skiing resort, has become a round-the-year centre for select conferences and international seminars in diverse fields: medical, economic, financial, etc. Nice, the capital of the French Riviera, which is a large and well-serviced centre of tourism, has attracted new industries, including the large laboratory of IBM at La Gaude, and a university; Cannes nearby, recently only a seaside resort, sees nowadays almost one hundred international congresses and conferences annually.

The quality of the environment, of local entertainment, of the services has become an important factor in city development; the success or decline of a modern city depends on a variety of considerations, among which the diversity and quality of the services locally available and the reputation they have, form the essential nucleus. These services were built up gradually in the past at major national and international crossroads; here were not only the best facilities but also the best and most abundant information which were traditionally gathered through large, tight, and far-flung transactional networks that were long established. Hence the attrac-tion of the old, great seaports and of the old capitals. The functions and com-petence inherited from the past are not easily transferable; rather they snowball.

That is why a metropolis like New York, London, Paris, Tokyo, Rome, Moscow or many others on a smaller scale cannot be decentralized easily, even when many of the factories and industrial plants, which used to make it prosper, migrate elsewhere.

The concept of 'the West' encompasses a considerable variety of national cultures which look in divergent ways on urban trends and facts. Tastes differ. France and Italy prefer life in cities, in dense settlements and go to the periphery only if forced to do so by overcrowding and economics. Haussmann, rebuilding Paris in the 1850s, pushed the working masses, the poor, out to the suburbs. In the United States the attitudes have been opposite: the middle classes have preferred moving 'uptown', which has come to mean scattering to suburban areas. Attitudes towards skyscrapers and tall skylines have also varied: they are popular in America, resisted in London, Paris and many other European capitals. The use of streets and markets also differ: these are much more popular as an addition to housing and indoor services in some countries than in others. The relationship between private and public spaces in cities is a basic element of local culture, expressing the aims of community life as locally understood.

The picture one observes today in Western cities is much more variegated within each city than it used to be, despite the use of similar architectural techniques. The variety is not only one of economic levels but even more of social, ethnic and cultural characteristics. Large cities, centres of power, wealth and industry, always attracted crowds of poor, under-privileged people from the countryside, who came in the hope of sharing in urban opportunity and obtaining a better life for themselves, or at least for their children. However, since 1945 massive flows from distant overseas countries have brought to Western cities millions of migrants of diverse origins. Partly the immigration was requested and organized by the receiving countries short of manpower. Partly, especially after 1970, it was caused by the inflow, legal or illegal, of newcomers from much poorer countries, in search of a better life. The migrations came from all parts of the world, and to Western Europe as well as to North America. The economic recessions after 1975, which followed thirty years of expansion in the West, increased the socio-economic tensions in cities. Nowadays there is hardly a Western country that does not claim to have thousands of illegal immigrants in its urban areas.

Urban futurology grows more and more complex and uncertain. But the past of cities has seldom been orderly: neither can we expect the future to be. How will sprawling, growing communities be administered when old structures become obviously outdated? The study of urban affairs will long remain a rich and exciting field.

References

Dogan, M. and Kasarda, J.D., (1988), *The Metropolis Era*, (2 vols), Sage, Beverly Hills and London, especially the chapters by M. Kasarda, Castells and I. Sachs in volume 1 and by E. Jones in volume 2.

Gottmann, J. (1961), *Megalopolis*, The Twentieth Century Fund, New York and, for more recent trends, Gottmann, J. (1987), *Megalopolis Revisited*, University of Maryland Institute of Urban Studies College Park, Md.

Gottmann, J. (1983), *The Coming of the Transactional City*, University of Maryland Institute of Urban Studies, College Park, Md.

Nagashima, C. (1981), 'The Tokaido Megalopolis', *Ekistics, 48, 289,* 280–300: this issue is a special one on 'Japan's organization of space'.

Index

NOTE: *passim* indicates the word so anotated can be found in scattered passages throughout the pages indicated; 'n' indicates a note and figures in italics refer to an article by the author mentioned.